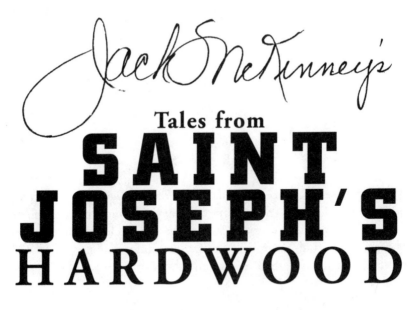

Tales from

SAINT JOSEPH'S
HARDWOOD

The Hawk Will Never Die

Jack McKinney
with Robert Gordon

Foreword by Phil Martelli

www.SportsPublishingLLC.com

ISBN: 1-58261-929-8

Publishers: Peter L. Bannon and Joseph J. Bannon Sr.
Senior managing editor: Susan M. Moyer
Developmental editors: Regina D. Sabbia and Doug Hoepker
Art director: K. Jeffrey Higgerson
Dust jacket design: Dustin Hubbart
Interior layout: Kathryn R. Holleman and Greg Hickman
Photo editor: Erin Linden-Levy
Director of marketing and sales: David W. Hulsey
Media and promotions managers: Kelley Brown (regional),
    Randy Fouts (national), Maurey Williamson (print)

Printed in the United States of America

Sports Publishing L.L.C.
804 North Neil Street
Champaign, IL 61820

Phone: 1-877-424-2665
Fax: 217-363-2073
www.SportsPublishingLLC.com

Contents

Foreword

As we prepare to celebrate 100 years of Hoops on Hawk Hill, it is important to look back before we move ahead.

Over the past 50 years Saint Joseph's University has changed in a cosmetic sense.

Women now make up more than 50 percent of the student body. The geographic profile of the student body has expanded as has the number of programs on campus. The footprint of Hawk Hill remains the same, while the additional facilities are both welcomed and have enhanced the look of campus.

As for Hawk basketball, the more things change the more they stay the same. The Fieldhouse still holds 3,200 rabid fans night after night, year after year. The passion for its team, which truly separates Saint Joseph's University from the rest has, if anything, grown and been fueled by alums and students alike. The spirit, that is evident to all—whether at the famed Palestra, the packed Alumni Memorial Fieldhouse, or one of the big arenas around the country—was, is, and will continue to be the fuel that fires the players and coaches. You feel that spirit when you're in one of those arenas. You can even feel it coming through the TV screen if you're watching at home. The pride that brings goose bumps to everyone who has worn the Hawk across his or her chest, pours forth at every opportunity.

Basketball at SJU is a shared experience. Fathers and mothers pass along pride and love of the Hawk to their sons and daughters. Seniors explain the responsibility of the "student section" to freshmen who eagerly carry on the tradition. Coaches from Ferguson to Ramsay to McKinney to Booth to Lynam to Boyle to Griffin have set a standard of excellence that must be maintained and upheld by the current staff. Meanwhile the players from all eras fervently encourage the current players to take their places in the history and lore of a proud tradition.

Any discussion of basketball at 54th & City Avenue must begin and end with the Hawk. The uniform is probably the same but more importantly tradition weaves its way through the fabric of basketball on Hawk Hill. So at every game in every season:

•The Hawk will always flap its arms
•The Hawk will always run figure eights
•The Hawk will always be considered a part of the team, not a mascot.

And

The Hawk Will Never Die!

For all who have experienced SJU hoops, you know that this is not a slogan but a way of life.

Enjoy and cherish.

—Phil Martelli

Photo courtesy of Saint Joseph's University/Sideline Photos

Preface

They've convinced me. The Hawk will never die. The "they" in this case is the entire Saint Joseph's University community, which comprises administration, students, alumni, volunteers, and staff—in other words, all the amiable and helpful people I met on this "project" (a word that belies the pleasurable nature of the endeavor). Wittingly or unwittingly—but inevitably with wit—they convinced me. They pounded or pampered that recurrent theme into my head—the Hawk will never die.

The theme is nothing if not recurrent. It's a mantra uniting every Hawk generation. They pound that theme home at SJU's home court, the Fieldhouse—a bandbox of a basketball arena swaddled in legacy and lore disproportionate to its modest dimensions. When I watch a game in the Fieldhouse, I'm constantly struck by the absence of pretension in the scene. The unabashed glee and pride the noisy—maybe a bit raucous—Hawk fans share with their team is a breath of fresh air in this age of shallow spectacle. Hawk rooters are not about spectacle. They're about fun that's unorchestrated, ingenuous and refreshing.

The players on the court don't strut like unapproachable media stars. They act like—get this—students—students who happen to play basketball very well for a school they love. What an archaic notion. The basketball players in the crimson and gray uniforms are students who live in the same dorm as the throng of crimson-clad crazies screaming behind the basket. They are not the stuck-up, uneducated golden boys marking time till the NBA drafts them (uneducated ... isn't that a sad commentary on the deceit and failure of many college sports programs ... athletes who leave universities without an education despite carrying a "student" ID issued by their benefactors for four years).

"The Hawk will never die" is not about a basketball team or a flapping mascot. Nor is it a rallying cry exclusive to the hardwood. The ubiquitous little anthem reverberates all over campus celebrating a spirit of community and continuity. Those five words span and bond generations. In this millennium, strong student-college bonds are giving way to blasé attitudes of the everyone-goes-to-college-so-this-place-isn't-very-special-to-me variety. St. Joe's students still feel their school is special. Their student body continues to embrace that vanishing I'm-blessed-to-be-here mindset. Talk to the new breed of Hawks, and you still detect a smidgen of the chest-pumped-out pride that second-generation Americans felt when they pioneered their family's initiation to the halls of academia.

Saint Joseph's University still seems caring. Sadly at far too many institutions nowadays, colleges give off a cold, big business-like, impersonal vibe. Many college campuses feel simply like a place—just any old place to hang out before plunging into the workaday world. At many institutions with successful basketball programs, students seem to love their basketball team on a less visceral level than the Hawks love their team. Big-program love seems more akin to an NFL fan's love of his or her city's team. The home team represents the city in some ambiguous, impersonal way. The players on the team itself exist outside the fan's world and certainly outside the fan's reality. Fellow students know their team's heroes only via SportsCenter.

The Hawk Will Never Die incorporates a lot of intangibles that relate to the school's student-team-alumni bond. You'll sense different nuances throughout this book. You'll get to know Jack McKinney, one of the Hawks' great coaches as Jack recounts an eventful life that saw him play and coach at St. Joe's, win an NBA championship, cop the NBA Coach of the Year award, and coach teams in dozens of countries around the globe. But beside Jack's story, the majority of the book deals with the lore and legend of St. Joe's basketball. And who better to share this rich legacy than Coach McKinney. Inducted into the SJU Athletic Hall of Fame in the fall of 2004, Jack maintains an extraordinary rapport with numerous generations of players, fans, and coaches on Hawk Hill. They've all shared their insights and memories with Jack and me in hours of interviews, conversations, and countless e-mails.

You'll chuckle over the travails of the earliest teams the Crimson and Gray (they weren't the Hawks then) trotted onto the hardwood. You'll learn more about the Mighty Mites, the team that introduced tiny Saint Joseph's College to the national stage. You'll whisk through the Coach Bill Ferguson era and read about the exploits of George Senesky, the first

Hawk (they were the Hawks then) player to feel the full national spotlight.

The hardwood history of the Hawks is told through running narrative—mostly by Coach McKinney—supplemented with scores of different Hawk Tales. Hawk Tales may take several different forms from humorous anecdotes and poignant reflections, to historical happenings. We kept the stories that appear to retain a grain or two of truth. A few may even retain several grains, but who's counting? Actually we're not as concerned with how truthful they are as we are with how entertaining they are. And they are entertaining.

Our excursion through Hawk history is organized chronologically by coaching eras. Why coaching eras? Hawk coaches have been an enormously successful lot. Did you know that Saint Joseph's University has sent more alumni into the ranks of NBA coaches than any other college in the nation but one? (Many people interviewed for this book would call that move a demotion—and you know who you are)? You'll learn a lot more about the Hawks coaching tradition in the upcoming pages and gain some insight into why it's so successful.

We profile several of the top players ever to cavort on the Saint Joseph's hardwood—like George Senesky (we cover his brother, too), Matt Guokas, Jr. (we cover his dad and uncle, too), Clifford Anderson (we cover his brother Lou Peltzer, too. Confused? You won't be when you read the book), Mike Bantom, Jameer Nelson, and Delonte West. You can read what their coaches and teammates had to say about them, and how they view life on and off Hawk Hill.

You'll read an extensive account of the Hawk mascot—the best mascot in college sports (that's not our opinion—although actually it is—but it's not *just* our opinion. Some pretty influential authorities in the world of sport share it, as you'll find out.) And throughout the book, you'll enjoy loads of great photos, including some rare oldies from way back when. The book is a must-read for sheer pleasure, but those photos make it a dynamite coffee-table book, too—one that every dyed-in-the-wool Hawk fan will be proud to show off. But you already know that. You're holding the book in your hands.

Buy it and enjoy it, but heed this one caution. If any of your Villanova, LaSalle, Temple, or Penn friends pay you a visit, don't leave them alone with this beautiful book. You know how childish those other Big Five schools can be. They might deface it. Jealousy can be such a destructive emotion.

—Robert Gordon

CHAPTER ONE

Saint Joseph's University

T he Hawk will never die. What Philadelphian doesn't know that? Every dyed-in-the-wool, cheesesteak-chompin', soft pretzel chewin' Quaker City native will tell you the Hawk will never die. St. Joe's and its beloved Hawk burrow deeply into the heart of Phillytown. The Hawk and Philly go together like milk and Tastykakes, like the Palestra and the Big Five. A Philadelphian is more likely to toss a snowball Santa Claus's way than diss the Hawk. Santa only comes to Philly once a year. The Hawk is a Philly homey. He might be flighty on occasion, but he never flies the coop. And the Hawk never dies.

Though he does flutter occasionally. From time to time over the past century and a half, the Hawk has gone into tailspins or hibernations. For you biology majors or *Jeopardy* wannabes, a hibernating hawk is an anomaly. But the St. Joe's Hawk isn't your run-of-the-mill hawk. Its nest, better known as Hawk Hill, is loaded with anomalies.

Anomaly number one is how the little ragamuffin school that perches atop Hawk Hill can be so consistently good in basketball. With a modest 3,950 students (who are anything but modest about their basketball team) and a modestly funded basketball program, St. Joe's consistently goes toe to toe with the NCAA's big boys—the deep-pockets programs that *should* be out of St. Joe's league. But they're not. That fact alone vaults St. Joe's basketball into a league of its own.

St. Joe's has consistently scuffled and scurried to the front and center of the college basketball limelight through little more than cussed determination and pluck. Time and again, little St. Joe's has socked it to

some of the most prestigious, high fallutin' teams around the country—
and around the globe as you'll read further on.

The Jesuits Come to Philly

Saint Joseph's College officially arrived on the Philly scene back on January 29, 1851. That's the date the Legislature of the Commonwealth of Pennsylvania granted the school its charter. However, the seeds of the institution were planted much earlier.

Saint Joseph's University of Philadelphia is a Jesuit college. St. Ignatius of Loyola founded the Catholic missionary order known as the Jesuits, and more formally as the Society of Jesus, in 1540. True to their role as missionaries, the Jesuits ventured to the New World from Great Britain.

In 1577, the Jesuits created the English Province of the Society of Jesus in Britain. In 1634, they established the Maryland Mission in the New World. Maryland, which was Lord Calvert's colony, was favorable toward Catholics in that era. Early on, the Maryland Mission identified Philadelphia as a propitious site to set up a second Jesuit foothold in the New World. Why Philly? William Penn and his fellow Society of Friends (more popularly known as Quakers, particularly to cereal lovers worldwide) granted religious freedom to anyone who worshipped one God. The Quakers happened to be one of the few groups in the New World who weren't openly hostile toward Catholics.

The Maryland Mission dispatched Catholic missionaries to colonize Penn's Province in the 18th century. Father Joseph Greaton, SJ (Society of Jesus), headed the small band of Jesuits whose charge was to minister to six colonies.

As early as 1741, Greaton planned to found a new Jesuit college in the Quaker City. In 1732 he started construction on the house that ultimately would become St. Joseph's first faculty residence more than a century later.

Greaton's proposed school would have been the first Catholic College in the U.S. But that's not what went down. In 1785, the Council of American Clergy tapped Georgetown for that distinction. Even rabid Hawk fans admit that Georgetown was a valiant first try. They hasten to add that by the time Saint Joseph's College made the scene in 1852, the Jesuits had ironed out all the kinks and got it right.

William Penn, SJ?

One old story has it that an unnamed Maryland Jesuit visited William Penn in 1683, presumably to talk about establishing a Jesuit mission in Philly.

Anyway, this visionary missionary's house call set the rumor mill spinning. Philly's founder was unpopular in his native Britain. And in that age, what better way to smear someone than to accuse him of being a Catholic? The rumor went around that Billy Penn had converted to Catholicism and died (the cause of death was not Catholicism). Penn squelched the rumor with this letter.

"I find some persons who have had so little wisdom and so much malice as to report my death. And to mend the matter, dead a Jesuit, too."

Billy closed his letter indignantly, "I am still alive and *not Jesuit.*"

Loosen those britches a little, Billy.

The Mass House Survives

On July 25, 1734, Governor Patrick Gordon announced to the Provincial Council of Pennsylvania that "I am under no small concern to hear that a house lately built on Walnut Street in this city [Philadelphia] had been set apart for the exercise of the Roman Catholic religion, and is commonly called the Romish chapel, where several persons, I understand, report on Sundays to hear mass openly celebrated by a Popish priest." Apparently the Governor liked run-on sentences more than Catholics. The Mass house referred to the original Saint Joseph's Church. Actually, Governor Gordon wasn't as concerned about Catholic bashing as he was about the authorities back in Britain. Pennsylvania was still a British colony, subject to the laws of the Crown. Whereas William Penn's Provincial Laws of Pennsylvania allowed Catholicism, the Penal Laws of London forbade it.

Anglicans had succeeded in overthrowing the Catholic charter in Maryland. They sought a reprise in Pennsylvania. To that end, Pennsylvania Anglicans dutifully reported Catholic activities back to English authorities.

Despite the charged atmosphere of religious intolerance, neither British nor colonial authorities disturbed Father Greaton's "Mass House" at Saint Joseph's.

The Jesuit Suppression

The Hawk temporarily stopped flapping at St. Joe's around the time of the Revolution. In 1773, the Society of Jesus—19 Jesuits in Maryland and five in Philly—was forced by the authorities to cease its activities. During the Revolution, the stock of Catholics rose significantly. Catholic France helped fund the Revolution. France sent the Colonies men and money (always a great influencer) to aid the revolutionary cause. Catholic Spain chipped in with war materials, and Catholic Poland sent soldiers.

By the end of the American Revolution, Catholics were gaining grudging acceptance by their fellow countrymen, and Catholicism began weaving its way into the American fabric. Notwithstanding those gains, the Jesuit suppression lasted in varying degrees till after the War of 1812.

Converting The Founding Fathers

On at least one occasion, both Washington and Adams attended mass at the Jesuit church that would become St. Joseph's College. The two future presidents were impressed. Washington scribbled this diary entry on October 9, 1774: "Went to Presbyterian meeting in the forenoon and the Romish [sic] Church [that would be Saint Joseph's] in the afternoon."

OK, so that account is pretty vanilla, but remember, George was a politician. John Adams's account was anything but vanilla, however. Adams's diary entry read: "Went this afternoon to the Romish chapel and heard a good discourse upon the duty of parents to their children, founded on justice and charity. The scenery and music are so calculated [back then, being calculated was a *good* thing—*calculated* meant well planned and precise] to take in mankind that I wonder the reformation ever succeeded."

Open for Business

It wasn't till September 15, 1852, that Father Barbelin SJ, opened Saint Joseph's College for business at 321 Willing's Alley. Willing's Alley was situated around 4th & Walnut. Father Barbelin along with Father Ignatius Brocard and three other Jesuits served as the first faculty.

First-year enrollment was 40 students (compared to 3,950 students today). Saint Joseph's University teaches the same values today as Father Barbelin and his colleagues taught then, except that the faculty places higher value on whipping other Big Five teams than it did in 1852.

St. Joe's tuition has also changed significantly. Today $12.50 will buy a great lunch for two at the campus café. Back in 1852, $12.50 bought a student one quarter's worth (11 weeks) of matriculation at Saint Joseph's College. Tuition for Saint Joseph's Preparatory school was $6 per quarter.

The price must have been right. St. Joe's attendance more than doubled its second year. Enrollment swelled to 126 students in the third year.

Things were going so well those first three years that on January 14, 1856, St. Joe's moved on up to more fashionable digs on Filbert Street. The move was short lived. Economics dictated a quick return to Willing's Alley a few years later.

Stiles Street

In 1866, College president Father Barbelin purchased a full city block. The tract ran from 17th Street to 18th Streets and fronted Stiles Street. Barbelin intended to use the grounds for the college. Unfortunately, that year the Hawk went into hibernation from 1866 through 1887. Notwithstanding the shutdown, Father Burchard Villiger, an original faculty member who became president in 1866, started construction on the Styles site. Funded by the estate of Francis Anthony Drexel, new buildings, including the Gesu Church, went up during the down time.

When the college resumed operation, it remained at Willing's Alley. Then on September 2, 1889, Saint Joseph's College moved lock, stock and barrel to the Stiles site. There it survived the vicissitudes of world wars, depressions, recessions, and other national and global events for the next 38 years.

The Current Site

Then-president Father Matthew Fortier, SJ, launched an aggressive million-dollar expansion campaign in November 1922 to acquire and develop land for a new campus. Saint Joseph's College wound up purchasing a 23-acre tract at the western limit of Philadelphia. Three years later, on November 27, 1925, ground was broken at 54th and City Line Avenue to erect the first building, which was dedicated on November 14, 1927. That's when Saint Joseph's College moved to its current site. The *Philadelphia Bulletin,* a now-defunct newspaper, occupied the vacated college site at 17th & Stiles.

In 1927, Saint Joseph's College had a small student body of commuters. Enrollment declined during the war and the Depression, then started to climb in the late 1940s as servicemen returned to post-war society. In 1943, the evening college was launched. In that same decade, Saint Joseph's, which had always been strictly a commuter school, acquired and converted a number of former neighborhood residences into student living quarters. A new campus life flourished.

The 1960s ushered in a decade of significant expansion. A science center, new library, six-story student dorm, student center, and other facilities were added. The campus boundaries expanded too. The school purchased the nine-acre estate on the Montgomery County side of City Line Avenue.

At the dawn of the 1970s the school transformed into a coeducational institution. Later that same decade, on July 24, 1978, the Secretary of Education of Pennsylvania recognized Saint Joseph's as a university.

Saint Joseph's University Today

As they say, all that preceding stuff—that's history. What is Saint Joseph's University today?

"It's a place that continues to grow in the love and loyalty it gets back from its people," Don DiJulia feels. Don is an ex-Hawk hoopster and longtime athletic director who has spent 22 of his last 29 years on Hawk Hill.

"I think we attract real people here," Don says. "We're on the very edge of Philly. We have an urban edge and a campus that feels suburban. We see that suburban-urban mix in our student body that's coming from a continually expanding geographical base."

St. Joe's used to be a pure commuter school. Philadelphia kids— especially in the Archdiocese of Philadelphia—grew up immersed in the Hawks culture. They watched them on TV and cheered them on at the Palestra. One of the "coolest" nights out for Philly high schoolers was to pack into dad's car and ramble out to Penn's campus to catch some Big Five action—all the while harboring dreams of starring on that same hardwood themselves.

The Big Five has lost a bit of that luster, the kind it enjoyed in the 1960s in the glory days of UHF. Commuter schools don't appeal nowadays, either. But Saint Joseph's has changed enormously over the past few decades, morphing from a liberal arts commuter college into a residential university—a small residential school with appeal to today's student.

"These days," Don explains. "About 55 percent of our students live in our campus residence halls, another 35 percent live in apartments near the school, and the rest commute. Of course, we've managed somehow to expand the acreage of the campus to allow those kinds of demographic shifts. We had 10 or 15 acres in the 1960s, and now we have something like 60 acres.

"Our student population is much more diverse as a result. Whereas we used to draw about 90 percent of our enrollment from the Delaware Valley, we now get almost 60 percent from outside the Delaware Valley."

"We're most certainly increasing in our appeal. We're also elevating the quality of our education," University president Father Lannon explains. "The applications we receive now double the number of students we accept. We received 9,400 applicants last year for 4,000 positions. Applications have been increasing by about 1,000 a year. Yet we're not expanding the undergraduate student body. We're limited by the size of the campus and the available housing, so we're maintaining the undergraduate enrollment where it is. Actually, we're planning to acquire 38 additional acres from the Episcopal Academy next door, so we'll gain some more valuable space. Our focus is really on educational quality, though, more than quantity—numbers of students. We're hiring 50 more full-time faculty to improve our instructor-student ratios. Meanwhile, we plan to expand our graduate school enrollment.

"I've been here on this campus in one role or another in each of the past five decades," Don DiJulia chimes. "We started admitting women during that period. At this point, we have more women students than men. We've built residence halls, gone from a college to a university, and switched from a predominantly Jesuit faculty to a lay faculty. That's a lot of change. The campus is more diverse, more cosmopolitan, and more vibrant now because we have a substantial student population of non-Philadelphians. But when you get down to it, the place retains the same flavor it did when I was here playing basketball for Jack Ramsay in the 1960s. It must be something in the drinking water that keeps it that way. No one gets away from here 'un-Hawked.'"

One More Page

University president Father Timothy Lannon was enthused about the Hawk project right from the start, *especially* when he found out Bob

Gordon had just written the book *Ed Pinckney's Tales from the Villanova Hardwood*.

Father Lannon has only been the "head hawk" for a couple of years. He may be new to the Quaker City, but he is wise to the ways of Philly hoops. As he flipped through the Villanova book, he settled on the final page—page number 186.

"Now tell me," he asked the two authors of this book, leaning forward. "How many pages is the Saint Joseph's book going to be?"

We said we really didn't know.

"As long as it's at least *187* pages long, you have my full support."

Make That "Saint Joseph's University"

You'll read the words "St. Joe's" a lot in this book. That's an official Saint Joseph's University no-no. Make no mistake about it: Saint Joseph's University is *Saint Joseph's University*. It is not *St.* Joseph's. It is not Saint *Joe's*. And it certainly is not *St. Joe's*.

In the tradition of the great Hawk coaches who instilled the sense that there are no shortcuts to success, Saint Joseph's University sanctions no shortcuts for its name. So we're guilty. You'll find lots of format violations in this book. But it's not just for convenience and not just to save trees. It's a matter of integrity. Given Father Lannon's "suggestion" to make the book at least 187 pages long, we don't want to inflate our page count somewhat artificially by writing "Saint Joseph's University" in each instance. That ploy alone could add as many as 30 pages to the book, a pretty flimsy way to top the 187-page challenge. Come to think of it though, a ploy like that does smack of the kind of stall technique a Hawk basketball-coach-turned-author resorted to on the court on occasion.

We promise *not* to stoop to that tactic—at least until page 180 or so.

CHAPTER TWO

Coach McKinney
In Coach's Words

The McKinney Clan

The Jack McKinney story started in Chester, a town about 45 minutes south of Philadelphia. In the 1940s, Chester was a wonderful place for a young boy to grow up, particularly a kid who lived for sports. As a young athlete in Chester, I had one big role model—big as in 6'3" big, big as in 240 pounds big. The role model was my dad. Paul McKinney was a local gridiron legend—a thundering fullback and crunching middle linebacker who was usually the biggest guy on the field. His exploits earned him a charter position in the Delaware County Hall of Fame.

My dad never played professional ball. He was a lifetime member of the Chester Police Force, beginning his career as a patrolman before being promoted to sergeant. When the Police Department expanded and started a vice squad, Paul McKinney was tapped to head it. When the detective bureau absorbed the vice squad, Joe Eyre, mayor of Chester, appointed Dad the captain of detectives.

After 10 years, my dad considered retiring. However the mayor offered him the position of chief of police. Paul McKinney, even in his fifties, didn't fancy sitting behind a desk all day, and he declined. He opted to run for sheriff and won by the biggest margin the county had ever seen. As fate would have it, he ended up reporting to the Delaware County seat of government in Media each day—and spending his day behind a desk.

Four years later, he was re-elected sheriff. Again he won in a landslide. A Delaware County law prohibited a sheriff from serving three consecutive terms. Wishing to keep Paul McKinney in public service, Delaware County created a position for him, director of courthouse security, which he held for eight years before hanging up the phone, gun, and holster and moving "down the shore" with my mom.

Jen and Joan McKinney

My mother, Jen McKinney, was pure stock Irish and a super-loving mother who loved to dote on her boy. She always referred to me as "my Jackie." I think sometimes she thought I was Jesus.

My mom played basketball in grade school, but singing was her biggest talent. She was plenty busy singing at weddings and funerals, and playing the piano at silent films.

My sister Joan was three years older than I. She spent a good portion of her youth rolling her eyes at her mother's constant fussing over her little brother Jesus. Joan was a basketball player, too. I used to travel to Notre Dame in Moylan, Pennsylvania, to watch her play. She wasn't much of a scorer, but it wasn't her fault. Back then in women's basketball, only forwards were allowed to shoot. Defensive players couldn't stray beyond half court (who would ever call them "the good old days!").

Joan and I always had a wonderful relationship. She went out of her way to visit Claire and me wherever we were living—just to see my kids (her children as she called them). Joan fought a valiant battle against cancer in her fifties and finally succumbed. I lost a sister, a supporter, and a friend.

Getting the Basketball Bug

I got my introduction to competitive basketball at St. Robert's Elementary School in Chester (now called St. Katherine Drexel Elementary School). One morning, Sister Edward Francis, my fourth-grade teacher, made an unexpected but enticing announcement to the class. Fifth-grade teacher Sister Michael Anita had challenged the fourth-grade to a basketball game the following Friday.

The big day came. Our team had done nothing to prepare, other than getting overly excited and anxious. We were playing this game for high stakes—neighborhood and school bragging rights. I knew I had to step up. I was the tallest kid in our class.

We gave those fifth graders all they could handle. Toward the end of the game, I got fouled. I went to the line to shoot two.

The Underhand Foul Shot

Does anyone remember Rick Barry? Barry was the last guy I can think of who shot fouls underhanded. Interestingly enough, he is second on the NBA all time list for foul shooting percentage at .900 for 15 years. Mark Price shot .904 for 12 years—but not underhanded. Hal Greer of the Syracuse Nationals and later of the Philadelphia 76ers revolutionized the style of foul shooting. Hal simply shot his jumper.

Call me old fashioned, but I can't help thinking the underhand foul shot is still the surest way to put the ball through the hoop consistently. It just lacks the all-important highlight-reel look, so it's been shelved.

Making a Point

Coolly I released the ball with a strong arch. It sailed to the rim—then beyond the rim, then beyond the backboard. It landed on the stage behind the baseline in St. Robert's gym.

Big deal, I thought. I missed. I still had shot number two.

I compensated on the second shot, throttled back on the oomph and cut down on the arch. This one hit the backboard—high up on the backboard. It banged hard back to the rim, bounced straight up for what seemed 10 seconds, and tumbled earthward again right through the hoop. Nothing but net.

The fourth grade went wild! The bench did a victory dance—which in that era would have been the Jitterbug (young readers, ask your grandparents). Unfortunately, my heroics were all for naught. My unpretty foul shot was our only point in a 12-1 loss.

The next day in class, Sister Edward Francis didn't stop talking about "our great basketball player, John McKinney." She was ready to canonize me for the greatest one-point performance of all time. My mother would have told Sister [had she asked] that I didn't need to be canonized. I was Jesus already—at least to my mom.

St. James and Saint Joseph's

In September of 1949, I left St. Robert's Grade School and walked a block and a half to St. James High School. I was now a high school student. When you came into an all-boys school as a freshman, you were not big time, buddy boy. The upperclassmen had their fun with the little squirt freshmen, but we all survived. It was a great experience, a great school, and a period of my life where I grew educationally, socially, and athletically. I thank St. James for showing the way.

I played on Joe Logue's freshman team. Joe had been my grade school coach at St. Robert's and moved up just as we did. In sophomore year, I made the jayvee team, coached by a newcomer to St. James, fresh out of St. Joseph's college. His name was Jack Ramsay.

In junior year, I played varsity on the first Bulldog team to play in the Catholic League playoffs. Coached by Ramsay and led by 6'6" senior center Bill Lynch, we had the thrill of playing on the Palestra floor—for one game. Bill Lynch went on to hardwood stardom at Saint Joseph's College.

With this success, Jack Ramsay moved on to greener pastures, and I missed having him as a coach in my senior year. My old coach, Joe Logue, became the head varsity coach. My team—I was voted captain—did not scare anyone. We were a good team but not good enough in the strong Philadelphia Catholic League to make it into the Catholic League Playoffs. So, my high school playing career, with no postseason play, was concluded, and I looked forward to going out for baseball. At the sports banquet later in the spring, I was awarded the Basketball MVP. Some consolation, anyway.

A Mother, a Father, and a Doctor

Three people that I came in touch with during my high school career influenced me forever: a mother, a father, and a doctor.

In St. Robert's Grade School, I belonged to a quartet of sports nuts who were never very far from each other. Jim, Bob, Joe, and Jack: we were the Four Musketeers, and we remained close all through high school. We'd play sports all week, go to the movies on the weekend, then watch the Bulldog football team every Sunday, wherever they were playing, so we could cheer on Dick Christy and Bob Mahoney and Ducky Van Horn.

One night, the spring of my junior year, after dinner, my mother said, "Son, I'm concerned about you. All you and your buddies ever think about is sports—all the time. You have no social life. So you are going to the junior prom. I said, "Mother, I'm not going to any junior prom. I don't even have a date." My mother said, "Well, I suggest you get busy and get a date. Sunday, go to the St. James dance and get a date for the prom." "But Mom, I—" "No buts, you are going to the prom." Earlier, I had learned, you don't mess around with assertive mothers who put great meals on the table every night. Get a date. Mother has spoken.

The next day at school, when the four Musketeers got together I said, "Guess what? My mother told me I'm going to the junior prom (which happened to be just three weeks away)." Bob and Joe and Jim all spoke at the same time, "Mine said the same thing." Without saying it, we knew four mothers had been busy on the telephone. We all had a great laugh. Now the hunt was on. So, the future Dr. Joe Pappano, Father Jim Delaney, business executive Bob McNelis, and Coach Jack McKinney all had to come up with dates for the junior prom, which was just three weeks away. That Sunday night at the St. James dance, I spotted this cute, little blond in a red jumper and asked her to dance. We danced and danced again. Then after the dance, I walked her home, where I asked her to the prom and she said yes. Not bad for a first try. In a few months, we—Claire and I—will celebrate our 48th wedding anniversary. *Thank you very much, Mother.*

When the basketball season was over, in my senior year, I was looking forward to playing baseball. The day after our last basketball game, I was walking through the hallway during the change of class, when I heard a very authoritative voice from across the hall say: "McKinney, I want to see you." I turned to see Father Wesolowski, my chemistry teacher. Father "Weso" was the moderator of sports and the track & cross country coach. He continued, "McKinney, I've been watching you all season on the basketball court. You can really jump. I want you out for the track team." I said, "Father, I don't have any interest in track. I want to go out for baseball. And besides that, I don't know anything about track." Weso said, "McKinney, I will teach you to be a high jumper, and you will be pretty good, too. Besides that, McKinney, you know you are not doing too well in chemistry." And I said, "What time is practice, Father?"

The next day, Coach "Weso" taught me how to high jump. Eventually, I won every meet, broke the school record, won the Catholic League Championship, and got a scholarship to Saint Joseph's College, which changed my life! Oh yeah, I also got a good grade in chemistry. *Thank you very much, Father.*

In high school, during my sophomore and junior years, I had the privilege of playing basketball for coach Jack Ramsay. I left St. James, went to Saint Joseph's College, and again had the honor of playing my junior and senior years for Jack Ramsay.

Upon graduation from St. Joe's, Jack Ramsay recommended that I take the offer from St. James High School as basketball coach. His exact words were, "Coaching basketball will be good for you, and you will be good for basketball."

After spending a couple of years coaching at St. James, Ramsay invited me to come back to St. Joe's as his assistant and freshman coach. Then, upon his retirement, he recommended me as head coach at Saint Joseph's College. About 10 years later, when Jack took the job as head coach of the Portland Trailblazers, he called me to be his assistant. The first year there, the two of us were fortunate enough to win an NBA World Championship. So, "Doctor Jack" was instrumental in developing my coaching skills. He was my coach, my advisor, my mentor, my very close friend, and the past few years here in Naples, Florida, two or three times a week he has become my golfing partner along with bulldog Tom Wynne and few other Hawks. *Thank you very much, Doctor.*

A mother, a father, and a doctor. Some guys are lucky enough to have one great person in their lives. I have three—must be my good Irish blood!

St. James and Saint Joseph's University had an astounding hardwood connection. Dudie Connors, Tom Brennan, Bob O'Neill, Dick Barr, Tom Wynne, Don DiJulia, Steve Courtin, Jack McKinney, Bill Lynch all came to Hawk Hill from St. James. If you consider a few other Chester ballplayers at Hawk Hill, Jameer Nelson and Dwayne Jones, I think we could field a nice Chester Hawks team. Jack Ramsay would coach and we could really win some games!

Getting the Coaching Bug

My college playing career is detailed in a later chapter on the Jack Ramsay Years at Saint Joseph's University.

After college, I coached at St. James High for a couple of years until Coach Ramsay offered me the job of assistant varsity basketball coach, freshman basketball coach, and assistant athletic director at St. Joe's. After pondering the offer as long and hard as a human being can in two and a half seconds, I accepted. I was 24 at the time—the youngest ever to hold an assistant AD position in the Big Five.

My most memorable year as freshman coach was in 1964. My squad of Clifford Anderson, Bob Brenner, Steve Donches, Vince Curran, and Al Grundy went 15-1. What a ride!

After a few years with the Hawks, I accepted the job of head basketball coach at Philadelphia Textile in 1965. Herb Magee was my assistant. We made the Eastern Regional NCAA College Division playoffs that year and finished the season 22-6.

Meanwhile, over at Hawk Hill, Coach Ramsay developed a retinal problem that forced him to step down as coach. He asked if I would like to succeed him. This time I mulled the question over for a full one and one-half seconds (my generation doesn't do nanoseconds) pinched myself, and said yes. Wow! Jack McKinney—head coach of the Saint Joseph's Hawks!

From Hawk Hill Onward

My days at Hawk Hill were among the best years of my life. You'll read about them in the "Jack McKinney Years" chapter. When I left St. Joe's, I started job hunting, interviewing for positions outside basketball. During that time, I was asked to speak at a basketball clinic at Kutchers, a popular upstate New York resort. Hubie Brown, the assistant coach of the Milwaukee Bucks, was also working at the clinic. When I told Hubie what had happened to me, he said, "Damn, you lose a good job and I get a great one! Crazy racket, isn't it?" It wasn't yet public, but Hubie was taking the head coaching job for the Kentucky Colonels of the ABA. Hubie continued, "Hey, maybe you'll be able to take my job with the Bucks! I'll call Larry Costello [Bucks' head coach] tonight and tell him you're interested."

Next morning I was off to Philly bright and early. When I got home, Claire greeted me saying that I was to call Larry Costello. I did, and two days later, I found myself on a plane to Milwaukee. Larry picked me up at the airport. We talked in the car on the way to his office. We stopped, had lunch, and I was ready to fly home again—as the just-appointed Milwaukee Bucks assistant coach. I thought, "The NBA doesn't fool around, do they?"

I started my NBA career in Milwaukee in the 1974-1975 season and stayed there two years. The Bucks had won an NBA championship back in 1971 with Kareem Abdul Jabbar and Oscar Robertson. Oscar had

Jack McKinney on the sideline as the Indiana Pacers' coach. *Photo courtesy of Jack McKinney*

retired by the time I arrived, but Kareem was in his prime, and we had a fine array of talent. Bob Dandridge was our finest. Super-shooter John McLaughlin complemented him well. The rest of the squad consisted of Jim Price, George Thompson, rookie Gary Brokew, big Kevin Restini, and even bigger Cornell Warner. Kareem missed most of the season with a broken hand. After a botched play around the basket, he punched the padding on the standards that support the backboard. He never recovered, and neither did we.

Before the 1975-1976 season, Kareem was traded to the Lakers for Junior Bridgeman, Brian Winters, and David Meyer—three quality players, but they didn't equal one Kareem.

I made a smooth transition from college to the NBA. The most startling difference was the number of plays the pros ran, at least on the Bucks. Actually, with a little experience, I discovered the Bucks' big playbook was not the NBA norm, just a Larry Costello thing. Larry wanted a new play every game. That may be somewhat an exaggeration, but my playbook that season stopped at number 73!

After my second year in Milwaukee, Jack Ramsay called me again (is there a pattern here?). He had just accepted the head coaching job with the Portland Trailblazers. Jack asked me to be his assistant. After a half-second of reflection, I accepted (is there a pattern here?).

Off to Portland

I moved the McKinney clan to the great Northwest and situated our kids in new schools (thank God for moms). Then Doctor Ramsay and I began strategizing for the upcoming season.

Despite the presence of Bill Walton, the Trailblazers never reached the NBA playoffs. Under Jack Ramsay, that changed. The Trailblazers kept improving all season and peaked near the playoffs. We scrapped our way through the competition in the west and beat the Lakers. That earned us the right to take on the Philadelphia 76ers.

What a homecoming! The Sixers featured Julius Erving, George McGinnis, Doug Collins, and Lloyd Free. Egged on by that Philly crowd (not literally, I'm happy to say), the hometowners jumped out to a two-game lead. We came back to Portland to a huge cheering throng at the airport. Driving to practice the next day, Jack Ramsay said to me, "We'll win this thing, and we're not changing a thing. We got here playing our game. We just have to play our game better." He told the team the same thing that day. Four games later, we were world champs—the highlight of my pro career.

Next season, we were the kingpins, and we played like it. We were 60-10 when fate dealt a disastrous blow. Bill Walton went down with a foot injury, and our hopes of a Portland dynasty vanished. That injury hobbled Bill the rest of his career. He never regained his form. We were a so-so team for the next three years and never mustered enough firepower to compensate for the loss of one of the greatest players I ever coached, Bill Walton. I say one of the greatest, because I'd be hard pressed to choose between Walton, Kareem, and Magic Johnson.

After the 1978-1979 season, Laker GM Bill Sharman contacted me in Maggiore, Italy, where I was running a clinic with Allesandro Gamba, the Italian National Coach. He said Laker owner Jerry Buss wanted to talk with me on Friday, so Friday I was flying into Los Angeles to meet with Jerry Buss. I walked out of our meeting as the new Laker coach.

I brought Paul Westhead onboard as my assistant. Paul was a friend and my former assistant at St. Joe's. Paul was La Salle's head coach at the time (he also replaced me in Italy when I jetted out of Maggiore).

As for the Laker job. ... It doesn't get much better. Kareem was center. The frontcourt was Jamal Wilkes and Jimmy Chones. The backcourt was Norm Nixon and Magic Johnson. Kareem, Jamal, and Norm Nixon had all made the previous year's All-Star squad.

Bringing out the Magic

Two weeks into training camp, I sat Magic down and asked him, "Magic, how do you feel about your performance?" In his usual cheery way, he said, "Coach, I'm starting to feel real good. My shot is coming around, and I feel good running the break, and I feel like I'm starting to flow. What do you think, Coach?" I frowned and answered, "Actually I'm disappointed. When we drafted you, I thought you'd take charge and direct the show." Magic said, "Coach, I couldn't tell Kareem, Jamal, and Norm what to do. These guys are All-Pros."

I countered, "Magic, somebody has to do it. Just yesterday after practice, Kareem said to me, 'Coach, when is that young buck gonna take over like you said he would?'" Magic's eyes widened, "Kareem said that?!" I said, "Yep, just yesterday." Magic said solemnly, "Well if Kareem said that, then I better do it."

The fact that Kareem had never so much as mentioned Magic or Magic's role, falls under the category, "Coach's prerogative."

I stretched the truth a little, but you can't dispute the results.

An Abrupt End to a Season

We started the season hot. Magic was improving daily at point guard, and we were riding high at 10-4 when we came back to LA for a home game.

We had landed at two a.m., so I slept in the next morning as much as I could. At nine o'clock, Paul Westhead woke me up. "Hey Action (my nickname was 'Action Jackson,' after the hero in a movie out at the time … don't ask)," Paul said, "I'm going to reserve the tennis courts for 10 o'clock." I said OK, showered and gulped down a cup of coffee. Claire had the car, so I grabbed my son's bike and peddled to the courts, about half a mile away. I never made it to the courts.

En route, the back gear on the bike froze and I was flipped over the handlebars. I landed on my head in the street and slid down the incline on my face. I was ambulanced to the hospital and placed on the critical list with a brain injury. I spent the next three weeks in a coma. My faithful wife stayed at my bedside the entire time, beating on my chest from time to time trying to keep me from sinking deeper into the coma. She returned home only to sleep. Our daughters flew in from college, Susan from the University of Wisconsin and Ann from Oregon State. Claire's sister Ann flew in from Pennsylvania to look after our teenage sons, John and Dennis.

A Day of Thanksgiving

When Claire walked into my room early on Thanksgiving Day morning, she didn't expect to see her husband propped up in bed reading an old newspaper. The old newspaper contained the account of my accident. Claire purposely left it by my bedside just in case. After a hello kiss, I said, "Is this me they're talking about?" I had no recollection. I still don't.

She told me it was Thanksgiving Day. Indeed it was. It was the best Thanksgiving Day I had ever had or would ever have.

The following week my broken elbow was set with a rod, and I had plastic surgery on my face. Then for the first time in more than a month, I went home. I spent the next four months in therapy, relearning how to walk and talk and think and—most importantly—how to smile and laugh. My recovery was more than a marvel of modern medicine and faith. It was a marvel of the triumph of wifely love and faith. I thank God and I thank Claire for my life.

The Aftermath

I had a long, slow recovery—during which I lost my Laker head coaching job. When that door closed, another one opened. The Indiana Pacers called, and I landed the job of head coach there.

The club made the playoffs for the first time in the franchise's history and I ended up winning the NBA Coach of the Year. I spent three more years in Indiana, a period that saw our talent erode drastically. We started losing, and after four years, I was out looking for a job.

I found one with the Kansas City Kings. The team had already announced their plans to move to Sacramento after the season. My heart wasn't really in KC, and after one month I turned in my coach's whistle. I think I left the profession prematurely, but I did feel more relaxed afterwards.

Post NBA

After resigning my coaching post at KC, I figured I'd take a year off and sort of loosen up mentally. I was sure I could land an assistant coaching slot somewhere in the league. But it didn't happen, so I turned my focus to the business world, the "real" world. I found a terrific company, Ampro Sports in Delaware County, Pennsylvania. Gary Huddell, one of the company's three founders, placed me in charge of supplying Philly's professional teams with their sportswear. The Sixers, Phillies, Eagles, and Flyers were my accounts. I also supplied most of the local colleges, including my alma mater.

I managed to keep my hand in basketball. In 1993, PRISM cable network inked me as their colorman for 76ers games. It was a fine job while it lasted. Unfortunately, the Sixers had a dismal season that caused them to sweep their house clean. They replaced everyone starting with the coach and extending to the broadcast team. Mark Zumoff and Steve Mix, were brought in and have handled the assignment ever since.

Fortunately I didn't quit the day job. I stayed with Ampro for 13 years. Gary Huddell was kind enough to allow me to continue accepting invitations to run overseas clinics. I ran clinics or coached in 17 different countries. My wife was with me on every trip but two—to Brazil and Lebanon (don't ask).

I did some of the camps/clinics (Brazil, Canada, Jamaica, Mexico, Portugal, Puerto Rico, Israel) as the sole U.S. coach on the staff. On other occasions, I teamed with other U.S. coaches like Jack Ramsay in

al times to Connie Mack Stadium to see the likes of Bob Feller, Ted
, Stan Musial, and Joe DiMaggio.

rove up to NYC for Babe Ruth's viewing at Yankee Stadium.
ht we went to the movies to see *The Babe Ruth Story* starring
Bendix as the Babe. The next day we went to St. Patrick's
l to watch the funeral procession. St. Pat's was sealed off to the
s of fans who circled the block. Never one to step back, Captain
d a very Irish-looking police sergeant, flashed his badge and
armest Irish smile told the sergeant how he had driven his son
y to New York from Chester, Pennsylvania, to see Babe Ruth.
Blarney Stone that my dad once kissed must have worked. The
eant took us in hand, walked us across the street, and the next
w I was standing in the back of St. Patrick's cathedral next to
pallbearers, William Bendix and Thomas E. Dewey.
th was filled with those kinds of special memories—wonderful
a wonderful father.

dult, I relished the opportunity to show my appreciation for
one. I took him to the Kentucky Derby and the Indy 500. I
to the Olympics in L.A. and the NBA championship game.
happiest moment was in Italy. I met my dad in Rome after
amps was done. Dad was then 83 and had lived alone since
passed away. He had successfully navigated from the airport
and was seated comfortably in the lobby when I arrived.
great week together. The highlight was an audience with
Paul II. We were among a throng of about 10,000
faithful as Il Papa said the Angelus. My dad was in awe. In
minute period, he probably blessed himself 17 times. All he
back home was "our audience with the Pope." After he and
ded that summer, Dad never complained that the Pope
to his Christmas card list.

Growing up with Father

n McKinney de Ortega, daughter of Jack McKinney

a kid, I wanted my father to come home from work in
a hat, like a proper dad, like Mr. O'Neill next door. I'd
oking fit and handsome as he pulled into the driveway at
day. Then he'd swing out of the driver's seat wearing
whistle. "He's a basketball coach," I'd explain to gaping
ids.

Denmark, Hubie Brown in Turkey, Billy Cunningham and Kevin
Loughery in Ireland, and the University of Delaware's Dan Peterson.

Like Taking Flowers from an Old Lady

While I worked the clinics overseas, Claire explored. She was always
curious to learn about every locale and the people.

Once we were in a small town in Sicily that reminded us of Sea Isle
City, New Jersey, with its promenade and the beach and sea beyond.

Claire was strolling along this scenic promenade. She was approached
by a woman clad in black carrying a large bouquet of flowers in her
outstretched arms. She was chanting and moaning and appeared
disconsolate and destitute. Claire pressed some liras into her hand and
took one of the flowers.

Immediately, the woman's moaning and shouting got louder and
more hysterical. Claire hurried away, puzzled and a bit frightened by the
woman's behavior.

That night at the game Claire related the incident to our interpreter.
He informed her that the lady was "keening," that is, grieving the loss of
a loved one. The flowers represented her memories. When Claire took her
flower she symbolically stole a memory of her deceased love one. Oops!

Topping off the Trip

My son John was a basketball player. When he was a college freshman,
he helped me with one of my clinics in Italy. We were staying at the
Grande Hotel, a spot that attracted Europe's beautiful people like Sophia
Loren because of its famous hot spring baths.

John and I weren't familiar with Italian customs at the time, not that
it would have mattered in this case, But you be the judge.

One of their customs was the siesta. Italians stay out of the sun from
noon until three. Everything shuts down, so John and I decided to use
siesta time to catch up on our reading. We headed down the hill to a
crystal clear swimming pool for a little peace and quiet.

We were relaxing on our lounge chairs when three very attractive
ladies got up from their chairs and converted their two-piece bathing
suits into one-piecers by removing their tops.

They dropped their top pieces into the chairs next to us and slid into
the pool. Meanwhile, two more lady swimmers went through the same
routine on the far side of the pool.

As the topless quintet floated by us on their backs for the umpteenth time, John leaned over and said, "Dad, I don't think you realize it, but that book you are reading is upside down."

Smart aleck college kid!

I Can't Swim

One of the finer perks of the NBA offseason for coaches was a little vacation jaunt arranged by Nike. Since I was a member of the Nike NBA Coaches Team, I had the pleasure of being part of the contingent each year.

One year we went to a vacation resort on the Sun River in Oregon where one of the big activities was a white-water rafting escapade. After a little familiarization course, we eased into our rafts. I was in Raft #1 with

Jack McKinney and Nike's Phil Knight lead their raft into the Class IV rapids.
Photo courtesy of Jack McKinney

Claire, coach Cotton Fitzsimmons from Kansas and Phil Knight along with his wife, Penny, founder and president of Nike. Raft No. 2 inc Phoenix Suns, his wife, Carol, and Coach Al his two daughters.

The "franchise player" in each raft, howev got us through the Class IV rapids. We got a hill where we could watch Raft No. 2 plus We could see right away they were overma dipped and next thing we knew, it flipped into the drink. Well, that's what we thou passed and each head bobbed up to the su back over right side up. To our amazement That was good news for his raft-mates. toughest players in the NBA. Al once down when Wilt tried to play peacemak Stilt, "Don't come any closer, Wilt, or opted for discretion as the better part of

Al lifted everyone into the raft one b gathered, the battered rafters floated ov Al, the hero of the moment. I yelled, raft?" Al looked at me and mumbled raft. I can't swim!"

We found out later that day that flipped over about a month earlier a

Travels v

I had a wonderful relationship lifelong love of sport. He was alwa took me to Shibe Park for the 19 Eagles won over the Chicago Cardi for 98 yards and the Birds won 7-0 *did* win some championships—ar Philadelphia Arena to see the Pl George Senesky. We saw Rocky heavyweight championship of t flashed two tickets to the *fifth* fans, we never got to use them. T

---

me seve
William
We
That nig
William
Cathedra
thousand
Paul four
with his
all the wa
Well the
police serg
thing I kn
two of the

My you
times with

As an a
all he had
treated him

But my
one of my
my mom ha
to the hotel

We had
Pope John
genuflecting
that brief 15-
talked about
the Pope bo
didn't add hir

by Sus

When I wa
an overcoat an
see my father l
the end of the
sneakers and a
neighborhood l

Being a basketball coach meant my father often worked on Saturday nights. It meant my mom would shuttle the kids off to McDonald's so Dad could crash out on the couch after a strenuous loss—make that *a* loss, any loss. All losses were strenuous. It also meant he took us to places like Puerto Rico in the summer and New York City and Hawaii in the winter for things called tournaments.

I was just enjoying the ride. I only knew two things about the place where he worked. One, there was a big hardwood floor for me to run around on, and two, there was a man-sized bird costume in his office closet. In my personal life, the first identification I had with my Dad's place of employment, Saint Joseph's College, came when I went to school. That's when I realized St. Joe's had enemies. "The Hawk is dead!" fellow students would yell at me. Most of the yelling came from the have-nots, the ones whose parents had gone to La Salle, or worse, Villanova. "The Hawk Will Never Die!" I yelled back, calling them the names under my breath that I wasn't supposed to say out loud. I didn't understand the word "rivalry," but I did have a feeling that the Hawk was something worth dying for.

Of course, not everybody wanted the Hawk dead. In first grade, when St. Joe's beat Villanova, Sister Virgo called me to the front of the room and told me the whole class was proud of my father. She licked a gold star and pasted it on my collar. Most likely she didn't see Michael Curley making a slicing motion across his neck at me while I was being honored.

Being the Hawk coach's kid entailed more than standing up for the honor of Saint Joe's. It meant that while other kids were home in their pajamas on Saturday nights, I was cavorting around the most glamorous place on earth—the Palestra. My dad joked with Yoyo (a rabid fan who attended every Big Five game) before the games. My mother let us eat lots of hot dogs and Cokes and some loud guy named Sam the Drummer made all the noise we wished my mom and dad would let us make. In my early years, I spent the games rolling the crepe paper the Booster Club threw back up. Then as I got older, I realized I was seeing some of the finest basketball the country had to offer. My dad and his Hawks would go up against big-name schools that they weren't supposed to beat. But they did. Afterwards my dad would act like the game went just the way he expected it to go.

Being the coach's daughter had other privileges too. I got to leave school early once because I had to go to a pre-Villanova game pep rally at the Saint Joseph's Fieldhouse.

For a time, I thought every kid's father won awards and was invited to speak at banquets. I went to some of those banquets with my father, until I knew his speeches by heart: the jokes ("I better let so-and-so get up here before his jacket goes out of style") and the themes ("Drive, Determination and Desire"). My sister and I would mouth those three Ds to each other while my dad was saying them and we were squirming in our seats.

By and by his words sunk in.

By the time I was in college, I'd long since realized how cool it was to have a basketball coach for a father. In 1977 when I was a freshman in college, my mother, sister and I rode with Dad in the NBA championship victory parade through downtown Portland. He wore hip, long sideburns, and I got to wave like a Miss America contestant. Frenzied people waved their arms and threw roses at us as if we were rock stars.

By the time I got out of college, I had long since realized that not everybody's father got his name in the newspaper several times a week. And I started pursuing my own dream—a dream I eventually achieved. I became a TV news reporter. I wondered if admiration for my dad as I was growing up motivated me to seek a job that put me in the public eye. I wondered if I landed my job because his "Drive, Determination and Desire" speech played on continuous loop in my subconscious. I wondered if it was because he taught me to have the same faith in myself that he taught his beloved Hawks to have in themselves.

Nowadays, my father brings a lifetime of positive thinking and optimism to his role as my family's number-one fan. He cheers my girls on as they ride their horse in competitions and reminds me he has faith that I will publish my book.

"You never say die, do you, dad?" I ask him.

"It's a Hawk thing," he says."

CHAPTER THREE

The Bill Ferguson Years

The Hawks Before Fergy

O K. So basketball didn't get off to a jackrabbit start at Saint Joseph's. The cagers lost their first official game 19-5 on December 10, 1909, to Catholic High. Before any naysayers (or California Governators) start taunting them as girly men, in basketball's halcyon era, it was not unusual for a college team to play a high school. A week later, the Hawks lost again, this time to LaSalle. That would be the Big Explorers, not the Little ones (for anyone still snickering). In this game, the St. Joe's squad managed to whittle the margin of defeat down to four points (LaSalle 22-St. Joe's 18). They were poised for their first victory in their next contest—a 31-13 shellacking of Mount St. Mary's. The Mount started Saint Joseph's College on a course that would lead them to 1,410 victories and counting by season's end 2005.

The Crimson and Gray, as the St. Joseph's quintet was called in pre-Hawk years, finished the season with a 10-6 record—all in all, not too shabby a start for a 96-year trek—and counting. But let's return for the moment to those thrilling days of yesteryear—more specifically to St. Joe's maiden season, just in case any Explorer fans might be gloating or snickering. St. Joe's avenged its loss to LaSalle that year not once, but twice. On the other hand, St. Joe's failed to overtake mighty (the evidence seems to indicate) Catholic High in two subsequent battles. A student—player-coach-student John Dever, Class of 1910—started the long line of St. Joe's coaches.

After the promise of its inaugural season, St. Joe's bball slipped a bit. They managed only a 6-6 log in season number two playing mostly local clubs and schools. Their farthest trek took them to Bethlehem. The star of Bethlehem that night was Bethlehem Prep who trounced them 58-11. That 47-point deficit represents the largest margin of defeat a St. Joe's basketball squad ever suffered, although the official record is the 44-point whupping Oscar Robertson and Cincinnati laid on the Hawks on December 11, 1959.

Edward Bennis, a 1906 Penn grad, took over for Coach Dever in year two. In the Hawks' 96-year history, Bennis is one of only three coaches who was not himself a St. Joe's graduate.

Forgettable Seasons and an Upsurge

St. Joe's third season, 1911-1912, turned out to be its worst basketball season ever. Under rookie coach John Donahue (class of 1908), the team sank to a horrid 6-22 record (a .214 percentage, which is officially the worst winning percentage in Hawk history). That same squad set the all-time record for losses in a single season as well.

We did find a silver lining in that bleak season, at least for the glass-is-half-full contingent. That season, for the first time ever, St. Joe's managed to top old nemesis Catholic High. Catholic High, who had whipped the boys from Hawk Hill twice in both the 1910-1911 season, and the 1909-1910 season would never again beat St. Joe's.

As for Coach Donahue, despite the abominable season, he became the first St. Joe's coach to coach more than one season. He actually posted some decent numbers for his career. His winning percentage over an eight-year span was .600. That percentage places him sixth (out of 14) on the SJU coach's list of best all-time winning percentages. In fact, take away his 6-22 rookie season, and his winning percentage zooms up to .705, second on the list only to Jack Ramsay (.765).

Starting in his second year, Donahue strung together six straight winning seasons, including a sparkling 14-1 campaign in 1914-15. Saint Joseph's .933 winning percentage that season stood as the school's all-time best record till Jameer and his cronies shattered it in 2003-2004.

In Donahue's final season at the helm, he managed only a .500 record, three wins, three losses, in a program that was drastically cut back because of World War I. In 1920, the program started to pick up again. St. Joe's, headed by new coach John Lavin (class of 1915), boasted a 9-6 season that included a win in the first ever battle against Villanova. Of course, that contest wasn't yet an authentic Hawk–Wildcat tilt. Saint Joseph's was still the Crimson and Gray, while Villanova was the Blue and White. The Wildcats didn't adopt the Wildcat nickname till the thirties.

With the 1917-1918 campaign, the basketball schedule started to resemble the kind of schedule we see today. Most high school opponents had dropped off the schedule, replaced by rivals like Muhlenberg College and Lebanon Valley College, as well as several military teams competing during the war. By the time 1919-1920 rolled around, the schedule included St. John's, Seton Hall Hall, Fordham, Navy, Loyola-Maryland, and Drexel.

Unfortunately as these changes occurred, Coach Lavin could not sustain his first-year success. He had only one other season on the desirable side of the .500 line.

Tom Temple (class of 1921) replaced Lavin and remained but two seasons. Both years his teams managed identical 6-11 records.

The 1928-1929 season brought Bill Ferguson to Hawk Hill. Fergy was destined to remain the Hawks head coach for the next quarter-century. Fergy was the head honcho who would bring Saint Joseph's College its first national renown.

The Penn Grad Gets the Hawk Post

After Bill "Fergie" Ferguson graduated from the University of Pennsylvania in 1920, he returned to his high school alma mater, Roman Catholic High School in Philadelphia, to teach mathematics. Bill had been a star athlete in his student days at Roman Catholic. He starred in basketball in 1914, 1915, and 1916 and was elected captain of the team his senior year. He was also the starting catcher and captain of the baseball team for three years. Bill was also senior class president (class of 1916).

After he graduated high school, the Chicago White Sox gave him a tryout, but he opted to attend Penn rather than pursue major league baseball.

When Fergie returned to Roman Catholic, he served as assistant basketball coach to Billy Markward, who was then the dean of eastern basketball coaches.

In 1928, when Tom Temple left the post, Ferguson was appointed head coach of Saint Joseph's College. He performed double duty for seven years—coaching Saint Joseph's basketball and teaching math at Roman Catholic High. In 1935, he resigned from his teaching post at Roman

Catholic. Eventually he would join the faculty at Saint Joseph's Prep. He stayed on as basketball coach at Saint Joseph's College. In fact, he stayed longer than any other basketball coach before or since. Fergy was the man till 1953. During his 25-year tenure, his teams racked up the most wins under any Hawk coach. Ferguson's lifetime won-lost record is a sterling 311-208 for a .600 winning percentage.

Like most of his predecessors, Fergie's hoopsters didn't blow out of the starting gate. His first season was a losing one. St. Joseph's hobbled in at 8-10. He followed up with two successful seasons. His boys went 12-9 in 1929-1930 before shooting out to a glittery 16-5 in 1930-1931.

The Mighty Mites Hit the Scene

Fergie's fortunes dipped a bit after that 16-5 season. In 1931-1932, the Hawks posted an 8-10 record. But the news wasn't all bad. Phil Zuber became the first Saint Joseph's player ever selected to the All-America team. Nonetheless, the team suffered through three successive losing campaigns. Then one of the most popular college teams ever to hit Philly burst onto the scene. They were known as the Mighty Mites.

Some of the Hawk faithful claim that no other college team ever had a nickname. That's stretching it a bit. Clyde Drexler's Phi Slamma Jamma Houston Cougars might take issue. Nevertheless, not many college teams boast a nickname. The Mighty Mites earned their tag because of their diminutive stature in a sport that, even in those days, was stacked against the vertically challenged. The Mighty Mite quintet was comprised of Matt Guokas, John McMenamin, Dan Kenney, Jim Smale, John Kenney, along with sixth man Joe Oakes.

The Mites played together from 1934-1935 through 1937-1938, posting a 54-17 record. As sophomores in 1934-1935, the Mites finished at 12-3. Guokas led the team in scoring (145 points). McMenamin had the highest single-game score, tallying a city-high 21 points in a win over Ursinus. In their second year together, they dipped slightly to 14-5, but two of those losses occurred while Guokas was injured. In their junior year, they went 15-4. Highlights included a 46-44 upset of Clair Bee's nationally ranked Long Island team in double overtime. Dan Kenney's follow-up shot in the final minute turned out to be the game-winner. They also scratched out a 37-36 come-from-behind win over Penn in front of a record crowd of 10,682 at the Palestra. Sixth-man Oakes calmly sank two free throws for the decisive points with 19 seconds to play.

Coach Bill Ferguson talks to his players before a game. *Photo courtesy of Saint Joseph's University*

The Mighty Mites bowed out of the Philly hoops scene in the 1937-1938 season on a 13-5 mark. Matt Guokas Sr. was selected as an All-American—the second Hawk to be so honored. Their victories included upsets of national powers Mississippi State, Creighton, North Carolina, and Duquesne.

The Forties

After the Mighty Mites departed, the Hawk basketball program declined. But it was brief. The 1938-1939 team had a losing record. Fergy's boys rebounded the following season before rolling up six straight winning seasons. During that time, St. Joe's produced its first bona fide national star, George Senesky.

Senesky played from 1940-1941 through 1942-1943. In his senior year, the Mahonoy City native averaged 23.4 ppg in leading his team to an 18-4 season. Senesky's heroics that year set the standard for highest single-season scoring average till Cliff Anderson broke it in the 1960s.

Prior to his super season, no St. Joe's player had ever put up numbers anywhere near Senesky's—nor would many subsequent Hawks. Senesky was a pioneer in a new era of basketball when the game started to take on more of the look of the game we see today.

One of Senesky's teammates, Jack Kraft, went on to local and national acclaim. Kraft performed on the Saint Joseph's hardwoods from 1940-1942. Later he became head mentor of the Villanova Wildcats and guided his charges to 11 consecutive postseason tournament berths. Kraft's Wildcats narrowly missed a national title in 1971 when they lost to UCLA.

After Senesky graduated in 1943, Jack Flannery (12.2 ppg) led the team to an 18-7 record. By the end of the decade, another Senesky—George's brother Paul—carried the team. Paul averaged 21 ppg in his junior year (1948-1949) and 22.8 ppg in his senior year (1949-1950). Like his brother before him, Paul Senesky teamed with a guy destined for national acclaim as a coach. The guy was Jack Ramsay, who averaged 11.2 ppg in 1947-1948 as a junior and 8.8 ppg as a senior when he captained the squad.

Alumni Memorial Fieldhouse

The Fieldhouse is the 3,200-seat, on-campus home of the Hawks, named in honor of the Saint Joseph's University graduates who lost their lives in World War II. The building was dedicated during Fergie's watch, on November 11, 1949. Two weeks later, the Hawks' new arena had an inauspicious christening as Rhode Island whipped the Hawks 62-46.

Johnny Hughes, who cavorted on the Hawk hardwoods from 1948-1952 recalls the night the Fieldhouse was christened: "With all the great basketball that place has hosted all these years, I'm thrilled to have had the honor of playing in the first game, although at the time, I was more surprised than honored. I had no idea I was going to be a starter till minutes before the game. Fergie never said a word. I hadn't practiced with the first string the whole week. When I finally found out I was starting, I was super nervous, because I knew how historic this game was."

The Hawks followed up that initial Fieldhouse setback with 23 consecutive victories. Since then, the Hawks have amassed a gaudy 292-71 record (80.4 percent) on Hawk Hill. They've had some spectacular runs along the way. They closed out the 1950s and rode into the 1960s

Eddie Garrity pumps away one of his patented jumpers against Westminster in 1952.
Photo courtesy of Saint Joseph's University

to complete a 34-game winning streak. In 55 seasons of competition at the Fieldhouse, the Hawks have suffered but two losing seasons there.

The facility was rehabbed, modernized, and spruced up from 1987 through 1991. New lower-level seating and scoreboards were added. A new roof and windows were installed. A new, more forgiving playing surface was laid. The lobby was overhauled, and new media and laundry facilities were constructed (the two are unrelated—the media doesn't do their laundry there, at least not as far as anyone knows). The locker room was spruced up and rebuilt as well.

As Johnny Hughes contends, the Fieldhouse has witnessed many historical basketball moments—starting way back on February 4, 1953, when Ed Garrity canned 40 points against Rhode Island, setting the single-game Fieldhouse scoring record that still stands. His 16 field goals that evening are still a Fieldhouse record. In fact Garrity's record for points and field goals are the longest-standing Fieldhouse records.

Fergie's Farewell

The decade of the 1950s limped in undramatically for the Hawks. They eked out a mediocre 13-14 record in the 1950-1951 season. The next season, however, they busted out of the doldrums by celebrating their first 20-win season ever. Led by Johnny Hughes, who averaged 15.5 ppg, they ended at 20-7. John Doogan was a close second in scoring with 14.4 ppg. The Hawks received their first invitation to a postseason tournament. They played in the National Catholic Invitational Tournament at Rensselaer Polytechnic in Troy, New York. They dropped a 65-56 decision to a fine St. Francis of Pennsylvania team led by the legendary Maurice Stokes.

The NCIT

Johnny Hughes played for the Hawks from 1948 through 1952. A mainstay on the Hawks' first ever tournament team, Hughes recalls that the tournament bid came as a disappointment.

"We lost to Temple at Convention Hall that year. We came back and beat them a week or so later, but it didn't matter. We had already lost our invitation to the NIT and NCAA, even though we had such a good year. I remember we lost to St. John's by only two points, and they were ranked number eight. We also split a pair of games with LaSalle, who was ranked number 13.

"We were disappointed, but I suppose the disappointment was lessened at least a bit when we got that invitation to the first—and I believe only—NCIT (National Catholic Invitational Tournament). Then we went up to Troy New York against a great player, Maurice Stokes, and lost anyway."

The following season, 1952-1953, was to be Fergie's final season as the Hawks' head coach. He bowed out with a 14-11 season.

Ferguson had coached Saint Joseph's College from 1928-1929 through 1952-1953 amassing a record of 309-208. His 309 wins remain an SJU record.

Fergie Frugality

David Dorsey, Class of 1954, tells how Fergie could stretch a buck, or squeeze a nickel till the buffalo did what buffaloes do when you put the squeeze on them. David Dorsey: "I was friends with Ed Garrity. Ed tells about the time he showed up for a game at Convention Hall only to discover he had forgotten his sneakers. Fergie metered out exact change for the bus. These were the days before you needed exact change. Fergie was just being frugal. He gave Ed exactly enough cash to get home and back. He told Ed to go home, grab his sneakers, and get back—and do it fast!"

Small Time

Ed Garrity, Class of 1953, recalls an era when Hawks' basketball was truly small-time (it was also a time when the world was less politically correct).

"Harry Weinmann, our team manager in 1952, was a midget. We used to stuff a load of basketballs in a couple of huge bags. Before the game we would open the bags at center court, let the balls loose, and start lay-up practice. One time I hauled the bags out to center court. I didn't know it, but Harry was hiding inside. When I opened the bag at center court, here comes Harry rolling out onto center court along with five basketballs. It's tough to surprise a Palestra crowd, but I think that little maneuver did."

World's Longest Home Run

Phil Martelli, Jack McKinney, Jack Ramsay—eat your hearts out. Sure, that trio coached the likes of Jameer Nelson, Mike Bantom, Cliff Anderson, and Matt Goukas. But former St. Joe's coach Bill Ferguson not only coached some of the Hawks' all-time greats like the Seneskys— Fergie also coached the Babe.

Jack Lister (1951): "Fergie was a good catcher in baseball. He played for Ascension Parish in the city. The pastor at Ascension was a good friend of Connie Mack, the Philadelphia Athletics' legendary manager. Ascension's baseball diamond was in bad shape, so the parish came up with a fund-raising idea to fix it. The parish asked Connie Mack if he would try to convince Babe Ruth to help out with a fundraiser. They planned to haul the Babe out to the Ascension field for an exhibition.

Ruth agreed he'd do it, so some of the parishioners drove down to Shibe Park (later called Connie Mack Stadium) after a Yankees-A's game and motored the Babe back out to Ascension's Field

"Hundreds of people showed up. The Babe donned an Ascension uniform. Fergie was the Ascension manager so he managed the Babe that day—if anyone was capable of managing the Babe. The first time Babe came to bat, he smacked a ball so far it cleared the field and bounced in the street beyond the field and into an open boxcar that was headed for New York City. We figure that had to be the longest home run ever hit. The ball traveled from Ascension's field all the way up to New York!"

CHAPTER FOUR

George Senesky

Note to the reader: Starting with this chapter, for clarification Jack McKinney's voice appears in a different typeface than co-author Robert Gordon.

The Mahonoy City Brothers

Before the 1940s, Saint Joseph's College didn't mine much turf outside of Philly when they looked for basketball talent. Locally grown hoopsters competed so well with the national powers that the provincial recruiting program didn't need much enhancement. When St. Joe's finally did peer out beyond the shadow of the Quaker City, the first out-of-towner they spotted became a sensation and one of the finest players in the school's history. What's more, St. Joe's bagged a two-fer in the process. The star had a little brother at home who was almost as good as he.

The prize out-of-towner was George Senesky who hailed from the coal-mining region of Mahonoy City in "upstate Pennsylvania." "Upstate" is the catchall term Philadelphians use for the Pocono Mountain region specifically and for practically any other spot in the rest of the state less specifically.

Senesky arrived on Hawk Hill in the wake of the Mighty Mites. The year after the Mighty Mites left town, the Hawks let down and slipped to 9-12. They closed each of the following three seasons with identical .666 winning percentages. The 1941-1942 season saw the unveiling of a major star, George Senesky, who averaged a sparkly (for the era) 12.8 points per contest. That was a good season, but it gave no hint of the monster year that was to follow.

In his senior year, George busted out to become the nation's top scorer—a feat no Hawk before or since has matched. Senesky averaged a (then) record-setting 23.4 points per game while netting a (then) record-setting 515 points for the year.

George's senior year exploits set the bar at St. Joseph's for decades to come. His mark for points in a season didn't last as long, but it did stay in the family. His brother Paul shattered that mark in 1949-1950 with 570 points. Paul needed 25 games to do it, however. George had played only 22 to set the record. The record stayed in the Senesky family till 1964 when Steve Courtin bagged it with a 579-point season. More than five decades later, Paul still ranks seventh on the Hawks' all-time single-season scoring list. Brother George is knotted with Mike Hauer at 23rd.

George Senesky, All-American

George Senesky set a new school record for points in a game when he poured in 44 against Rutgers-Newark on February 3, 1944. His 19 field goals that evening remains the SJU record for most field goals in a game.

For such exploits George Senesky was selected All-America in 1943—the second Hawk ever chosen for the All-America squad. He received the prestigious Helms Foundation Player of the Year Award that same year. He remains the *only* Saint Joseph's University player who ever led the nation in scoring.

George Senesky was 6'2". That was a decent size at the time, but not unheard of. He was a deadly outside shooter. Statistically, he represented a bigger part of his club's scoring arsenal than any other Hawk in history. Consider this: George's 515 points accounted for a whopping 41.6 percent *of all the points the Hawks scored that season.* No one ever came close to that—and likely never will (although Marvin O'Connor had his miraculous minute that you'll read about later). Senesky's junior year wasn't too shabby, either. George bucketed 217 points for 22.8 percent of his team's offense.

Professional Success

George moved up to success in the professional ranks as well, although more as a coach than as a player. The Philadelphia Warriors of the old Basketball Association of America, forerunner of the present

National Basketball Association, signed George in 1946. He played eight years for the Warriors, tallying 3,455 points for an average of 7.2 points a game. His best season was 1951 when he averaged 10.4 points a game. He averaged a respectable 9.0 ppg in 49-50 and 8.3 ppg in 1950-1951.

His most successful professional season was his rookie year. George was a starter for the newly formed Philadelphia Warriors. Angelo Musi, Howie Dallmar, Ralph Kaplowitz, and Joe Fulks completed the quintet. George averaged 6.3 points a game with that quintet. The big news, however, was that his team won the first NBA championship ever played.

The Hawks' Most Successful NBA Head Coach

Seven Saint Joseph's alumni have gone on to coach in the NBA. The latest, of course, is the former Philadelphia 76ers head coach, Jim O'Brien. His predecessors include George Senesky, Jack Ramsay, Jack McKinney, Matt Guokas Jr., Paul Westhead, and Jimmy Lynam.

George Senesky was the first to enter the professional coaching ranks, and in terms of winning percentage, he remains the most successful, although Jim O'Brien, despite his premature departure from Philly, is keeping pace with him, so stay tuned.

Senesky's career .551 winning percentage edges out runner-up Jack Ramsay's 525.

An Explorer Leads The Way

George Senesky replaced Hall of Fame coach Eddie Gottlieb, a cigar-chomping, Damon Runyanesque character, as the skipper of the 1955-1956 Philadelphia Warriors. George played on Gottlieb's final Warrior team in 1954-1955. That season was also Senesky's swan song as a player. He saw limited action and averaged only 1.9 points a game.

George inherited a last-place team, despite boasting the league's top two scorers. Neil Johnston averaged 22.7 points, and teammate (Villanovan) Paul Arizin averaged 21.0, but the best the team could do was a 33-39 log.

Senesky broke his charges out of the gate fast as they rocketed to a 12-4 start. The Warriors finished 45-27 and went on to beat their longtime nemesis, the Syracuse Nationals (who later became the Philadelphia 76ers) in the playoffs. They steamrolled the Fort Wayne (later Detroit) Pistons four games to one to cop the championship.

Senesky kept a local stamp on the Philadelphia Warriors. In the 1955 draft, three of the top five draftees were Big Fivers: Tom Gola of LaSalle, and Bob Shafer and Jack Devine from Villanova. George always credited rookie Tom Gola for Philadelphia's turnaround from worst to first. Gola averaged 9.1 rebounds and 5.9 assists per game and supplied the missing links that unchained the club the previous year. So when the new champ was crowned (and there have only been *two* NBA champions since), the coach was a Hawk, the big scorer was a Wildcat (Arizin), and the floor leader was an Explorer (Gola).

Senesky coached only two more seasons. In 1956-1957, the Warriors barely made the playoffs before Syracuse eliminated them. In 1957-1958, they got by the pesky Nats and into the playoffs, only to get trounced four games to one by the Celts. The following year, Senesky was gone. Al Cervi took the reins, and the Warriors returned to the basement.

As Saint Joseph's University Athletic Director Don DiJulia sums up, "George Senesky is the only guy who ever won college basketball's MVP Award, graduated number one in his class, and was the class valedictorian. I guess you can throw in coaching an NBA champion, although we have Hawks who can say that. We still present the George Senesky Award yearly to the basketball player with the best academic record."

George Senesky died on June 26, 2001, in Sea Isle City, New Jersey at the age of 78.

Brother Paul

COACH McKINNEY:

George's brother Paul enjoyed a career that rivaled his brother's. Unfortunately Paul played on some so-so teams that diminished his legacy. In his junior year, St. Joe's barely eked out a .500 season, finishing at 12-11. Paul Senesky's statistics were anything but so-so. He averaged 21.0 ppg. In his senior year, though the team faded to 10-15, Senesky scintillated with a 22.8 per-game average.

Those accomplishments put Paul Senesky in a unique—and exalted—place in the annals of St. Joe's hoops. Paul is the only Hawk ever to average more than 20 points a game in a season twice. His senior year average of 22.8 ranks third on the school's all-time list, right behind brother George. His 20.7 ppg career scoring average tops the SJU all-time list.

Paul ended up trailing his brother into the SJU Basketball Hall of Fame. George was inducted in 1973, Paul in 1976. As of yet, Paul has not followed George into the Hawk Athletic Hall of Fame. George was accorded that honor in 1999, when he and Jack Ramsay were each inducted.

When Paul Senesky left Hawk Hill, he held the school's all-time career scoring record with 1,471 points over 72 games. Currently he ranks 17th on that list. He averaged more points per game over the course of a career than any Hawk ever. The 570 points he bucketed in his senior year ranks ninth on the single-season scoring list. He is one of only a handful of Hawks ever to lead his team in scoring for three consecutive seasons.

Paul was the fourth-round selection of the Philadelphia Warriors in the 1950 draft, but he didn't latch on with the squad. He had to compete with a pretty impressive class. The Warriors nabbed Paul Arizin in the first round. Meanwhile the Celtics locked up two future Hall of Famers, Bob Cousy and Bill Sharman in their first two rounds.

CHAPTER FIVE

The Flap About the Hawk

The Hawk Will Never Die

T he Saint Joseph's community insists that no other college can match the intensity and complexity of the bond between its mascot, team, and student body. The three link in a trinity/unity that not even the Jesuits can fathom, and they handle trinity issues as a matter of profession. The Saint Joseph's Hawk bond might be mysterious, but one thing's for certain: if the Hawk ever *did* die, St. Joe's would follow.

Opponents know how much the costumed avian with the nonstop flap means to St. Joe's morale. Over the years, the opposition has tried everything to vanish the mascot. They've stolen the Hawk costume and intimidated, maimed, kidnapped, and outlawed the Hawk—all to no avail. None of their dastardly deeds work, because some opponents simply don't get it. The Hawk will never die.

The Birth of the Hawk

The year was 1929. Wall Street laid an egg that year—the very same year that Saint Joseph's College laid a Hawk egg at 54th and City Line Avenue. While Wall Street's egg scrambled off into history, Saint Joseph's egg hatched into something Saint Joseph's University considers immortal.

Here's how the Hawk hatched. Charlie Dunn, the yearbook editor at Saint Joseph's College, held a contest in 1929. He challenged the student body to come up with a symbol for the school. From the hundred or so submissions he received, Dunn narrowed the field down to two: a Hawk and a Grenadier. Hawk was chosen because the contest organizers felt the animal represented the fighting spirit of the school. Besides hawks were often seen circling above the campus (well sometimes seen ... occasionally seen ... OK, one student once swore that the bird he saw circling the Philly sky was a Hawk). The college occupies the highest promontory in the region.

The other finalist, "Grenadier," is the French word for a soldier who tosses grenades. Fortunately, grenadiers were not seen circling the campus, nor did anyone lob grenades at Barbelin Hall—dirt bombs yes, but not grenades.

The nickname "Hawk" won out. John Gallagher, 1931, was declared the winner. Gallagher caught on for the Saint Joseph's College baseball team. His prize for the winning submission was a sweater monogrammed with Saint Joseph's College.

The students of the era said "Hawk" was an appropriate nickname because it related to the "aerial attack which has made our football team famous." Not that famous, though. The football team flew the coop for good 10 years after the Hawk nickname was adopted.

Crimson and Gray

Prior to voting the nickname Hawk in, Saint Joseph's College was known as the Crimson and Gray. Lore has it that in the 1880s, a theologian, while delivering a speech to the student body, gazed down and saw a crimson and gray book, and decreed that the college would henceforth be known as the Crimson and Gray. Crimson and gray remain the school colors.

There is no truth to the rumor that, in the 1960s, there was a campus movement to change the colors to Crimson and Clover. That way, rather than chant, "The Hawk will never die" over and over, the fans could chant, "Crimson and clover, over and over, crimson and clover, over and over ..."

Animating the Hawk

The idea to animate the Hawk traces back to Jim Brennan during the 1954-1955 season. Brennan, an ex-marine and SJU cheerleader, at first envisioned a real live hawk. The Palestra didn't seem a very good habitat for a hawk. So he opted to costume a *homo sapiens*. Brennan spearheaded the effort to raise the staggering sum of $120 necessary to buy the first costume. That costume was made by designers at Philly's Trocadero. Old-line Philadelphians might remember the Troc (or claim that they do not if their wives are within earshot) as the burlesque theatre in center city. When Gypsy Rose Lee came to town, you could catch her act there.

Brennan debuted as the Hawk at a January 4, 1956 win over La Salle (69-56) at the Palestra. He continued the gig for the next three years. Since Brennan started the flap, 23 other SJU students have donned the feathers. The Hawk's string of basketball games, which started on January 4, 1956, remains unbroken. The mascot has *never missed a men's basketball game* on any continent.

The Hawk's stature over that stretch rose exponentially. The Hawk mascot is endowed with a scholarship these days. Jack Gallagher is the man behind that endowment. Jack is a Class of '63 grad and the son of the same John Gallagher who gave St. Joe's its Hawk nickname back in 1929. Jack himself was never the Hawk, but he felt the tradition and importance of the mascot merited an endowment.

That endowment validates the place the mascot occupies in the hearts of Hawk fans. There are 325 Division I men's basketball programs in the country. Allegedly the Hawk is the only program that provides its mascot with a full free-paid ride (or flight, as the case may be). Jack himself is a member of the Selection Committee that chooses the mascot.

Mascot Recognition

The Hawk is the most decorated mascot in the country. St. Joe's flapper has garnered numerous accolades. *Sports Illustrated, Street & Smith Basketball Yearbook* and *ESPN College Basketball Magazine* have all selected the Hawk as the nation's top mascot. *Eastern Basketball* tagged the Hawk as the Atlantic 10 Conference's best mascot. In January 2001, *The Sporting News* named The Hawk as the Nation's Best Mascot in its "Best of College Basketball" issue.

Speaking of tags, remember the original price tag of $120? That price has inflated to $10,000! The current costume is made of dried ostrich feathers.

At this point, the adventures and misadventures of the Hawk mascot within the Saint Joseph's University community have taken on the proportions of the Arthurian legend, although the latter might be more credible.

The following Hawk Tales recount a bit of the color, and maybe a pinch of the off-color lore of St. Joe's renowned Hawk.

And Now a Word from The Phillie Phanatic

A celebrity author who knows a lot about the Hawk and a lot about the fine art of mascoting has agreed to conduct a guest interview of the 2004-2005 Hawk. Our celebrity author is Tom Burgoyne, the "best friend" of the Phillie Phanatic, professional sport's most popular mascot for the past 11 consecutive years, according to *USA Today*. Tom will share some personal reflections on the St. Joe's Hawk. The Phanatic knows the Hawk because Tom Burgoyne *was* the Hawk at Saint Joseph's Prep. Tom knows a bit about authoring, too. He was Bob Gordon's co-author in two top-selling books about the Phillies: *More Than Beards, Bellies, and Biceps: the Story of the 1993 Philadelphia Phillies and the Phillie Phanatic Too* and *Movin' On Up*.

And now, "Heeeeeere's Tommy!"

The Phillie Phanatic: My Life As A Hawk

For the past 17 years, I've made my living dressing up in a green, furry costume. So I have to admit to a soft spot in my heart for any individual whose life, like mine, is a perpetual Halloween. But I have a special place for the Hawk mascot, because the Hawks are in my blood.

I spent my high school years at Saint Joseph's Prep. My alma mater, located in the heart of North Philly at 17th and Girard Avenue, churns out Jesuit-educated men year after year. It's a school that revels in traditions. A spirited and dedicated alumni base supports the school.

I suppose I'm connected to that alumni base more than the average Prepper. My father attended the Prep. So did my three brothers. It was in the cards that I'd be a Prepper, too. I didn't feel any pressure to attend. Honest. My parents always emphasized that the choice of high school was mine and mine alone—as was my choice of eating or not.

With due respect to Bill Cosby, I could have gone anywhere, but I chose the Prep. Admittedly the deck was stacked in the Prep's favor. As a young kid, I tuned in early to Prep spirit by attending football, basketball and soccer games with my family. To me in those days, Prep football was as big-time as Eagles football. I guess it helped that some of those Mike McCormick-led Eagles squads would have struggled to beat the Prep.

I used to cheer for the Crimson and Gray while sitting on the fringes of the rowdy student section as close to the Mini Band as I could get. The Mini Band was a quirky Prep tradition. Too "cool" to field a marching band, Prep musicians dreamt up the idea of a Mini Band—a student-run,

The flapping Hawk runs a figure eight. *Photo courtesy of Saint Joseph's University/Sideline Photos*

rag-tag motley crew of 10 to 20 instrument-toting guys. No uniforms, no conductor, no baton twirling—just a bunch of idiots blending into the crowd, playing tunes in subfreezing temperatures, and trying to will their team to victory.

Those games had a lasting effect on me. I enrolled in the Prep and immediately signed up for the Mini Band my freshman year. I was a clarinet and tenor saxophone player. Since I never got a chance to jam with the Stones, this was the next best thing. I was in the Mini Band for three years. I played in just about every stadium in the Catholic League at that point, so when my senior year rolled around, I was looking for a new gig.

Enter the Hawk.

St. Joe's Prep boasts a proud Hawk mascot tradition of its own. Dan Brennan (no relation to Saint Joseph's College's first Hawk mascot Jim Brennan) was a longtime teacher/principal/administrator at the Prep. In the fall of 1970, Dan was scratching his head for gimmicks to spruce up the Prep's football game-day experience. His quest led him up Hawk Hill where he begged a retired Hawk costume for the Prep. He secured one, and the Prep's Hawk tradition, despite having a liftoff that was pure hand-me-down, soared from that day forward.

By the time my senior year in high school rolled around in 1983, the Hawk had undergone a complete featherlift (I guess that's what you would call it). The familiar brown-, black- and rust-colored feathers were history, replaced by a new red, furry plumage with bright orange feet. It resembled a character in a Muppet movie or a Hollywood Boulevard pimp. Anyway, to my delight, my classmates voted me in as the guy to wear it. Little did I know at the time that the experience would set my career as a mascot off and running. I moved on up to the job of Phillie Phanatic (sorry, but for that story, you're gonna have to buy our books, *More Than Beards, Bellies, and Biceps* and *Movin' On Up*).

Phillie Phanatic Interview:
Mike Tecci, The Golden Jubilee Hawk Mascot

St. Joe's has a wonderful basketball tradition. Many great players have come and gone. Championships have been won and lost. Yeah, yeah, yeah—this we know. Yet for a growing army of fans around the country, the school and the basketball team's renown stem from a different tradition. They know St. Joe's for its Hawk—its unflappable and continually flapping big bird.

As the Phillie Phanatic, I have to deal with my share of birdbrains. Cardinals, orioles, eagles, falcons, ravens, jayhawks and yes, even dreaded blue jays (especially the yellow-bellied Joe Carter species... Joe, if you're reading this, "yellow-bellied" is a figure of speech reserved for only the greatest of the great) wing their way into sporting events around the country. None, however, match the grandeur and sheer majesty of the St. Joe's Hawk. I'm not schmoozing—honest.

Jim Brennan played Dr. Frankenstein to the Hawk mascot. He dreamed up the idea and brought it to life. He also played the monster itself. When he was a St. Joe's sophomore, Brennan figured that if college football teams could have a sideline mascot, then why couldn't the St. Joe's basketball squad? He convinced the student government to donate $80 to the cause and wheedled 40 bucks from the athletic department. Jim was a finance major—a business guy who figured that his Hawk needed a trademark, something unique in mascot-dom (which was a very small kingdom in those days). That trademark became the non-stop flap. The true Hawk, he decreed, would flap his wings nonstop from warm-up drills to the final buzzer.

Brennan's brainchild caught on. For 50 years now, the Hawk has been present at every man's basketball game flapping his wings and running figure eights on the court during time outs. Besides all the national awards already mentioned, he even won the "Best Mascot in Philly" award in 2004.

About that ... I've got something to get off my chest, Hawk fans.

The Phillie Phanatic spends the whole game falling down steps, walking into walls, wrestling baseball players, dodging thrown baseballs, buffing bald heads, spilling popcorn, shooting hot dogs and t-shirts into the crowd, dancing and gyrating his big belly on top of the dugout and generally wreaking havoc wherever he goes. The Hawk flaps his wings a little bit and *he* gets the Best of Philly award?

Actually, the Hawk flaps those wings more than just a little bit. A couple of years ago, the folks at ESPN, bless their souls, had nothing better to do on a slow sports night. They introduced a "Flap-O-Meter" during a televised St. Joe's game and calculated that the Hawk flaps his wings over 3,500 times during a regulation game. No one ever hung a flap-o-meter on any of our local sportscaster's mouths, but you've got to figure that, at 3,500 flaps a game, the Hawk holds his own with any of Philly's top jaw-flappers. In this town, that's sayin' sumptin'.

Flapping is a sight that native Philadelphians take for granted, but it's becoming familiar to the rest of the country, thanks to ESPN and other round-the-clock, round-the-nation sports stations. Switch on the highlights of the St. Joe's game anywhere, and in the upper right portion of the TV screen you'll spot someone in a brown-feathered costume waving his arms up and down nonstop like he's attempting lift-off.

If the Hawk were ever caught napping rather than flapping, the St. Joe's student and alumni body would have his head. Trust me, I know quite a bit about losing my head. Read *Movin' On Up*. You'll see.

I've witnessed how seriously the Hawk takes his nonstop flapping. Over the years, the Hawk has joined me for some Phillie Phanatic birthday parties. The whole cadre of local mascots comes out to celebrate. I've never seen the Hawk slip out of character. Never. Even when the entire gang of mascots is just chillin' in the locker room far away from the eyes of the public, the Hawk flaps away.

One time, the Hawk and I were waiting together to take the field to do a little routine. "Yo Hawk," I yelled. "Nobody's looking. You can give it a rest now."

The Hawk never even fluttered, and never missed so much as a flap.

"It's understood that under no circumstances can you stop flapping," says Mike Tecce, the 28th student to wear the Hawk costume. "It was a little tough at first to make it through a whole game, but now it's second nature."

Mike grew up in Chalfont, Pennsylvania, in Bucks County and was such a diehard Philly fan, he applied only to Big Five schools—LaSalle, Villanova and Temple (sorry, Penn). But once he set foot on the campus at St. Joe's he was hooked as a Hawk.

"I knew right away I wanted to go to Saint Joseph's. From the day I first laid eyes on the campus, I knew it was the place for me."

Mike is more than just a guy covered with feathers and fur. On Hawk Hill, Mike has been president of the Student Union Board. He has also been active in the campus ministry program, a residence assistant, and an orientation leader. He has won the Reverend Edward Brady Scholarship for service leadership and dedication to the community, the Achievement Award Scholarship, and the Sons of Italy Scholarship. He has also volunteered time in Virginia and Kentucky building homes for "Project Appalachia."

Mike underwent a progressive selection process to earn the mascot mantle. After composing an essay about why he wanted to be the Hawk, he advanced to the next phase of the competition, an interview with the athletic department. Men's basketball coach Phil Martelli went one on one with Mike in the interview.

"After the interview, Coach Martelli called me and asked me to meet him outside the chapel. My stomach was doing flips. I was praying for good news. When Coach said that I got the job, it was my second best moment in college. My best moment was my first official appearance as the Hawk. I'll never forget that day. Coach Martelli called me into his office and gave me some last-minute instructions. Then he got up from his desk, put out his hand, and said, 'Welcome to the team.' It was the best feeling ever."

That first game happened to be against the perennial powerhouse Kansas Jayhawks at their gym, the Allen Fieldhouse.

Mike recalls: "All I could think of was, 'What if I somehow stop flapping? What if I'm so tired I can't run my figure eights?' When I first went out onto the court, I ran to center court, just trying to soak it all in.

There were 16,000 screaming Kansas fans. They all looked like they wanted to kill me. It definitely pumped me up. Dick Vitale was broadcasting the game. I went over and shook his hand. I kept my one arm flapping all the time, so it was OK. The Jayhawks mascot got right in my face, but I just kept on flapping. In the training, they stress that if a fan or another mascot wants to mix it up or get rough with you, you can't retaliate. You can defend yourself, but you can't retaliate."

Mike realizes that wearing the Hawk costume in its Golden Anniversary year makes his experience as the mascot even more special. He says, "It makes me feel an even greater responsibility to represent not only the basketball team, but the students, faculty and every person involved with St. Joe's. To carry all that on your shoulders is really amazing, the coolest thing I've ever done."

Did Mike say cool? Getting back to my Philly's best mascot flap—hey Mike, try flapping while you're running around at a Phillies game in August when temperatures reach the triple digits and it's stickier underneath those feathers than the Senate hearings about steroid use in baseball.

Ah, you know what? Somehow I think Philly summer heat wouldn't faze Mike Tecce the Hawk one bit. He's a man on a mission. No matter where the Hawks are in the standings, no matter where the team is playing, no matter how hot it gets, Mike's gonna see to one thing. The Hawk will never die.

Boy Sweat

COACH McKINNEY:

Sarah Brennan is the first and only Lady Hawk. She recalls watching college basketball on the tube in Point Pleasant, New Jersey, when she was still in high school. Her mom, Corrine, said, "Wouldn't it be fun doing that when you grow up?" Sarah asked, "What?" Her mom said, "Flap."

So she did. As she said in an ESPN interview, "The costume smells pretty bad. It's 10 years old. That's a decade of—yuck—boy sweat."

Quaker Gloats

Sarah Brennan says she got her rudest reception from the Penn students. Sarah chuckles: "They had a sign that said, 'The Hawk has no balls.'"

In The Trunk of The Wildcat

Al Pastino who served as Hawk from 1961 through 1964, passes this story along:

"In 1962, we found out that Villanova cheerleaders were planning to steal the Hawk uniform, so we hid it in the trunk of Bob and Jack Gottsman's car. Jack happened to be one of the guys trying to steal it. They never found it, and the Hawk flew!"

The Headless Hawkman

In 1965, Charlie Wieners was the Hawk. Georgetown cheerleaders stole the suit and stashed it in a locker. That didn't deter Charlie. But it did blow his cover. Wieners had to perform all night without a head. So the Hawk did not die, but presumably he couldn't squawk.

A Hawk Walk

From Bill Berner, the Hawk mascot from 1968-1970: "My first year as the Hawk was also Jack Ramsay's first year as 76ers head coach. The Sixers' season started before ours, so the Booster Club organized a 7.6-mile march down Broad Street to Dr. Jack's first game at the Spectrum. I was worried about being a white guy walking through North Philly in a funny suit. I thought I'd be safest once I was on Temple's campus. Was I ever wrong! North Philly people were curious and hospitable. Temple was loud and adversarial.

"I learned two things on that walk. First, sports can be a universal language and a great unifier. And second, if sports fail as a universal language, you can't do better than having Sam the Drummer and the Booster Club share the mob's antagonism with you."

Combat Pay

According to Bill Berner, "Games against teams with mascots that are pirates, musketeers, or other swashbucklers should include combat pay. Also the suit should include chain mail shorts to protect against tail-feather thrusts during figure eights on the court."

Off with The Wildcat Head

Bill Berner says, "By the time the Villanova game came around, I was getting comfortable with the job. I had been thrown at, swung at, wrapped in toilet paper—and I was still alive. I knew the history of the Villanova game

(Knew? Hell, it was the reason I rejected my acceptance at MIT and came to St. Joe's) and I welcomed the week of bodyguards who made sure I wouldn't be kidnapped prior to the game. One of my best friends in high school had become the head of Villanova's spirit club. When I led our team onto the floor into the pandemonium of the Palestra, Villanova's first roll-out appeared. It read, 'Bill, this is war.' I thought that was fun. I took it as friendly jousting.

"Most of my figure-eights brought on a hail storm of rubber chickens. I dodged most of them. I didn't want to give any Villanova fans the satisfaction of hitting the target. In the middle of the second half, there was a time out. A rubber chicken whizzed past my head and hit the floor like a depth charge. It was filled with a couple of pounds of pennies. I decided it was time to go on the offensive. The Hawk suit had a form-fitting head that gave me a lot more flexibility than the papier mache head of the Wildcat. When the 'Cat made—let's call them politically incorrect gestures— in front of our stands, I tore off his head and tossed it to the crowd. That caused a scene and brought Philly's Finest [the police] into the fray. A couple of Philly cops grabbed my arms and arrested me for "inciting a riot." College president Father Toland stepped onto the court and used his considerable influence to get me released in his recognizance. The Booster Club carried me out of the Palestra on their shoulders even though we lost the game."

Paybacks

"The year after I graduated," Bill Berner says, "Saint Joseph's President Toland invited me to the Villanova game at the Palestra. I watched my successor John Donnelly, zoom out onto the court for his first season and reflected on what a fast learning curve the mascot faces.

"At half time the new Hawk flapped over to the Wildcat for what he expected would be a press photo-op. Next thing John knew, he was lying flat on his back at center court—the result of a Wildcat roundhouse punch. Father Toland was shocked, especially when I told him that punch was meant for me. I reminded him of when he rescued me from the police after I had decapitated the 'Cat two years before. As for John Donnelly, he got up off the floor and flapped for the next two years."

Heeding The Hauer Household Head

Bill Berner says, "I was doing a halftime figure eight at Hofstra's Fieldhouse when a football player from my high school trudged out onto the court. I thought he was my friend, so my guard was down. The next thing I knew, he was carrying me over to the Hofstra stands on his shoulders. The fans were holding me aloft and passing me up and down the stands.

"I was on my third unappreciated trip to the top of the Hofstra cheering section when Mike Hauer's father waded into the chaos and bellowed that the next guy that manhandled the Hawk was going to have to handle him. Everyone in the stands froze. I got dropped down on the floor. I straightened out my wings, got back on the court and didn't worry one more second about anyone messing with me that night. I also never again wondered who was in charge in the Hauer household."

Plucky LaSalle Fans

"We were playing Seton Hall in a rough game that ended up in a bench-clearing brawl," Berner says, "I was in a neutral position when I saw Coach McKinney being held by one Seton Hall player and punched by a second. There was no way the Athletic Department could complain about the Hawk coming to the aid of the Coach! I bolted across the court and put a shoulder into the attacker. I drove him off the court and planted him in the stands. But I had failed to cover all the bases. The stands were full of LaSalle fans waiting for the second game. Before I escaped they had plucked most of the feathers from my suit."

Maryland Is for Crabs

Bill Berner tells another Hawk story: "The Booster Club had gone down to Georgetown, in big numbers. The Hoya rooters noted where we'd be seated and they rigged up tubs of water over them. They ended up deluging our section with cold water. On the floor we resolved to avenge the indignity. I crowded their mascot, ran through their cheerleaders, and ignored the traditional mid-court mascot boundary. Georgetown sent its women's field hockey team to attack me. Bottom line was: we won the game. The trip home was a little overly—well—exuberant. We cleaned out the Maryland House on I-95 like a swarm of locusts. Besides food, though, we cleaned some other things out that we weren't supposed to. It was bad enough that the Maryland State troopers stopped the buses just before the Pennsylvania state line. We returned all the silverware, condiments, and potted plants. The St. Joe's Booster Club was given a lifetime ban from the Maryland House—at least for the foreseeable future."

Draft Night

Bill Berner says, "I'll never forget the Albright game my senior year. Not because of the game. It happened to be the night of the first ever Vietnam draft lottery. Both coaches understood the significance of the lottery to the college kids. By mutual consent, the coaches agreed to pull each player out of the game as his number was drawn and give him the news. Our manager, Lee McLain, and I were given a portable radio and the date of each player's birthday. You can see how important that lottery was when you look at the 1970 yearbook. Under each graduate's photo, not only does a name appear, but a draft number as well. No address, no quote, no awards—just the draft number.

One Nation Under God

"I found out what a big country I live in when I was the mascot," says Bill Berner, "I remember playing in Evanston, Indiana, where the arena was filled with mature adults all dressed in fire-engine red clothes. We lost the game and all went out afterwards to see *Easy Rider*. I had seen the movie already in Philly.

"The audience watched the shocking ending of that movie where some good ole boys casually shot Dennis Hopper. Our Philadelphia contingent watched in stunned silence, but we were even more stunned when the rest of the theatre erupted into cheers at the murder.

"I doubt if any college social studies course could have opened my eyes more quickly or indelibly to the huge diversity of opinion that existed in this one nation under God that I had grown up believing in."

The Lobo Tournament

Bill Berner says, "Unlike the big cities in the east, Albuquerque had no professional teams to complement what was happening on the college scene. The Lobo Tournament was the biggest sports event of the year, and it was obvious by the crowds and media hype. The arena was called the Pit because they built it by digging a hole out in the desert. The building was shaped like a pyramid. They put a roof over the top and a basketball court at the bottom. The effect was like a funnel that focused what seemed like a square mile of screaming fans onto a little postage stamp of hardwood.

"St. Joe's finished third in the Tournament. At the awards ceremony, the announcer called each guy out to get a watch. After all our guys were honored, the crowd, which at first had been hostile to the Hawk, wouldn't let the ceremony continue. They kept chanting 'The Hawk.' The organizers quickly located another watch and called me to center court simply as 'The Hawk,' because they didn't know my name. I got a standing ovation from a crowd that had previously been hostile. From then on, I knew what took *Sports Illustrated* another 30 years to recognize—the Hawk was the Mascot of the Century."

The Hawk and The Hair

From Randall Kiernan, the 1982 Hawk macot: "In my first appearance, we played at Cleveland State, the year after they knocked us out of the NCAA tournament. Each time I came around for a figure eight, an elderly woman sitting courtside was shaking her fists and sticking her foot out like she was going to trip me. On each pass, she edged closer to the court until finally I knocked off her wig with one of my 'flaps.' It was pretty comical."

Auburn Allies

Kiernan says, "I represented St. Joe's at the Auburn-Mississippi State football game. Saint Joseph's University had adopted Auburn as its 'football team,' and the Auburn coach Pat Dye offered free tickets to any St. Joe's student who came down for the game. Former Saint Joseph's athletic director Mike Schultz booked me on a flight.

"I ran out of the tunnel on game day with the Auburn football team into a stadium overflowing with 80,000 screaming fans. I flapped the entire game, as well as at halftime, and had a wonderful experience partying with the Auburn people afterwards. They were all wondering who the 'idiot was who refused to stop flapping.'"

Tales from the 1990s

From Dan "Tripp" Gallagher, Hawk mascot from1993-1994: "My fondest memory was the day Mr. [Don] DiJulia told me that I had been selected as the Hawk. He told me I had to keep it quiet! Me—be quiet?! I ran to the Bluett Theatre and grabbed a payphone. I *had* to tell my parents. My father knew I had applied for the Hawk position. My mother didn't know, and she was the one who answered the phone.

"I was going crazy. On the other end, my mom really didn't seem to be too wild at all about the news. She was like, 'This sounds great and all, but let me get one thing straight. Haven't you *always* been a Hawk?' I was at a loss. I responded, 'Yes,' and she was like, 'Tripp, I know you aren't the world's best student, but you're definitely not the world's worst. And you're always reminding me how hard you're studying, but you can't tell me that after being at Saint Joseph's for over THREE YEARS, you're just now figuring out that your school is called "THE HAWKS!"'

"My jaw dropped when she said that. So did the phone. I explained the whole thing over again—that I was chosen as the Hawk mascot and everything that meant. When it hit her, she was so excited, she couldn't wait to tell everyone.

"She begged me never to reveal the conversation we just had. She was so embarrassed. I assured her the secret was safe with me.

"Sorry, Mom! Ha, Ha, Ha! But hey, at least it's not like I sold you out for money!

"Overall, Dad was happy. Unfortunately, he reminded me that my grandfather, a Penn alum, would be looking down from heaven in anger. You see, when I decided to go to SJU in 1993, my grandfather was so upset he didn't speak to me for a month or so, because I went to SJU. I guess that was my first taste of the Big FIVE!"

Handcuffed in Tulsa

Bobby Gallagher, the Hawk mascot in 1997-1998 says, "We were playing the Golden Hurricanes in Tulsa. The locals were heckling me (what's new?). They claimed I was blocking their view. The local sheriff agreed. He approached me and told me to stop flapping or get off the court. I declined, and he pulled his handcuffs out saying, 'Then I'll have to take you out of here.' Only the intervention of Don DiJulia stopped me from having to run around the Reynolds Center to avoid getting pinched by the local sheriff."

The Two-Hour Death of The Hawk

The Atlantic 10 Conference had just spent the morning session adopting a cost-cutting measure to outlaw bands, cheerleaders, and mascots for road games. Don DiJulia, St. Joe's AD who bleeds Hawk blood was shaken. The measure meant that St. Joe's revered mascot who had attended every St. Joe's game since 1956, now had to be absent at half the team's contests.

"It was a rough morning," DiJulia recalled. "It's easier to replace me than the Hawk." Don spent his lunchtime lobbying to resurrect the Hawk.

Don recalls: "I lobbied with the schools I thought I could persuade to change their votes—the ones who knew a little about the uniqueness of our Hawk."

Don's lobbying earned him a chance to present his case again at the afternoon session. He hammered on the facts: the Hawk serves as a team manager. He dresses with the players. He has his own locker. He sits in on strategy sessions. He is part of the inner sanctum. And he's on full scholarship.

When the afternoon session ended, the athletic directors in the Conference granted the Hawk a waiver. He's the only mascot in the conference permitted at road games.

"The Hawk was dead for two hours," DiJulia smiles now. He wasn't smiling that day, however. And with good reason. When he related the ominous events to the university's president, the Reverend Nicholas S. Rashford, Father Rashford said succinctly: "You're lucky. You're very lucky."

You can figure out yourself what that means.

Returning The Wright Stuff

Jay Wright passed this story along about his first season as Villanova head coach.

"I was in a restaurant the night before we played St. Joe's, eating and watching the news on TV. They reported that the Wildcat mascot uniform had been stolen. It was my first year back and I was thinking, 'Wow. This is wild.'

"The next morning, while I was driving around the Villanova campus, I spotted Don DiJulia. When I got to my office, I found out that Don had stopped by to return the stolen Wildcat costume. I thought, 'Only in the Big Five do you bump into a rival Athletic Director on your campus returning the mascot uniform the day of the game.'"

Final Flap

Every legend has its doubters. Although Jim Brennan is recognized officially as the first Hawk, the innovator—the guy who gave life to the Hawk, a couple of conflicting accounts fly around occasionally. One alumnus, Bill Dietzler (1954), says he wore the Hawk costume at Madison Square Garden in a game against St John's. Hmmm …

Charles Reilly, 1950, maintains that an ROTC student held the position a decade before Brennan began his college career.

CHAPTER SIX

The Jack Ramsay Years

Coach John J. McMenamin

John McMenamin was Saint Joseph's seventh coach—the guy sandwiched between two legends, Fergy and Jack Ramsay. McMenamin took over the head-coaching position at age 38 and held it for only two seasons (1953-1954 and 1954-1955).

McMenamin was introduced to organized basketball as a youngster when he took "Beginner's Classes" sponsored by the Big Brother's Association.

He attended Francis Xavier's Parochial School in Philadelphia, graduated from Roman Catholic High in 1934, and graduated from Saint Joseph's College in 1938.

At Catholic High, his coach was Billy Markward. The voluntary assistant coach for the Roman Catholic High five was Billy Ferguson, head coach of the Hawks.

McMenamin played four years of varsity basketball at Roman and was selected All-Catholic as a junior and senior. He went to St. Joe's with his teammates Dan Kenney (who served as McMenamin's assistant when McMenamin rose to Hawks head coach) and Matt Guokas Sr.

At St. Joe's, Kenney, Guokas, and McMenamin joined forces with Jimmy Smale of Northeast Catholic High, and Joe Oakes and John Kenney of Saint Joseph's Prep to become the Mighty Mites.

John McMenamin was the co-captain of the Mighty Mites in his junior year (1936-1937). After his years on the Hawks hardwood, he served 39 months with the U.S. Army Air Corps during World War II.

He returned from duty in 1938 and became Saint Joseph's freshman and junior varsity basketball coach as well as Bill Ferguson's assistant coach. In his years as freshman coach, his teams won 97 games and lost 42 for a .676 average. He lost three years to military service in the early 1940s.

His record as Hawk head coach was a respectable 26-23 (.531).

Jack Ramsay's Early Years

COACH McKINNEY:

The arrival of Jack Ramsay in September 1955 ushered in the modern era of coaching at Saint Joseph's College. Jack combined the science and art of coaching as well as anyone I've ever seen.

Jack was young when he landed the Hawks head-coaching job. He had never before coached a college team.

Of course, the future Dr. Ramsay was no stranger to Hawk Hill. Jack had performed on the Saint Joseph's hardwoods for four years, though not successively. His college career was interrupted when he enlisted in the Navy for World War II. He was ticketed for Officer Training School and emerged as an ensign. He served with the Underwater Demolition Team, UDT #30 as a Frogman (these days Jack lives in Florida and probably swims as much as he did in his Frogman days).

When Jack returned to Saint Joseph's after the war, he pondered pursuing a medical career but wound up opting for coaching.

Jack's Hawk mentor, Bill Ferguson, saw promise as a coach in his young player. Fergy was a pretty good guy to have in your corner if you had coaching aspirations. Fergy had been a mainstay on the Philadelphia hardwood scene for a quarter-century and was well connected. One of the people in his network was Father Adolph Baum, principal of St. James High School. Fergy recommended Jack to Father Baum for the school's head-coaching job. Jack interviewed and walked away with the job.

Jack's St. James teams didn't set the world on fire, but he still managed to attract attention and interest from the sports community. Mt. Pleasant High School in Delaware offered him a head-coaching job. It was an offer Jack couldn't refuse. Looking back over his career, Jack credits Mt. Pleasant as the post where he started fine-tuning the coaching art.

While he was teaching and coaching at Mount Pleasant, Jack was also playing for Sunbury in the Eastern League—a semi-professional roundball league of the early fifties.

A reporter for the Sunbury daily newspaper was impressed with the supercharged schedule that Jack maintained and penned a column about it. The *Philadelphia Inquirer* carried the piece as well.

A few weeks later, Jack happened to be at a Phillies game where he bumped into Father Geib, Saint Joseph's athletic moderator. Father Geib mentioned that he had read the newspaper article and inquired about Ramsay's long-term ambitions. Two days later he called Ramsay to ask him if he was interested in coaching the Hawks. "Interested? I almost jumped through the phone," Dr. Jack chuckles as he recalls the conversation.

Father Geib asked Jack to come to campus and talk. The two sat under a tree outside Barry Hall and chatted about basketball, particularly Saint Joseph's basketball. Father Geib parted with the promise that he'd "call Jack tomorrow."

He did. He offered Jack the job. The young high school coach eagerly snapped it up and signed a one-year, $3,500 contract—despite the fact that he was receiving $5,500 a year at Mt. Pleasant High School.

Obviously Jack didn't accept the Saint Joseph's offer as his road to riches. Nor did he snap it up because of the glitzy facilities he was moving into. For five years, Coach Ramsay and his two assistants had to crowd into a small room under the stands. That single room served as office, dining room, and shower. The occupants ended up posting one-way signs and issuing mock fines for U-turns, but somehow the staff survived.

After five years in those crowded quarters, longtime Hawk athletic director George Bertelman retired, and Jack was named to replace him. I was on Jack's coaching staff by that time. We were all movin' on up, but not exactly to a dee-luxe apartment in the sky. Jack wound up with a bigger office. He *had* to. There were closets bigger than his original office. But I don't know that he really gained any space. With his promotion, he now he had to share his office not only with his two assistant coaches but also with an assistant athletic director. It was sort of one step forward and two steps back for Jack—at least as far as space was concerned.

Jack Ramsay was a busy man in those days (and all the other days of his life). His responsibilities included: athletic director, head basketball coach of a Division I school, head of the education department for both the day school and the evening school, and supervisor of studies. Did I mention he was also a doctoral degree candidate at the University of Pennsylvania? In 1963, Jack Ramsay became Dr. Jack Ramsay.

Jack Ramsay, Rookie Coach

As a rookie Hawk coach in 1955-1956, Jack didn't inherit a super talented squad. I can say that authoritatively. I played on it. Ramsay built his team around Bill Lynch, a 6'6" center he had coached back at St. James. Lynch was a senior who had played on the St. Joe's varsity the previous three seasons. Mike Fallon had come out of the Army the year before. Mike was about four years older than the rest of us. He brought maturity to the team mix. Those few extra years helped make him a quiet leader. He and Lynch were the co-captains. We had three juniors who handled the inside duties: Kurt Englebert, Ray Radziszewski, and Alphonse

Juliana. Danny Dougherty teamed up with Mike Fallon in the backcourt. Jimmy Purcell and I backed them up.

Coach Ramsay got off to a magnificent start in his rookie season. We trekked up to the Big Apple to take on Fordham University, the top team in the east. No one expected us to smash them 89-71. As Ray Radziszewski recalls, "We walked into the gym, and all the local gamblers were sitting in the stands telling us, 'You should have stayed in Philly.' Ramsay had already included the full-court press—the defense that brought him national renown—in our defensive arsenal. But we dominated this particular game so much we didn't have to use it. We were in control the whole game."

What's Up, Doc?

This tale begins in high school in the 1951-1952 Philadelphia Catholic League season. Dan Dougherty (Doc) was the starting guard for Saint Joseph's Prep when they took on the Bulldogs of St. James High in Chester. Jack Ramsay coached St. James. One of Ramsay's guards was Jack McKinney. Doc frames the scene:

"My teammate Fran Daly dove for a loose ball. The Bulldogs' forward Bob Wise jumped on top of Fran. I tried to pull Wise off Franny, and someone grabbed me from behind. I turned around and took a swing. Fortunately I just grazed the guy's head. The guy turned out to be coach Jack Ramsay. I was thrown out of the game and got reprimanded at school the next day. Then I worried because we had a return match with St. James—in Chester. Fortunately, the return game went without incident.

After his days at the Prep, Doc went to Saint Joseph's College. In his junior year, Jack Ramsay stepped in as the Hawks' new head coach. Doc tells the story this way:

"I got scared about Ramsay coming! What if he remembered? I was relieved after a few days cause he didn't seem to remember. Practice sessions went well, and I started to relax. Then one day, only 11 guys came to practice instead of 12. So when we split up for one-on-one drills, like we did every day, Ramsay said, 'C'mon Doc, I'll be your partner.' I got a little nervous. No, make that terrified. I had the ball first and tried to drive on the Coach. Jack put a hit on me that knocked me to the ground and left my ears ringing. He clobbered me! Then he grabbed my hand, helped me up, and whispered, 'That's for two years ago. Now we're even.'

"Let me tell you. I spent the two most wonderful years I could ever hope for as Coach Ramsay's starting guard. Coach Ramsay was the toughest and at the same time the warmest coach I've ever known. He was also the best."

Tie and Teeth

Some guys would forget their head if it weren't attached. Ask any nun. Nuns were always saying that to their students. More accurately they were always beating that into heads of kids who wished that they did not have a head while the beating proceeded. Bob McNeill recalls one of his teammates beset with a head forgetfulness syndrome.

"John Hoffacker [played 1960] had a set of false teeth that he took out when he was at practice or in a game. We were on the bus one night on our way to Easton and a game against Lafayette. John discovered he had forgotten his teeth. It was too late to go back and get them (note to young readers: this was the stone age—there were no cell phones).

"John also had a problem remembering to wear a tie when we were traveling. It was Coach Ramsay's strict rule to wear coat and tie when we traveled. Of course, forgetting your coat and tie was easier to spot.

"Coach Ramsay made it a practice to give us logistical instructions at the last practice session before a game. The instructions were always the same: 'Don't forget your ties.' He made a slight change after the Lafayette game. He continued to give the team the same instructions, but then he started adding, 'Hoffacker, don't forget your tie and teeth.'"

New Sneaks

Speaking of forgetting heads and sneaks, Joe Spratt showed up for a game at the Palestra without sneaks. Right Joe?

Joe Spratt: "I was captain of the team at the time. Hey, what do you expect from a young married guy in love? Who needs sneaks? It ended on a good note. Penn had NEW sneaks for me, and we won the game."

Breaking Training

Joe Spratt recalls telling Jack Ramsay that he was married.

"Joe Spratt: "I was a sophomore. It was really funny. It was the first time I ever saw Coach Ramsay speechless. After I was married, Jack pulled me aside before the season and told me abstinence was necessary the day before games. I looked at him and said, 'Uh huh. Right, Jack.' My wife, Donna, laughed hysterically when I told her. All I can tell you is my game improved. Our two children were both born in April right after March Madness. That was the best we could do to accommodate Jack!"

Grin and Beer It

When we went to board our bus after the Fordham game, there was a car full of delirious Hawk rooters parked next to us. The car happened to be filled with cases of beer. The Hawk students were trying to push cans of beer to the team through the open bus windows. Dan Dougherty canned the operation, "If Coach Ramsay catches you, you'll be wearing that beer." So they hustled the beer back into their car and headed back to Hawk Hill. So did we—just without beer.

A Radd Decision for St. Joe's

Ray Radziszewski ("Radd") didn't take the standard path to the St. Joe's hardwoods:

"I was the first athlete north of Jersey City to play for St. Joe's. I got a call from LaSalle, but they never followed up. I would have accepted an offer from LaSalle because I had watched Tom Gola and LaSalle play in the NIT on TV. When I was a kid, I knew nothing of St. Joe's, never heard of them, and could care less if they threw a fish onto the Garden floor (you'll read about "Throw 'em a fish" later).

"I didn't get any basketball scholarships coming out of high school. I was only 16 when I graduated. After graduation, I worked for a brokerage house in NYC. The company had a team in New York and Philly, too.

"We played a home-and-home series against the Philly branch. The Philly team had some former LaSalle hotshot on it. I forget his name. But he couldn't stop me in this series. A few Hawk alumni happened to attend the games. One guy was named Lynch, and he arranged a tryout for me with Coach Ferguson. As it turned out, I had just received a scholarship from St. Michael's in Vermont, so I figured I had nothing to lose. I was loose at the tryout, and St. Joe's offered me a scholarship.

"Anyway, I wound up choosing St. Joe's because George Bertelsman visited our house and did some serious drinking with my father. St. Joe's was also closer for my parents to visit."

Honey Sweetens The Victory

Ray Radziszewski "Radd" got an extra kick out of beating Seton Hall.

"I had extra incentive against Seton Hall in the NIT. When I was in high school, their coach, Honey Russell, called and invited one of my teammates and me to a tryout on the South Orange campus. After a long train ride and two bus transfers, Coach Russell was a no-show. Scratch Seton Hall off my list! That victory was sweet!"

Two Points In No Time

One of our toughest opponents in the MAC was Muhlenberg. We had to get by them to win the conference and ensure a postseason bid.

With three minutes to go, we were nursing a small lead when Dan Dougherty, our hard-nosed guard, got rocked taking a shot. Doc landed on the back of his head. They had to carry him off the floor and take him to a nearby hospital. But he had two foul shots coming. Coach Ramsay substituted sophomore Jack Savage to shoot the fouls. Jack sank both. After the second shot, the horn sounded for a substitution and Coach sent Jim Purcell in for Savage.

The two points Jack scored took no time at all. Literally. No time ran off the clock. The St. Joe's philosophy department might argue whether he was actually in the game or not, but we won't. The only thing that mattered was that Savage's points counted. We held on and won 76-71. Jack's point total for the game and the year always appears with an asterisk (Trivia question: What do Roger Maris and Jack Savage have in common?) ... and a question mark.

Now let's return to Doc, our fallen comrade. The medics shaved the back of Doc's head in a circle and stitched him up. Unfortunately, the circle of hair they cut off never returned. Unfortunately or fortunately—take your pick—most of the rest of Doc's hair has also disappeared. It's less likely to make a comeback than Michael Jordan as an outfielder. Still, Doc insists that *the Muhlenberg game* is the culprit for his hair loss.

After the game, the team stopped by the hospital to pick Dan up. His first question was, "Did Savage make my two foul shots? He did? Great, that'll help *my* average."

Doc suffered a double loss that night—hair and points—and both of them were permanent.

A Foul In No Time

Not only do Hawks need no time to score, they need no time to foul, either. Joe Spratt recalls:

"I fouled Oscar Robertson at the Palestra when we were lining up for the center tap to start the game with no time off the clock! I was scared to look at the Coach because as we were heading out to center court before the jump ball, Jack was screaming, 'Remember, no fouls!' After I fouled the Big O, I managed to sneak a look over at the bench. Jack had grabbed his forehead and was looking to the heavens.

"Needless to say, I did foul out of the game. But at least it happened while the clock was ticking."

Winning the Big Five

Ramsay's first season witnessed the official birth of the Big Five. It was poetic justice for Jack and the Big Five to start their illustrious runs the same year. We whipped Villanova 83-70 in the first ever Big Five game at the Palestra. We had several big wins that year. We topped St. Francis of New York 80-76 to snap their 17-game win streak. We beat No. 10-ranked Temple 77-68, and we won the first ever Big Five Title. Jubilant fans hoisted Coach Ramsay on their shoulders and carried him around the Palestra floor the night we won the championship. One of the coach-carriers was my dad, Paul McKinney.

The Big Five Championship Flu

Ray Radziszewski recalls: "After we beat Temple for the first Big Five championship, the professors called off class, and the whole school marched down City Line Avenue to the TV station."

Radd fails to mention that the St. Joe's student body marched before the game as well. The student body rumbled en masse from campus to the Palestra.

Both teams entered the deciding contest for the first Big Five crown with identical 3-0 records. Temple that year was considered one of Philly's top all-time teams. The Owls were led by Guy Rodgers and Hal Lear, which was long considered the Big Five's best ever guard tandem till Jameer and Delante came along. Jay Norman, Harold "Hotsy" Reinfeld, and Tink Van Patton rounded out the Temple quintet.

NIT-Picked

To sweeten the season further, we got an invitation to the NIT. For the edification of young readers, in those days the NIT, not the NCAA, was *the* postseason tournament. And only eight teams participate. Getting an NIT invitation was tantamount to making today's Elite Eight.

In the NIT, we took our first-round game against Seton Hall. We lost the next game to eventual-champ Louisville but came back to top St. Francis of New York for third place. That win made the final line on Coach Ramsay's rookie season 23-6, with a third-place national finish in the NIT. And he accomplished it all with a team of unknown players and coaches. The 23 wins set a new Hawk standard for victories in a season. All in all, not too shabby a start.

We witnessed some outstanding individual performances that year. Kurt Engelbert scored a season-high 36 points against Davidson, and Ray Radziszewski pulled down 25 boards against PMC. In fact, Ray still holds a half-share of the Saint Joseph's University record for average rebounds per game (15.3) for a season. Cliff Anderson holds the other share.

No Soph Slump

In 1956-1957, Coach Ramsay leaned on the inside strength of Radziszewski, Juliana, and Englebert. The backcourt consisted of Dougherty, McKinney, and Spratt. Jack Savage, the foul-shooting specialist, and Al Cooke, the super shooter, backed us up.

Spratt was our best guard, but Ramsay opted to start the two seniors, Dougherty and me. The squad clicked, and we rolled. The LaSalle game was a gem. The Explorers were leading by 20 at halftime when Ramsay put us into his 3-1-1 full-court press and forced them into turnover after turnover. With six ticks left, we were down by two and had the ball under our basket. As referee John Stevens handed the ball to Doc (Dan Dougherty) for the inbound play, Stevens whispered, "Now don't screw it up." Doc didn't. He got the ball in to Al Juliana, who made the shot and forced overtime. From then on, it was all Hawks. We won going away, 97-85.

We also beat Manhattan 70-65 at Madison Square Garden where the ritual of the "throwing of the fish," (story is later in the book) was observed.

I Wouldn't Change a Thing

Jack Savage, 1958, remembers some instances when Al Julianna got the best of Coach Jack: "Jack was starting to get really irritated because Al Julianna refused to wash his practice shirt. When Coach challenged him on it, Al said he was trying to make it smell bad to keep defenders away so he could get his jump shot off easier.

"That's not all Al did that drove Jack nuts. Jack used to make every guy sit down and say what he needed to improve. Everybody had something to offer but Al. Al sat there and sat there. Finally he told Coach he couldn't think of anything. Dr. Jack went bananas!"

The Ramsay Recruiting Machine

Philadelphia's North Catholic High School produced two of the finest players in Philadelphia that year: Bobby McNeill and Joe Gallo. Ramsay wooed each to Hawk Hill by tapping into the relationship he had developed with North's coach, Ed Scullin. A former Hawk player himself, Scullin praised the value of a Saint Joseph's education to his two youngsters. He added that going to St. Joe's would also give them the opportunity to play for the top young college basketball coach in the area.

Driving the Recruiting Budget

One negative aspect about inking these two big names was the huge dent the transactions put in the recruiting budget. Just kidding. Jack Ramsay's recruiting budget was essentially the gas money it cost him to drive from West Philly to Northeast Philly (for young readers, gas in those days cost about 15 cents a gallon). To recruit, Coach Ramsay basically just drove around to different parts of the Quaker City.

The Falcon-turned-Hawk backcourt duo carried Ramsay's quintets for three years. But Ramsay didn't overlook the frontcourt in building his team. Uncharacteristically though, he beefed it up by looking outside the Philly area.

Ed Lassner, a friend of Jack's from his old Eastern League days, tipped him off about a couple of high school kids in Scranton: 6'10" Bobby Clark and 6'9" Jim Coolican. Jack contacted their coaches and invited both kids to campus to work out with the Hawks team.

Ramsay arranged for them to scrimmage with some varsity players. The season was over at that point, and scrimmages like that were not only legal but also common practice. The campus grapevine spread the word about the two upstate "giants" who were on campus working out. Excited Hawk basketball fanatics showed up in droves. Going back to the Mighty Mites era, St. Joe's teams usually came up short in the height department. At that point, the last Hawks center who topped 6'6" was John Doogan in 1953.

Coolican and Clarke accepted their offers and fit right in. They teamed up with Gallo and McNeill on a superb freshman team. Along with vets Joe Spratt, Al Cooke, John Hoffecker, and Jack Savage, they won 60 games over the next three years. The team received one NIT invite and two NCAA berths.

McNeill emerged as the ideal point guard. He left an indelible mark on the Hawk basketball legacy. He still ranks in the Hawks' top 10 for free-throw percentage, career assists, and assists per game (including the school's all-time single-game high of 13). His three-year assists-per-game average was a phenomenal 6.50. To put that accomplishment in perspective, McNeill rates ahead of Jameer Nelson on the Hawk all-time list. Jameer's average was "only" 6.45. After he made All-American, Bobby was drafted and played for the Knicks.

McNeill wasn't the whole Hawk show. Gallo averaged a career 14 ppg. Joe Spratt was a take-care-of-business player who coaches appreciate more than fans do. Joe contributed a respectable 11 points per game over his three-year career. But Joe did so much more. He could shoot, rebound, pass, and defend. He could play guard or forward. Best of all, he could shut down the opponent's best player.

The following season, Jack recruited another talented trio: Jack Egan, Vince Kempton, and Frank Majewski. The 1958-1959 quintet won 22 games. The 1958-1959 campaign included a heartbreaking loss in the

NCAA Tournament at Charlotte, North Carolina, to West Virginia University led by All-American Jerry West. The following year (1960), they lost by two to Duke.

In 1961, the Hawks were bested by a great Ohio State team that featured future NBA Hall of Famer John Havlicek, along with two other future NBA stars, Jerry Lucas and Larry Siegfried. There was also a little-known substitute guard on the squad named Bobby Knight. I wonder whatever became of him? The Hawks followed up the loss with a victory over Utah, led by Bill McGill. The victory netted them third place.

When the 1960-1961 season rolled around, senior Jack Egan had emerged as a major force. He averaged 21.9 points a game while pulling down 12.1 rebounds. The trio of seniors—Egan, Kempton, and Majewski—averaged 41 points per game. The squad was one of Ramsay's most powerful ever. They won not only the Big Five crown but also the first round of the NCAA Tournament in Charlotte to advance to the Final Four in Kansas City.

The 1959 team leaves for the NCAA playoffs. *Photo courtesy of Saint Joseph's University*

Muhlenberg

During the 1959-1960 campaign, the Hawks were ranked in the top 20. They had to get past Muhlenberg to nail down their NCAA Tournament bid. Doug Leaman remembers: "After we ate in the Saint Joseph's cafeteria, the team boarded a bus and headed to Muhlenberg. I was the 'goofball' of the team. No one's gonna take issue with that. John Hoffacher passed that title on to me after he graduated.

"While we were on the bus, I started to laugh. I have no idea why, just for the hell of it. Then Harry Booth joined in, then Joe Gallo. Within minutes, the whole bus was in an uproar, and the laughing continued most of the way.

"This was a major game, and Mark Kessler on Muhlenberg was averaging close to 30 points a game. These guys were no pushovers. So Ramsay heard all the laughing and began to stew. He sent Dan Kenny back to quiet us down. Apparently the laughter was getting way out of hand, and Coach Jack thought we were losing focus.

"Well I couldn't stop, and neither could the rest of the team. When the bus pulled into Muhlenberg, Ramsay gave me a dirty look. I was the heavy. I felt my scholarship was riding on us winning.

"It turned out to be a close game. Dr. Jack put me in as a substitute for Bob McNeill when he got in foul trouble. I had a decent game and we won by eight or 10 points. We also held Kessler in check.

"The ride back to campus was wonderful. Jack Ramsay was all smiles. And my Saint Joseph's career continued unabated."

Jack's Jacket, The Final Fling

The Hawks were on a roll. They had just beaten Villanova 72-70 on January 28, 1961. They were putting their 13-3 record on the line against number-eight-rated Wake Forest three days later. The game had a happy ending for the Hawks. Vince Kempton hit a baseline jumper at the buzzer for the Hawks' second straight two-point win, 72-70.

Ramsay was jubilant. He raced down to mid-court to shake hands with his buddy Bones McKinney, Wake Forest's coach. Dr. Jack sped off court, flinging his sport coat off and into the stands in the process. He motored past his players, ran under the Coliseum through the tunnel, and into the area of the Hawks dressing room. He went airborne to swing through the dressing room door. Unfortunately the door was locked, and Dr. Jack ended up crumpled on the floor. Embarrassed, the coach eventually picked himself up and limped into the locker room, which was opened shortly after he tumbled. He was still ecstatic, celebrating the V with the team when suddenly he whitened. He gasped, "The money—all the money is in my coat pocket!" He immediately dispatched the managers to recover his discarded coat, which contained the cash stash for the rest of the trip. The managers dashed out and immediately came upon a young Wake Forest student standing outside the dressing-room door. He was holding a jacket and an envelope of money.

Later that season, in the NCAA Tournament at Charlotte, Saint Joseph's College again toppled Wake Forest, 96-86. The Hawks' traveling stash wasn't threatened this time. Jack's jacket had already taken its final fling.

Goin' to Kansas City,
Philadelphia (?) Here I Come

St. Joe's took off for Kansas City and the Final Four in a pouring rain. As they prepared for a landing, the stewardess made a mistake and announced, "Please fasten your seat belts. We're approaching *Philadelphia*." She meant to say Washington. One of the St. Joe's players wisecracked, "Well, everyone said this team wasn't going anywhere."

An Historic Game

Utah was led by All-American Bill "the Hill" McGill. This particular game was meaningless. Both sides had already been eliminated from the tournament. Yet the Utah game went four overtime periods before Saint Joseph's finally came out on top, 127-120. Egan tallied 42 and sophomore Jim Lynam 31 to counter McGill's 34 in the highest-scoring NCAA championship game ever. The game set records for the most extra periods (four) and the highest combined point total (247) in the annals of the NCAA Tournament.

Need I mention it was also the longest game ever? The game featured just about everything, including a neighborly basket by Hawk Billy Hoy. Hoy grabbed a pass from Kempton off the opening tap at the start of the third overtime. He took a few dribbles and launched a jump shot. Score! Nothing but net! The problem was ... it was the wrong net. In a wild-scoring game, Hoy was the only guy who scored for both teams that evening.

Because of the four overtimes, the start of the championship game was delayed about 45 minutes. The two opponents, Ohio State and Cincinnati, spent their time sitting in the locker room, most likely cussing out Saint Joseph's and Utah. That lengthy delay precipitated some rule changes. After the Saint Joseph's College–Utah skirmish in 1961, the consolation final was permanently dropped from the NCAA tournament.

Scandal

It was only a few days after the season finale against Utah. Jack Ramsay had just switched hats from head basketball coach to Saint

Joseph's athletic director and was busy preparing for the spring sports season.

His phone rang. It was Father Geib, moderator of athletics, demanding to see Jack immediately.

The coach walked over to see Father Geib, who immediately hit Dr. Jack with some devastating news. Father Geib had just spoken with Frank Hogan of the district attorney's office in New York. Hogan revealed that his office had evidence that Jack Egan, Frank Majewski, and Vince Kempton had all accepted money from New York gambling kingpin Jack Molinas. The St. Joe's guys had shaved points in certain games this past season.

Jack faced the heartbreaking task of confronting each of the three. Initially each guy denied the allegations and the crisis stalled for a few weeks. Jack mentioned the allegations to nobody. After Easter, however, all hell broke loose.

That's when I was sitting watching a Hawk baseball game. Jack Ramsay sidled over to me. He wore an uncharacteristic anxious look. He told me to meet him in his office early next morning. He said he needed to share some disturbing news with me.

Jack wanted to tell me the news before it broke in the media. With dry lips, he related that Jack Egan, Frank Majewski, and Vince Kempton had fixed the outcome of the Dayton game that year—a game we lost by two points at the Palestra. They had also shaved points in the Seton Hall game— a game we won by a point.

In exchange for supplying evidence against Jack Molinas, the kingpin of the operation, our players were not being formally charged.

The NY DA office was determined to put Molinas away. They succeeded in doing so, in large part due to the evidence a host of college players provided, including Egan, Majewski, and Kempton.

Years later, I spoke to Frank Majewski. Frank told me how this life-altering episode came to pass.

"Some local gambler in New Jersey approached me about shaving points. He assured me we wouldn't lose any games. No one would know what we were doing and we would get 'nice money.'"

The money part sounded good. Frank's family was having tough times. His father had died and his mother was home in Jersey City alone, taking care of the other children while Frank was in college. Very little money was coming into the family till. Frank thought agreeing to the scheme gave him a way of helping pay the family bills.

The *Sports Illustrated* Article

Sports Illustrated covered the scandal in its May 8, 1961 edition. The article contends that Frank Majewski accepted $2,750 to shave points in three games and caused Saint Joseph's to lose two games it should and would have won.

The article was somewhat sympathetic to the plight of the young athletes ensnared in this web. Much of the article was a portrait of Frank Majewski, an industrial management major who maintained a C+ average. As a high school senior, he received queries from scouts for several teams, including West Point, Seattle, North Carolina State, Manhattan, and Navy. Eventually he took a scholarship to Holy Cross. However, it was "too far away," and he flunked out as a freshman. As a sophomore, Majewski's dad died. The next year, his mom had a heart attack. He was portrayed as a kid troubled by the hard times his mom and family had to face.

The article was positive toward Saint Joseph's College. The school had only 1,450 students at the time with only 150 living on campus. Compensating its athletes was unheard of in the Saint Joseph's program. St. Joe's had given the players hats as gifts for their good season. "Even that modest purchase made Ramsay wince!" the article said. To underscore how unslick and provincial the St. Joe's program was, the article stated that six members of the 11-man squad went to high school within two miles of campus.

Before jetting off to the Final Four, the team went across 54th Street to Sam Fishman's restaurant for a good luck banquet. The scene was described as follows:

"Sam Fishman is the Toots Shor's of 54th Street. A piece of cut-down net, a souvenir of a big Saint Joseph's College victory, hung from the ceiling and patrons weren't arguing about whether Saint Joe's would beat Ohio State, but by how much. Sam himself was renting two TVs so his customers could watch the championship games. He told the team to eat all it could. It was all on the house. 'These are great boys, just great,' said Sam Fishman."

The account went on: "At a much smaller and less gala lunch at Sam's that day, Jack Ramsay had shared little of the local enthusiasm, openly confessing concern about his opposition and less openly worrying about the basketball scandals. He lowered his voice once, ran a hand through his thinning hair, and confided: 'If one of my players were ever involved, I guess I'd just quit. You watch them and watch them, but you can't know all the people they meet, or all the things they do. What's more, nobody can tell when a player is shaving points. Nobody!'"

Frank Majewski Looks Back 45 Years

"I recognize I made a mistake," Frank Majewski states with conviction. "I'm disappointed in myself. I'm disappointed in what I did to my team and Coach Ramsay, and I'm disappointed in the disgrace I brought to Saint Joe's. But it's water over the dam now. I had to get over it and get on with my life. Ultimately it made me stronger and forced me to focus on new goals.

"The school was super nice in helping all three of us get back on our feet again. I was grateful they permitted us to come back and graduate. The stipulation was that we had to sit out two years before we could come back. Saint Joseph's College was nothing but charitable.

"I can honestly say the incident made me a better person and has helped me appreciate how great life is now. I have a wonderful wife [a Villanova grad], who stood by me all the way. All my soul-searching has also helped me do a better job raising my own beautiful children.

"For a while, I was an officer in a corporation, but if you know the corporate world, you know nothing like that lasts forever. But I've done very well and we are very happy. And I look forward to retirement and golfing and skiing."

Vince Kempton Reflects

Vince Kempton, who had to forsake being drafted by the Knicks, looks back on his darkest chapter this way.

"It was unmitigated selfishness on my part. I had no pressing need for money. I had no idea when I got into it how it would change my life and limit my options. I was looking forward to a chance to teach and coach. But I soon realized those dreams were never going to come true.

"I had to step back. I grew up that one week, all at once. It may have been a blessing in disguise. I may have made that kind of a mistake later in my life. Instead I made it then, and it forced me to turn my life around. I just hope my experience helps somebody else down the line.

"Saint Joseph's College was terrific. We met with Father Sullivan, dean of students, and he told us we couldn't stay at Saint Joseph's College, but we could return in two years and get our credits to graduate. That's what we did. So my wife and I and our baby came back to Saint Joseph's University in 1963 and I graduated. So did Frank and Jack."

A few years back when Billy Packer and Al McGuire were TV analysts for Nike, they asked Vince if he would be willing to make an instructional film outlining what he learned from his tribulations. The purpose of the film was to caution college athletes about the dangers of getting involved with the wrong people. Vince agreed to do the film, but it never got off the ground.

Jack Egan's Plight

Jack Egan was perhaps dealt the cruelest blow, because he had the most to lose. At that point, Egan was one of the best basketball players ever to came through the Saint Joseph's program. In his senior year, he averaged 22 points a game on a team that was loaded with good ballplayers. There is no doubt in my mind that Jack Egan was a surefire NBA player who was destined for a nine- or 10-year professional career.

But Jack had a major problem when he returned to campus his senior year. His wife was pregnant with their third child, and Jack had no income.

He elaborated his money crisis to Coach Ramsay and told him he needed a job. Ramsay promised him he'd get him a job and passed the request on to Jack Van Belle, president of the Basketball Club. Meanwhile, Egan says he grew desperate. Saint Joseph's did not find him a job, so he found one himself as a bartender, earning $40 a week. When Ramsay heard about the bartending job, he told Egan he had to quit it. Egan told him, "Then I won't play basketball. I need the money." Ramsay told him he'd lose his scholarship if he quit basketball.

Looking back, Jack Ramsay wishes he had handled the matter differently, "I didn't do right. I wanted to let Jack keep the bartender's job. But I couldn't. When I look back, I wasn't caring enough. I let Jack Egan down."

Getting Involved

Here's how it played out for Jack Egan. In his senior year, Frank Majewski approached him and gave him the lowdown on what the gambler was proposing. Frank tried to lure Egan into the scheme. Egan declined saying, "No. I always get caught whenever I do something wrong."

Tragically, Jack reconsidered.

"I couldn't get a job. My wife was calling me with money problems three times a day. I thought this might be a way out. So when Frank asked me a second time, I agreed.

"We only shaved points in three games. We could have done it in 10 more. But I said no. I wouldn't do a Big Five game and I wouldn't do a [MAC] Conference game. All in all, we just made a few bucks and that helped me make it through the year financially.

"When the bubble burst, I was humiliated. I couldn't get a job. I would take an interview and all they would want to talk about was the point-shaving scandal. They'd say, 'We'll call you.' Of course they never did."

Bad Times

Jack Egan recalls: "I knew the NBA wasn't interested in me anymore [the Warriors had drafted Egan] so I tried to catch on with a team in the Eastern League. I played on a local team. I think it was Allentown. I played one game and they asked me to leave. I was in deep despair. I took another job in Bethlehem for two years. Then I moved to New York and moved in with Vince Kempton, who got me a job working for his father, who managed a grocery warehouse. After two years, I was still in deep despair since my family was in Pennsylvania and I had to work in New York. After two years I came back home and worked at Atlantic Richfield for 10 or 11 years.

"Then I came back to Bethlehem and opened my own business, brokering for a trucking company for 24 years. I had to stop work a few years ago. All those years of playing basketball took their toll. My ankles gave out in the mid-1990s, and I haven't worked seriously since. Right now, I'm either in a walker or a wheelchair all the time.

"I'm desperate and angry about doing those things. Saint Joseph's didn't do anything wrong. The school was great to me and Frank and Vince. I watched the Hawks' big march in 2003-2004 and it was exciting. I was really happy for them."

Teammate Jim Boyle offered this: "When the news broke, I was distressed for them and myself. When I matured, I mellowed. I realized people make mistakes. Those three have paid their dues and have gotten on well with life."

Jim Lynam says, "It was tough to hear when it happened. But over time, I think all has been forgiven. They paid their dues, that's for sure."

Teammate Harry Booth says, "We were all in shock at the time. But we've all matured and see how those things can happen. All three guys have handled a bad situation well."

Weren't You a Blonde?

Until a few years ago, Frank Majewski hadn't seen Jack Ramsay for decades.

"I lost contact with Jack Ramsay for more than 35 years. We had the opportunity to have dinner in Charlotte, North Carolina, a few years ago. I felt compelled to spend an evening talking about old times and reacquainting with the 'Coach.' Funny part was when we first saw each other that evening, Jack didn't recognize me. I walked up to him and let him know who I was. He said to me, 'What happened to your blonde hair!?' I answered, 'It's gone, but I've still got a lot more than you!'"

Life Goes On at Hawk Hill

Though shaken to the core by the scandal, Coach Ramsay's fundamental values remained rock solid. He mulled over quitting. After endless soul-searching, he decided to keep on keeping on. And keeping on is what he did.

Jack had lost five seniors and three juniors from the Egan squad, but he patched his 1961-1962 club together on heart and hustle. Most of the year, the Hawks pressured opponents with Ramsay's celebrated 3-1-1 zone press. They managed to chalk up 18 wins and earn another NCAA bid.

Tom Wynne (left), Jack McKinney (second from left), and John Tiller (right) surround Jack Ramsey at his 80th birthday party. *Photo courtesy of Jack McKinney*

The 1962-1963 fivesome of Jim Boyle, Jim Lynam, Steve Courtin, Billy Hoy, and Tom Wynne came up huge. They matched the 25 wins of the scandal-scarred season to share the Hawk record for most wins in a season. They earned their fourth consecutive berth in the NCAA Tournament.

Their first opponent in the NCAA Tournament was the Princeton Tigers led by All-American Bill Bradley. This contest will forever be near the top of my "I'll always remember" list. Bradley dominated. He burned the cords for 40 points and grabbed 16 rebounds in regulation before he fouled out and then we won the game in overtime.

Wally's Dummy

Bill McFadden talks about how high Jack Ramsay got the Hawks for Villanova.

"All week before the Villanova game, we drilled to force Wally Jones to his left. Wally didn't like to go left. If you forced him left, he'd always try that spin move and come back to his right. That's the side he got that jumper off on.

"I knew we were up that night! The Palestra had swinging doors that the team came through from the locker room. That night when Bo [Jim Boyle] led the team out to the court, he blew the doors off the hinges!"

Different Strokes for Father Stokes

Former hoopster Bill McFadden tells this tale: "St. Joe's didn't give us special treatment. We had to compete in the classroom same as everyone else. But I'll let you in on one student secret. I found out the way to get an A in Father Stokes's Shakespeare class. All the upperclassmen said, 'Just give him Webster Golden Weddings with your blue book in the first test.' I did and got two As!"

Webster Golden Weddings are cigars. More accurately they *were* cigars. They're no longer made. When McFadden was telling this campus tidbit about cigars, John Tiller and a few listeners insinuated that Bill has been known to blow smoke himself.

Not Quite First

John Tiller was the first African American to receive a St. Joe's basketball scholarship. *Some* people think he holds that same distinction at Philly's LaSalle High School as well.

John Tiller: "I was a speaker for a certain affair one time and was introduced as the first African American to get a high school basketball scholarship to LaSalle High. I told them I *wasn't* the first. There was an African American before me named Ford Anderson. He fooled them. They just thought he was white!

"At LaSalle, I got scholarship offers from all Wake Forest, North Carolina and all kinds of southern schools. All they saw was '6'8" All-Catholic in Philadelphia. They figured, since I played for LaSalle I had to be white!"

Money Talks

John Tiller recalls playing in the south in the 1960s: "Villanova was playing in the same tournament we were, so Jack Ramsay telephoned one of the hotels near the arena down there in Winston Salem and asked if Villanova was staying there. The guy at the hotel said, 'Oh no, sir, they can't stay *here*. They have all them *Negroes* on the team!'

"We had to stay at another hotel. On that same trip, we were eating at a private club when in walks this guy wearing a big cowboy hat and smoking a big cigar. He looks around and sees me and his eyes almost pop out. He points to me and asks the owner, 'What is *he* doing here?'

Then he says, 'I'm not gonna stand for this.' The owner tells him, 'You don't have to. You can leave.' Ramsay had told the owner that I was the guy who was going to pay our bill."

Over the Top

John Tiller says, "We were playing Wake Forest down south and killing them all game long. Then the refs started calling fouls for everything. I stopped getting rebounds, and Ramsay called timeout.

"In the huddle, he got on me about not rebounding, 'What are you doing out there?' I told him the ref had told me, 'If you grab the ball over the rim, I'll give points to the other team.'

"Coach went ballistic. That's the day Billy Packer started his St. Joe's thing. The refs fouled seven of our guys out of the game. At the end of the game, Billy Hoy was on the foul line. We were up by one. There were only *two seconds left*, Hoy missed, and Packer drove the length of the floor and scored. *All in two seconds.* They never started the clock again till he scored."

Tiller Time

Back to that Princeton game, with Bradley gone, we went into our 3-1-1 press and set traps and double-ups every time the Tigers pushed the ball past mid-court. John Tiller was our "number five" man, or the "guardian of the hoop." Tiller spent the entire frame blocking shots. The box score gave him three blocks, but I swear he blocked 10! Three blocks in one overtime is awesome, and those blocks were the key to our eking out a one-point victory.

We scored an even bigger win on December 26, 1962, in the Quaker City Holiday Festival. The headliner was the No. 1 team in the nation, Bowling Green. They were the Hawks' opening-round opponent.

Bowling Green was led by seven-foot center Nate Thurmond and Howard Komives. Both were All-Americans. Thurmond became a huge NBA star with the Golden State Warriors and Cleveland Cavaliers.

Bowling Green held a 57-56 lead near the end of the game when Jim Boyle took a pass in the high post. Running a designed play, Boyle bounce-passed a beauty to set up a layup for Jim Lynam, who had beaten his man going back door. As Lynam cradled the ball, I figured, "That's it. Game over." Lynam and Jameer Nelson were the two best Hawks ever at taking the ball to the hoop in a crowd.

As Lynam recalls now, "I backdoored my man pretty well on that play. I started up for the shot, when all of a sudden, I couldn't see anything at all in the Palestra except Nate Thurman. He was in front of me—alongside me, above me—everywhere. Out of the corner of my eye I noticed that Boyle had stayed right at the top of the key. I don't know how, but somehow I flipped the ball to Jim. As I did, I noticed that the clock said three seconds.

"Boyle grabbed the toss, immediately leaped into a jumper, and launched one from about the hip, trying to beat the clock. It bounced around the rim about a dozen times—or so it seemed—and finally dropped down through the hoop as the gun sounded. Final score: 58-57, St. Joe's.

Courtin' Disaster

Tom Wynne and Steve Courtin, two stars of the team that toppled Bowling Green, were friends and neighbors from grade school through college. Wynne was one year senior to Courtin. Each had starred at St. James High in Chester.

Both were potent offensively. Wynne averaged 19 points a game in his junior and senior years, while Courtin chipped in with 16.5. Wynne is one of the most gifted athletes Saint Joseph's University ever produced. His mate, Courtin, earned a spot in the school's Basketball Hall of Fame.

At that point in the season, Wynne was a senior, averaging 20 points per game. Courtin was a reserve guard averaging about seven points a game. Billy Hoy started ahead of Courtin, but Hoy broke his ankle in a game at Madison Square Garden prior to the Holiday Tournament.

Wynne usually drove Courtin to the city games. Courtin recalls their conversation on the way to the Bowling Green game.

"We were riding in from the Milmont Park/Woodlyn area [outside Chester, Pennsylvania] for our pregame meal. When we were approaching West Chester Pike on City Line Avenue—I can remember the exact spot to this day. Tom said, 'Are you scared to be starting today against mighty Bowling Green? We might get our asses kicked.'

"I had two choices—to agree or get bold. I came back: 'Tom, I've got some information for you. I'm going to tell you who's going to win today. We are.'

"Tom laughed. Then I added, 'I have some more news for you. I'm going to be high scorer.' Then he really laughed.

"He had every reason to. Tom had been a supersub on the Final Four team as a sophomore. He made All-Big Five as a junior and was the Hawks' top scorer as a junior and senior.

"I was on a roll, so I kept going. 'Tom, I've got more news for you. We're going to win this tournament. And I'm going to name the all-tournament team.' I rolled off four players from our team. I know he was expecting me to save his name for last. Wrong! I said, 'Tom, the last member is me.'

"He was roaring at this point. So I finished strong, 'And now for the tournament MVP. It's yours truly—me.'

"Funny, but I was correct on practically all counts. We upset Bowling Green on Jim Boyle's buzzer bomb and won the tournament. My Saint

Tom Wynne drives with authority through the Dayton defense.
Photo courtesy of Saint Joseph's University

Joseph's career changed as of that tournament—and probably my path in life as well. I went from the sixth or seventh man in December 1962 to the 26th guy picked in the NBA draft 16 months later."

Ramsay's Final Two Years

Let it never be said that Dr. Ramsay didn't know how to close out a game—or a career. Jack's final two squads were probably the finest in his Hawk tenure. Their two-year record was 50-8. They had strength in both the frontcourt and backcourt. Cliff Anderson, Tom Duff, Marty Ford, and Charlie McKenna handled the boards with Matty Guokas, Jr. and Billy Oakes patrolling outside and averaging 31 points a game. Toss in a deep bench, and Dr. Jack had a bona fide NCAA contender.

Actually it was a member of that backup crew, Steve Donches, who provided arguably the biggest moment in Ramsay's glorious two-year final run.

On a Sunday afternoon, the Hawks and the Villanova Wildcats were squaring off at the Palestra, which was packed with 8,700 nutso spectators. Villanova's match-up zone defense was giving the Hawks fits. Besides, the Hawks were off their game and trailed through most of the match. Near the end, when the Hawks started changing defenses and confusing the 'Cats into some critical turnovers, they knotted the score at 69.

St. Joe's was playing for one last shot. They were getting frustrated trying to penetrate 'Nova's D. As the clock wound down to zero, the ball found its way into the hands of Steve Donches, who hailed from Bethlehem, Pennsylvania, the Christmas City—home of Philadelphia Eagle Chuck Bednarik and Lehigh University. Steve was standing practically in front of Coach Ramsay near the Hawk bench when he got the ball with two ticks left on the clock. Steve popped a 25-foot jumper that seemed to stay airborne for 15 seconds (I know the math doesn't make sense). It looked like the guiding star of Bethlehem as it traced across the Palestra "sky." With the horn sounding, the ball sailed through the cords for a Hawk victory.

Leaving Hawk Hill

Jack was having problems with his eyesight, suffering from edema in the retina of his left eye. He could only see dark spots in front of that eye. After a visit to the ophthalmologist and a lot of reflection, Jack decided to step down as coach. The basketball world, however, would have none of his departure from the game. The Philadelphia 76ers snarfed him up as their general manager. When Sixers coach Alex Hannum retired two years later, Dr. Jack's eyesight problems had been rectified, and he embarked on a long, fruitful career as an NBA coach.

Jack's coaching career in the NBA took him to Buffalo, Portland, and Indiana. Not surprisingly, he excelled as a professional coach. His NBA

Jack Ramsey calls him "safe" in his usual sideline manner. *Photo courtesy of Saint Joseph's University*

teams won 864 games. When he left the pro coaching ranks, Jack trailed only Red Auerbach on the list of all-time wins. Furthermore, he re-created the postseason success he enjoyed in college. Jack led his NBA teams to the playoffs 17 out of the 20 seasons he coached.

Ramsay's mark is forever emblazoned at his alma mater. The memory of the Coach on one knee in front of the team bench at the Fieldhouse or the Palestra will never die—just like the Hawk. Jack Ramsay has come to epitomize everything about which the Saint Joseph University basketball program has to be proud.

The Ramsay Lineage

Ramsay's influence continues to resonate at Saint Joseph's University. His influence on the Hawk basketball program transcends the 12 seasons he spent there as head coach. His disciples—the guys he groomed and shaped into coaches—have populated Hawk Hill ever since Dr. Jack's departure. Here's the Ramsay legacy of Hawk coaches who played for Dr. Jack or coached with him.

- Jack McKinney—Hawk coach from 1966-1974; played for Ramsay in 1957
- Harry Booth—Hawk coach from 1974-1978; played for Ramsay in 1962
- Jim Lynam—Hawk coach from 1978-1981; played for Ramsay in 1963
- Jim Boyle—Hawk coach from 1981-1990; played for Ramsay in 1963
- John Griffin—Hawk coach from 1990-1995; played for Lynam in 1978

The Ramsay lineage arguably includes Phil Martelli. Phil was an assistant coach for John Griffin who played for Ramsay and coached with Boyle. Suffice it to say, when it comes to Saint Joseph's University basketball tradition, Dr. Jack has left a Hawk-print that goes deeper than the talons.

It's not serendipity that sustains Jack Ramsay's 50-year grip on the Saint Joseph's University basketball program. It's success. In 11 years, Ramsay's teams rolled to a 234-72 record for an astounding winning percentage of .765. Perhaps even more incredible, Jack's teams were invited to 10 postseason tournaments in 11 years—seven NCAA Tournaments and three NITs.

What remains with his players and staff were his human qualities—qualities his staff sought to emulate. He was a mentor and a quiet leader, coupling an uncanny knowledge of the sport with the communication skills to convey that knowledge. He was a marvel at game preparation. He was better still at reacting and improvising during the course of a game.

A sentiment I've heard over and over from former players is, "After my dad, Jack Ramsay was the most influential man in my life." Jack motivated. Players busted their butts because they didn't want to disappoint him. Jack could get people to reach deep down inside and come up with their personal best. He gave each guy the personal strokes he needed. He encouraged his players and made them feel good about themselves.

I had the privilege of learning from the master, first as a player and later as a coach. As a player, after Coach Ramsay talked with me, I felt inspired. I felt he could get anyone to go the extra mile and give every ounce of effort they had.

The record shows Jack had that effect on players everywhere he coached. When Ramsay coached the Portland Trailblazers, his superstar Bill Walton once remarked, "Whenever we were losing by six points with five seconds to go and Coach Ramsay called a time out, I still fully expected him to dream up some kind of a six-point play that would give us the win."

Jack Ramsay was special. He was Dr. Jack. He was Coach.

Family Ties

Former 76ers coach, Jim O'Brien is Jack Ramsay's son-in-law.

"Jim has wanted to be a coach, right from the beginning," Jack chuckles.

Still, Jim O'Brien has a much tougher job impressing his father-in-law than most of us.

CHAPTER SEVEN

Matt of The Family Guokas

The Family Guokas

L ike a few other names at Saint Joseph's University, "Guokas" pops up quite a bit. Look at it this way, you'll find a lot more "Guokas" listings on the SJU all-time roster of basketball players than you'll find in your typical phonebook.

"Guokas" on Hawk Hill has a number of different faces associated with it. The most familiar is probably Matt Guokas, Jr. who starred for Jack Ramsay's squads in the mid-1960s. However, Matt's dad, Matt Sr., was instrumental in ushering Saint Joseph's basketball into national prominence. Matt Guokas, Sr. was the little big man of the Hawks' Mighty Mites squad.

Matt Sr.'s brother, Al Guokas, started for the Hawks of the late 1940s. One of his teammates was Jack Ramsay.

The last Guokas name (so far) is Matt Guokas III, Matt Jr.'s son, who wore the Hawk uniform for three years in the late 1980s.

Hawk Names

Another name that pops up throughout the Hawks' basketball annals is "Oakes." There were four different "Oakes" who played for the Crimson and Gray: Bill Oakes, 1926-1929; Billy Oakes, 1964-1966; Joe Oakes, 1935-1938; Johnny Oakes, 1922-1926.

Those four Oakes hoopsters match the Guokases in number. But they're not all the same family. Billy Oakes on the 1964 squad is not related to the other Oakes on the list. But Guokas and Oakes appeared on the rosters of two famous Hawk teams. Joe Oakes and Matt Guokas Sr. teamed together for three years on the Mighty Mites. Almost 30 years later, Billy Oakes and Matt Guokas Jr. partnered in the backcourt on Jack Ramsay's powerhouses of the mid-1960s.

Speaking about Hawk names, all you Hawk fans, here's a trivia question for you. What surname appears most on the Hawks' all-time roster? If you said "Brennan," you're wrong. "Kelly?" Nope. "Kenney?" Good guess, but wrong again. "H-A-double-R-I-G-A-N" might spell Harrigan (there has *never* been a Hawk player named Harrigan), and the "whole town might be talking about the Jones boys (there have been two players named Jones including Dwayne on the current team) but the correct answer is "Murphy." [Note to younger readers: both references— "Harrigan" and "The Whole Town's Talking About the Jones Boys"—are old, old songs …ask your grandfather].

Anyway, here's the list of Murphys: Bob Murphy, 1943; Ed Murphy, 1939; Frank Murphy, 1958; Joe Murphy, 1911-1912; John Murphy, 1917-1919; Tom Murphy, 1936.

Three names—Gallagher, Martin, and O'Neill—tie for the runner-up slot for most listings on the all-time Hawk roster. The Gallaghers were Ed, Jim, John, Pete, and Tom; the Martins were Jack, Maurice, Ray, Sam, and Sean; and the O'Neills were Harold, Bob, Jim, Joe, and Mike.

Hope that information helps in your "who buys the next round?" arguments.

Four for Four

The Hawks retired jersey number four in honor of four different greats who wore that number: George Senesky, Paul Senesky, Jim Lynam, and Billy Oakes.

Jersey number four has undergone two remarkable successions. First, the jersey was passed, after a brief hiatus, from George Senesky to his brother Paul. George Senesky is second on the Hawks all-time list for points-per-game. When brother Paul got the jersey, he gunned his way into the number-three slot on the points-per-game list. The second noteworthy succession for jersey number four came with the handoff from Jim Lynam to Bill Oakes. Lynam graduated in 1963. The next year Billy Oakes was wearing his jersey.

In addition to the four players who wore number four, three other St. Joe's greats have had their jerseys hoisted to the Fieldhouse rafters: Cliff

...rson (#30), Mike Bantom (#44), and Jameer Nelson (#14). That's four guys. There's that number again. Yeah, and every jersey that has been retired has at least one four on it, except Cliff Anderson's. Get with the program, Clifford.

More on Retired Jerseys

The only time in Hawk history that two players whose jerseys would eventually be retired played on the same squad were Cliff Anderson and Billy Oakes. The two teamed on the 1964-1965 and 1965-1966 squads.

Matt Senior

Matt Guokas, Sr. was the Mighty Mites' leader and top scorer. The dean of the clan Guokas was a consensus All-American in 1938—the second St. Joe's hoopster to be so honored. He averaged double figures in his senior year. His team generally held opponents below 40 points. The Mites seldom scored more than 40 points themselves. However, their gritty defense and scrappy team play set the tone for all the generations of Hawk teams that followed.

Matt Sr. left the hardwoods after his Mighty Mite days. There were no successful professional basketball leagues in those days. However, he resurfaced, Roy Hobbs-like, in 1946 to play for the Philadelphia Warriors in the newly formed BAA, the precursor of the NBA. The Warriors won the league championship that year, recognized as the first ever NBA championship. Twenty years later, his son Matt earned a championship ring with the Philadelphia 76ers. That makes the Guokases the only father-son duo ever to have each played on an NBA championship team.

Matt Junior

Matty Guokas Jr., in contrast to his dad, grew up in a basketball-crazed town (Philly) and basketball-crazed era (anytime after the 1950s). Matty was a high-profile Philadelphia star in his high school days at Saint Joseph's Prep. He averaged 16.3 ppg and earned Philadelphia All-Catholic honors along with Prep teammate Tom Duff, who averaged 17.1 His Prep team won the Catholic League championship but fell to West Philadelphia High in the city championship game at the Palestra. West Philly, led by Ken Morgan (17), Deforia Coleman (15), and Frank Card (14) topped, Prep 61-52, despite Matt's 15-point effort.

Matt was highly recruited while he was at Saint Joseph's Prep. He eventually accepted a scholarship to Miami, where he matriculated for a year before transferring to St. Joe's.

The Prototype

COACH McKINNEY:

I look on Matty Guokas as the precursor to Magic Johnson, and I coached them both. Though Matty stood 6'6", he was a precision passer who could shoot, penetrate, and take charge of a game. In Matty's college heyday, a 6'6" guy was supposed to station himself somewhere around the bucket and put the ball on the floor as little as possible. Not Matty. He changed that paradigm. He played point guard and turned out to be a prototype big guard—the kind of guy who was instrumental in changing the professional game. The things Matt Guokas was doing in the sixties were the kinds of things that Magic notched up years later when he played for me on the Lakers.

Fans nowadays might not realize that moving Magic to point guard was a controversial move at the time. I knew a talented big guy could play the position, though. I watched Coach Ramsay put Matty there during his first year of eligibility. And I've got to tell you, the superb way Matty handled the point guard position at St. Joe's influenced my decision about Magic.

Matt was fabulous in a transition situation. He shifted from defense to offense at the drop of a hat. His instinct on the court was matched by amazing peripheral vision. He saw everyone and everything on the court. If he couldn't actually see them, Matt had an uncanny ability to "feel" where they were. When he ran the break, if he didn't find Oakes, Duff, or Ford in good position for an easy layup, he brought the ball back out and set the offense up again. Then he'd look for a way to set up Cliff Anderson for a bucket.

Matty had to sit out a year at Saint Joseph's because he transferred from Miami after his freshman year. The biggest problem Matty faced was getting his teammates to catch up to his quick basketball mind. They weren't used to the slick passes that he tossed their way. Matty was always surprising his own teammates—almost as much as the defenders—with his uncanny ability to hit the open man. He hit them with passes from every angle and every direction. His favorite target was Cliff Anderson. Cliff was the greatest raw talent we had in those years—or any years for that matter. Matty knew how to exploit Cliff's talents to the maximum. He was always looking for him and usually he found him. Recently I asked Matty how the court relationship between Cliff and him developed.

Matty says, "I didn't know what to expect from Cliff at first. He was a Public League guy that I wasn't familiar with. It didn't take long to find out he was something special. He was the perfect outlet for me. Cliff always

On the court, Matt Goukas Jr. shared much in common with Magic Johnson.
Photo courtesy of Saint Joseph's University

managed to get open inside or running down on the break. I had great confidence that if I got him the ball in good position, Cliff would take care of the rest."

Matty, of course, was no stranger to the Hawk program. Besides the fact that his father was one of the greatest Hawks of all time, Matt Jr. was joining Tom Duff and Billy McFadden, two of his mates from St. Joe's Prep. As Matty recalls:

"I know it's overused, but we had chemistry. I was playing with two guys I played with all through high school. I was also playing with lots of guys I had played against at the Prep. But everyone quickly settled into his role. Because we knew each other so well, we all felt comfortable. We considered it our personal Catholic League All-Star squad. They were pretty impressive credentials.

"That chemistry and comfort helped in so many ways. I always think of Billy Oakes as 'Mr. Cool.' Whenever I got upset or excited, Billy cooled me down. Billy McFadden was the opposite. Whenever I got down on myself, Billy built me back up."

Matt's record speaks for itself. He had a great college career and played for some of St. Joe's greatest teams. Dr. Jack Ramsay still calls the Guokas-Anderson squad his greatest. That observation is pretty tough to dispute.

Show You're Human—Or Not

Jack Ramsay is still in awe of Matty Guokas's talents as a passer at Saint Joseph's College. As Jack puts it, "His passing was sharp and accurate. You wanted him to make a bad pass once in a while just to prove he was human—well in practice, not in a game."

High-Priced Recruiting

Not surprisingly, Jack Ramsay recruited Matt Guokas when he was an All-Catholic at St. Joe's Prep. But Jack wasn't successful. He didn't convince Matt to come to Hawk Hill, and Matty set off for Miami. In the spring of the following year, Matt Guokas, Sr. telephoned Jack and confessed that his son was unhappy in Miami. Would Jack consider taking Matty at St. Joe's?

Jack's answer was a definite yes.

That was it. When Matt Jr. returned to the Delaware Valley, he met with Jack Ramsay and became a Hawk despite having to sit out a year.

Matt practiced with my freshman team the year he came to SJU. That frosh squad was led by Cliff Anderson and they went 15-1. Imagine what we could have accomplished if Matt had been allowed to play!

Matt scrimmaged with us daily against the varsity. The freshman team consisted of Bob Brennan, Al Grundy, Stever Donches, Matt Guokas, and Cliff Anderson. We gave the varsity all they could handle. Jack Ramsay used to watch Anderson and Guokas and drool over the prospects of the future.

Anyway, that was the high-priced, sophisticated recruiting drive that brought Matt Guokas Jr. to Hawk Hill—a phone call from his father to the coach.

Home Boys

Matt Guokas was the playmaker and leader of Jack Ramsay's talented 1965-1966 squad. Athletic director Don DiJulia played on that team. He recalls a conversation Matt Guokas and he had prior to that season.

"Matt and I were checking the schedule out," DiJules says. "Nationally nobody knew Matt at that point. He had transferred from Miami and sat out a year. He and Cliff Anderson had never played varsity, so nationally no one knew Clifford, either. Anyway, Matt was so confident all the time, it was amazing. He was sure nobody on the schedule could beat us! We were scheduled to play some big teams—Bowling Green, Providence, Illinois—as well as the Big Five teams.

"Matt understood the individual court style of every guy on the team. He was comfortable with everyone and fit right in. Actually growing up in CYO and neighborhood basketball and the Catholic League, Matt had played with most of those guys all his life. Matt's confidence proved not to be hollow. We had a great season. They knew St. Joe's nationally the following year! Do you know that the following year in the 1965-1966 preseason, we were ranked number one by *Sports Illustrated?* But here's what's really amazing. *Every one of our starters that year grew up within a six-mile radius of the school!* Cliff Anderson went to Edison High, Marty Ford to West Catholic, and Billy Oakes to Bishop Neuman. Matty and Tom Duff both went to the Prep.

"Now I ask you: was there *ever* a No. 1-ranked team that could make that claim?"

Most likely, there is not—but without doubt, there will never be another.

In Summary

Matt Guokas Jr. merits a spot with the greatest Hawks of all time. Matt was co-captain of the mighty 1965-1966 Hawks that averaged 91.1 ppg en route to a 24-5 season where they established the St. Joe record for most points in a season (2,642). Matty belongs to the charmed circle of Hawk hoopsters who scored 500 points in a single season by tallying 508 that year. He also dished off 176 career assists, fourth best in Hawk history. Matt ranks fourth (1965-1966) and 11th (1964-1965) for most assists in a single season. On the Hawks all-time list for most steals in a single season, he holds down two slots: fourth (1964-1965) with 90 steals and seventh (1965-1966) with 76 steals. He ranks 10th on his college's all-time list for best career field-goal percentage with an accuracy of .482.

Matt became Saint Joseph's seventh All-American in 1966 and was drafted in the first round by the Philadelphia 76ers. He was a reserve on the 1966 76ers championship team and played 10 years in the NBA. He followed up with a seven-year stint as an NBA coach. He broke in with a stellar 54-28 season with the 1985 Sixers. He was let go by Philadelphia in 1987 after 43 games. The following season, he was named the first coach for the Orlando Magic where he remained at the helm till 1993.

Today, Matt continues a successful broadcasting career.

In 1975, Matt Guokas Jr. was inducted into Saint Joseph's University Hall of Fame—right on the heels of his father who was inducted in 1975.

The Guokas Succession Continues

Matt Guokas III played for the Hawks from 1988-1989 through 1990-1991. Unfortunately, Matt III hit Hawk Hill during a down period. He suffered through three successive losing seasons. Individually, his finest season came in his senior year when he averaged 7.0 ppg for a 13-17 squad that went 3-1 in Big Five competition and gained a half share of the Big Five crown.

Brother Al

Al Guokas always managed to get his thunder stolen. Al was a starter on a fine 1946-1947 Hawk squad that went 16-6, beating some fine teams like Temple, St. John's, and Utah State along the way. In his senior year, he averaged 10 points a game. Sophomore newcomer Paul Senesky who averaged 18.3, however, overshadowed his fine season.

Al graduated and was drafted by the Philadelphia Warriors. Unlike Hawk teammate Paul Senesky, who did not make the professional ranks, Al Guokas did—at least for a year. He played 16 games for the Philly Warriors, averaging 1.1 points per contest when he was shipped off to the Denver Nuggets. He finished the season out in the Mile High City where he played 41 games and averaged 4.8 points.

That Denver Nuggets franchise lasted only one season, 1949-1950. Denver finished sixth with a record of 11-51, and with their demise, Al's professional basketball career came to a close.

CHAPTER EIGHT

Clifford Anderson

C liff earned All-America honors as a senior in 1966-1967. He still holds the SJU season records for scoring average (26.5), rebound average (15.5), field goals attempted (605), free throws made (204) and attempted (279), as well as the all-time career marks for rebounds (1,228) and rebounds-per-game average (14.6).

How awesome are those stats? It's not often that the same guy holds the record for most points and most rebounds. Sure it can happen, usually the guy who does it is a dominant seven-footer who camps out near the basket, grabs the misses, and converts them into points. That was not the case with Clifford Anderson. Cliff was a slender 6'4" guy who constantly gave up half a foot or more to opponents he went up against.

Cliff's accomplishments go on and on. He shattered the SJU career scoring mark in his senior year, but has since slipped to fifth (1,728). Remember that freshmen were not eligible in his day. Guys who benefited from playing all four years eclipsed a lot of his records. Cliff also set the single-season record for points in a season (690), which was eclipsed by Marvin O'Connor in 2001. He grabbed 32 rebounds in a win over La Salle at the Palestra—which is still the second best rebounding effort in school history. He led the Hawks in scoring *and* rebounding all three seasons he played, and he was instrumental in helping his team achieve a No. 3 final AP ranking in 1964-1965 and a Number 5 in 1965-1966.

Cliff played a combined four years in the NBA and the ABA. He donned the uniform of the L.A. Lakers from 1967-1969, Denver in 1969-1970, and Cleveland and Philadelphia in 1970-1971.

Sight Unseen—Dr. Jack's Greatest Buy

COACH McKINNEY:

Jack got word that Edison High had a young kid named Clifford Anderson who seemed ideal for the Hawk program. He was a good student, a good kid, and a promising talent. Jack's friends in the Philadelphia Public League gave nothing but rave reviews of this Anderson fellow.

Jack invited Clifford and his mother, Cleo, to campus. The trio hit it off immediately. Jack discovered that Cliff had passed his PSAT exam, read books, and was well situated in his graduating class.

Sold! Before Cliff left campus, Ramsay had a new player, and Cliff had a new coach. And Cliff's new coach had *never seen him play basketball!* Not live, not on film. Jack Ramsay signed Cliff on faith.

But Jack soon *did* get a chance to see Cliff play—up close and personal. Coach Ramsay and I were running the Jack Ramsay Basketball Summer Camp in Canadensis in the Poconos that summer. Cliff Anderson became one of our counselors.

The highlight of the day was the counselor's game at day's end. Jack Ramsay was still in his thirties and in great shape, so he often played in the game. And that happened to be the first time Jack caught the Cliff Anderson Show act on the court. As Jack remembers it:

"I moved in to get a rebound when I felt someone go up, fly overtop of me and everyone else, grab the ball, come back to earth, slither through everyone around the basket, sky up over us again, and lay it in. Pretty impressive stuff—but even more impressive considering that he did it from the foul line. I thought, 'Wow! I got a good one here!'"

That's the story of how Cliff Anderson was recruited and introduced to his coach. Just another big dent in the Ramsay recruiting budget. As Jack Ramsay puts it: "Yeah, we had a huge recruiting budget of $300 a year, but we were careful not to spend *all* of it!"

What a Find!

Cliff led his freshman team to a 15-1 record, which set a school freshman-team record. In his sophomore and junior years, he and Matty Guokas teamed to lead their teams to 50 wins. As a senior, Cliff was astonishing. Working under a rookie coach (that would be me), Cliff hoisted a so-so team on his shoulders and led them to a 16-10 record.

That same year, he smashed George Senesky's 24-year scoring record for average points per game by more than three points per game. That's domination! Cliff's mark of 26.5 points per game still stands. Senesky remains second on that list, with an average of 23.4 ppg. In 1964-1965, Cliff tied the standard (15.5) for most rebounds per game in a single season that Ray Radziszewski held.

Cliff played three years of varsity ball and led his team in scoring and rebounding every year. Did I mention that the team he led was ranked number three in his sophomore year and number five in his senior year? Undeniably, Cliff put up All-America stats and boasted All-America credentials. Unfortunately, Cliff was snubbed for that honor, but he was All-America to us.

Today, still spry and athletic at age 61, Cliff looks back on his days at Saint Joseph's University with gratitude and happiness.

Cliff tells me: "I have so much to be thankful for. I grew as an individual during my college years. For one thing, you guys—Jack Ramsay and Jack McKinney—were so great to me. My education was invaluable. My Jesuit education at Saint Joseph's College taught me how to live, and on a personal level, my relationship with Al Grundy has been a lifelong blessing as well as rich and fulfilling."

Al was a 6'5" African American center from Ridley Township who became Cliff's teammate in college.

Cliff continues: "I was a 6'4"forward from North Philly. Al and I came from different backgrounds, but we clicked and we helped each other. Al was more ... I guess you'd call it orderly than I was. He was more sure of himself. He fit right into St. Joe's lifestyle—a lot more easily than I did. I had a completely different style than Al's. I was the big-city boy. I was more footloose and fancy-free. But what an experience I had at that campus! I loved the school, loved playing basketball there, loved playing in Philadelphia, loved Coach Ramsay and Coach McKinney, and loved playing with Matty Guokas."

A Style All His Own

Cliff had a style all his own, just like he says. But he had a style of his own on the court, too. It seemed like he was moving and jumping endlessly somewhere in the vicinity of the hoop. He'd be tapping a rebound three or four straight times, purposely tipping the ball so it bounced back toward him if he couldn't grab it or control it on the first jump. Then he'd somehow close the whole play off with a miracle follow-up bucket on the third tip. You got the sense he was controlling the whole action until he could finally manage to get himself a high-percentage shot—which for Cliff was a twisting, turning, spinning, over-one-guy-under-the-next-guy move that brought the whole crowd to its feet.

That's what I remember of Clifford Anderson on the basketball court. When I asked him what his most vivid memory on the court is, he came back with a surprise.

"I think the thing I remember most—or got the biggest kick out of—was the time I threw up about an 80-footer and sank it to end the first half against Temple. I remember running off the court laughing like hell!

"When I look back," Cliff says, "I have to give a lot of people special credit, like Dr. James Iannucci, head of the language department at Saint Joseph's College. He taught me French. But the most important thing he taught me in that course was *proper English*. I had communication deficiencies from my environment growing up. He explained that I needed to grow culturally and socially. He instilled me with confidence as a public speaker and helped shape me into a more rounded individual and a better person. That's a lot of growth and a lot of mileage from one French course.

"My mom, Cleo Anderson, was always my biggest role model and inspiration. Did you know she was the first woman journalist for the *Afro American Newspaper*? My mother was the one who helped me develop effective study habits and helped shape me as a communicator."

Cliff had some positive influences early in life as well. He speaks highly of Mr. Edward Davis, his sixth-grade teacher at Ferguson Elementary School in North Philly. Mr. Davis convinced Cliff that developing the habit of reading would improve his diction.

"Mr. Davis was always on me, trying to get me to read more. So I did. He eventually challenged me to read Tolstoy's *War and Peace*. And I did. I read the whole book cover to cover at age 13, which pleased Mr. Davis no end. It also gave me a sense of accomplishment."

The same kind of passion Cliff cultivated for reading burned when he was on the court. He funneled that passion into rebounding. As a rebounder, Cliff had no peer.

"I played with Trooper Washington and a couple of other really good players in high school," Cliff relates. "We were a good team, and those guys could really shoot! So I concentrated on rebounding. Rebounding became my first love."

Dropping Igor

Cliff's toughness under the boards shaped his on-court persona. Cliff wasn't mean, just determined, but he could step up to the enforcer role when he had to.

"When I was playing with the Hawks, we played Brazil's National team in Brazil," the Hawk great recalls." They were a good team, and they had this big tough guy who was manhandling our guys big time. I figured I had to do something to stop him, so I signaled our guys to go "four corners" on offense and get me the ball. Everyone did. Matty Guokas got the ball into me on the high post. I pump-faked this guy—got him into the air, then waited. As he came down, I went up, cracked him in his throat and rearranged his teeth. I think he's still gagging! But I had to protect my team!"

Matt Guokas recalls: "I remember that guy and I remember the play. We nicknamed the guy Igor. The way I remember it, Cliff called for that four-corners offense, then did a finger roll. While the ball was arching toward the bucket, he jammed a fist into Igor's face that laid him out. Igor

Left to right: Clifford Anderson, Coach Jack Ramsay, Tom Duff, and Billy Oakes celebrate after winning the Quaker City Tournament in 1965. *Photo courtesy of Saint Joseph's University*

turned beet red all the way down to his ankles and called time out. Cliff came over to the bench and said to the team, 'All right, forget about Igor. Now we can play.'"

Style and Substance

"Jim Boyle helped me develop as a rebounder," Cliff relates. "He pushed me in practice and showed me some great little tricks.

"As for our team, I think I brought a bit of creativity to the team offense. On defense, I was a bit of a thug, a tough guy. I'll let you in on something. I would love to have played with Mike Hauer. Could you see that! Hauer was a great rebounder and a bit of a thug, too, a good thug, you know what I mean—definitely my kind of player. Yeah, St. Joe's was a great experience. But without you two coaches, Dr. Jack and you, without the direction you provided, it would never have happened for Clifford Anderson."

I can't begin to tell you how rewarding it is to hear a quality person like Clifford Anderson make that statement. Don't let Cliff's sensitive side throw you off track, though. Cliff Anderson was one tough customer on the court, as Matty Guokas confirms: "If I could get him the ball, it was usually like money in the bank. Cliff always wanted me to bring the game to him. He had supreme confidence in himself. What a competitor! Cliff wanted to excel in every aspect of the game, and for the most part he did. His biggest weakness was foul shooting. He was not the best foul shooter. He never quite got the knack of it, even though he worked at it [actually, Cliff sort of got the knack, at least according to the record book. Cliff holds the all-time record for free throws made in one season with 204 in 1966-1967]. It would frustrate him when he missed a foul shot. He would get upset and Jack Ramsay would have to talk to him. Our teammates would pump him up so he didn't lose his focus. He never did. Cliff had tremendous mental toughness. He grew up on the mean streets of North Philly, and when he got to St. Joe's he didn't forget how to be tough on the court."

Matt relates that Cliff had to suffer some indignities and unpleasant experiences in the tumult of the 1960s.

"We were warming up before a game against Wake Forest in Winston Salem North Carolina. There was a section of fold-up chairs near the court that a group of Wake Forest students filed in and filled up. They started screaming nasty stuff about the 'Catholic school from the big city.' Then they shifted their target and started harassing Cliff and Al Grundy, working them over by hollering racial slurs. We all pretended not to hear, which ticked these jerks off all the more. Finally, Cliff and Al couldn't take any more. They rushed toward the stands and started climbing over the chairs to get to the obnoxious 'good ole boys.' Fortunately the rest of us got to Cliff and Al first and pulled them back. Those fans should be forever grateful. The rest of the Hawks saved them from a lot of physical pain.

"The officiating that game was disgraceful, too. There was a local Southern ref whose style of officiating was so biased it was like giving them an extra guy or two. We had brought Philly area referee Steve Honzo along on the trip to try to balance things out—to try to offset this—let's call it—peculiar brand of such southern 'hospitality.' Steve helped keep the game somewhat under control. It all came out in the wash, anyway. We won big and Cliff had a huge game."

After Hawk Hill

Added to all his other accomplishments and honors, in 1966, Cliff Anderson became the first African American captain of a Hawk basketball team. After three stellar years at St. Joe's, he was drafted in the first round by the Pittsburgh Pipers in the ABA. Cliff never played with the Pipers. He went to the Lakers prior to the season and spent the 1967-1969 campaign in a Lakers uniform. He played for Denver in the 1969-1970 campaign, and in 1970-1971 he split the season between Cleveland and Philadelphia.

Cliff was elected to the Saint Joseph's University Basketball Hall of Fame in 1973. In 1999, both he and his first coach, Jack Ramsay (as well as Jim Brennan the original Hawk mascot and George Senesky), were inducted into the Saint Joseph's University Athletic Hall of Fame.

CHAPTER NINE

The Jack McKinney Years

Textile Days

COACH McKINNEY:

In 1965-1966, the curtain dropped on Jack Ramsay's coaching career at Saint Joseph's. Of course, Dr. Jack's coaching career was far from finished. Enormous NBA success lay ahead. But the college hardwoods were behind him for good. As for me, for the second consecutive year, I found myself in the enviable/unenviable position of following a legend. Let me backtrack a year to explain.

The previous year, Harry Pure, the athletic director at Philadelphia Textile called me and asked if I might be interested in the head coaching job. The incumbent coach, Bucky Harris, was calling it quits after a 12-year career. Bucky himself had tipped me off about his upcoming retirement, so I wasn't hit cold. Incidentally, Textile is now known as Philadelphia College. Philadelphia College/Textile has been a big part of the Philadelphia fabric for a century.

At the time, I was one of Jack Ramsay's assistant coaches, a position I had held for five years. Jack enthusiastically supported my pursuing the Textile offer, so I accepted.

Herb Magee was my assistant. I couldn't have done better. I think history bears that out. Now (2005) in his 38th year at Textile, Herb is one of the sport's most respected mentors.

One Who Flew Over the Hawk's Nest

Herb Magee still rattles on in good fun about not becoming a Hawk. Herb was the backcourt mate of Jim Lynam at Philly's West Catholic High School. Both Herb and Jim were selected to Philly's All-Catholic squad in 1958. But only Lynam got a scholarship to Saint Joseph's.

Though he was disappointed, life went on for Herb Magee. He accepted a scholarship to Philadelphia Textile and enjoyed a stellar career, both as a player and a coach. As a player, he tallied 2,235 career points, had a scoring average of 25.6, and set a one-game scoring record of 50 points against Wilkes College. As a coach, Magee's Textile/Philadelphia University log is a glittery 772-298. He also boasts one NCAA Division II title.

Herb was probably the finest shooter I've ever seen. He used to shoot jumpers from the top of the key before practice while I camped out under the twine retrieving the ball. He'd can about ten straight and taunt, "Eat your heart out, McKinney!" If he missed, he'd yell, "Bad pass!"

When I coached Indiana in the NBA, I sent for Herb to come to summer camp and work with our guys on shooting fundamentals. When I introduced him to the team, the guys were skeptical. They were thinking (and some were saying aloud), "Who the hell is this skinny little creep, and what the hell is Philadelphia Textile? A mill?"

They soon found out that Herb could make baskets a lot better than shirts and pants. He spent a week with us before returning to Philadelphia University. Our guys were going to physically restrain him from going to the airport! They all wanted me to hire him permanently on the spot.

Coming to Hawk Hill

Even though I had been Jack Ramsey's assistant coach all those years, I was basically starting from scratch. At least it seemed so on paper. Six of the first seven players from the previous season were lost to graduation. Clifford Anderson was the only one on the squad with any legitimate experience. The frosh from the year before were considered one of the weaker crops of the recent vintages. But the season turned out great.

We put a pretty tough quintet out on the court with Clifford. Bob Brenner, Mike Kempski, and Dave Pfahler rebounded, and the backcourt of Steve Donches and Billy DeAngelis stepped up to the challenge. Buddy Gardler and jumping jack Al Grundy were our backups. Al was 6'5" and could leap as high as Cliff at 6'4". Of course, Al didn't have Cliff's uncanny rebounding instinct. Few did. However, our small frontcourt of 6'5" Grundy, 6'4" Anderson, and 6'3" Brenner more than held its own against bigger front lines all season long.

We ended the 1966-1967 season a respectable 16-10. We had some great highs, like the Holiday Tournament at Madison Square Garden. We fought our way to the finals and then lost the championship game 82-76 to star-studded Providence featuring Ernie "D" (Ernie DiGregorio), Marvin Barnes, and Kevin Stacom. We beat LaSalle 96-83 later in the season. However, the Explorers bounced back a week later and beat us 73-70 for the MAC Conference Championship and an NCAA berth. Season over.

The McKinney Peanuts Gallery

In my first year as Hawk head coach, I brought my whole family to the Holiday Tournament in NYC. Actually, I met them up there. I boarded the team bus and they came up by train. I warned my family that I'd be busy and wouldn't be able to spend much time with them. We had to face some stiff competition like Brigham Young, Rhode Island, and Providence, who had Marvin Barnes and Ernie DiGregorio.

We won our first two games in the Tournament and then had a day off. We designated the day off as "family day." All six of us in the McKinney household—Claire, our eight-year-old, six-year-old, four-year-old, and two-year-old (is there a pattern here?) and I—headed to the Rockefeller Center to see the Rockettes and a movie. The movie was *Charlie Brown's Spelling Bee* (or something like that). The show ended with Charlie Brown losing the spelling bee. Ol' Charlie acted as though it was the end of the world. He slinked away and sulked all alone by himself. Lucy sought him out. When she found him, she told him compassionately, "It's all right, Charlie. The sun'll come up tomorrow anyway."

By the time we got back to Philly, the movie was the high point of the trip.

We lost our final game that season 73-70 against LaSalle. I was crushed. Our season was over—boom, just like that.

I brought the whole family to that season-ending game. We drove home together as a family. I didn't say a word the whole way. When we got home, Claire took the children upstairs to bed. I was alone downstairs on the sofa staring at the ceiling when my brooding was interrupted. My eight-year-old daughter Susan had sneaked downstairs and climbed up on my lap. She put her arms around my neck and said, "It's all right, Daddy. The sun'll come up tomorrow anyway."

My daughter's words were just what I needed—a dose of perspective from my very own peanut gallery. You're a good man, Charlie Brown.

Avoiding the Sophomore Jinx

In my second year coaching, I was blessed with one of the Hawks' greatest tandems ever—Mike Hauer and Danny Kelly—gems we mined from Philly's Catholic League. We rode their coattails for three years. Billy DeAngelis—known as Billy D, where "D" stood for "Defense"—was another star. Billy had the quickest hands this side of Willie Sutton. Billy's 104 steals in 26 games (an average of four per game for the mathematically challenged or lazy) is still the Saint Joseph's University record. Steve Courtin, Bobby Gormley, Mike Moody, and Harry Booth are the only others I've seen with hands anywhere near as quick as Billy D's.

Rider

Mike Hauer—all 6'3" of him—was, pound for pound, the toughest basketball player I've ever seen. On talent alone, Mike could never have averaged 12.5 rebounds per game (with a high of 25 against Wake Forest) or averaged 19.6 points per game over a three-year career. Hauer's tenacity scared opponents. It scared us sometimes! His mate, Danny Kelly, was a pinpoint marksman who chipped in with 19 points a game over his three-year stint.

Hawk fans saw lots of great ball movement with that duo. It wasn't necessarily fancy stuff. In fact, our most successful play was drop-dead simple. It was also a teeth rattler. I dubbed the play "Rider"—a tribute to Rider College and their coach, John Carpenter. I watched Rider run it when I was scouting them.

Our guys didn't go for the name "Rider," so they changed it to "Two"— the two referred to Kelly and Hauer. What we did was clear out the right side and get the ball to a forward who was on the left side. Kelly would set up at the left low post and Hauer on the right low post. As the forward turned toward the basket, Kelly would swing baseline around Hauer, who set up a pick. Kelly would usually be free for a 15-foot jumper. If he was not, he'd look inside for Hauer, who would be licking his chops awaiting a short high-percentage bucket.

Usually Kelly wound up with a wide-open shot, because whoever was unfortunate enough to be guarding him collided with Hauer and ended up checking the floor for his teeth.

I'm sure a lot of Hawk fans remember the "Two Play." What they don't know is that Mike added his own little gimmick once in a while. At least once a game, he would signal me on our bench by holding two fingers on his jersey. That meant, "I've got a fish on the line. Let me reel him in." I'd signal the "Two Play" to Kelly, who would call it on the court, dish the ball off to the other guard, and set up in the low post. When the forward got the ball on the high post, Kelly would cut past Hauer as close as possible, elbow to elbow. As Hauer was about to make contact, Hauer would yell, "Switch," and Hauer's man would go with Kelly. That left Hauer with a skinny, little guard on him. Hauer would roll on the guard, throw a Shaq move, slide into the lane in front of the hoop and take a pass from Tommy Lynch in the high post. Then Mike would turn, face the defender, give him a pump fake, go under him—that's when he'd rattle the guy's teeth—lay the ball in, then nonchalantly walk to the foul line to complete the three-point play. On the way to the line, he'd wink at us on the bench. I've only seen one other Hawk with a comparable move. That was Alphonse Juliana on my 1957 team. We used to call it "the Fonzi" (from Alphonse) Fake as in, "Did you see that move? He really Fonized that guy out of his jock." Of course, the 76ers had a guy named Chet Walker who was making what should have been a Hall of Fame career on that same move in that era.

Coach McKinney shares his wisdom in the time-out huddle. *Photo courtesy of Saint Joseph's University*

Number Two was our play for crunch time. I've run Two (or Rider) successfully on every team I ever coached, and I've watched some great threesomes: McFarland off Bantom with Moody as passer; Norm Nixon off Kareem with Magic as passer; and Lionel Hollins off Maurice Lucas (Ooh, could he set some crunchers) with Bill Walton as passer; Billy Knight off George McGinnis with Mike Bantom as passer. McGinnis and Bantom could switch roles, too. All those trios were good, but the best was Kelly off Hauer with Tom Lynch as the passer. That play was meant for those Hawks.

Winning the Gator Bowl Tournament

Holiday season found us in Jacksonville Florida for the 1967-1968 Gator Bowl Basketball Tournament, which was played on the Thursday and Friday before the Saturday Gator Bowl Football game. We won the tournament by beating Washington, though we weren't supposed to (so what else is new?) Washington was favored. They had a 6'10"center named Neil Walk. Neil was a great college player. Besides scoring 20 points per game, he was the nation's number-one rebounder. Our "big" guy inside was 6'3" Mike Hauer. Mike was ranked 16th nationally in that category. The press really liked that matchup. When they asked Mike what his strategy would be against a 6'10" guy, Hauer replied, "Well, we are not a very good shooting team, so I'll be concentrating on pulling down a lot of offensive rebounds." I think that answer meant, "Watch out Neil, I came here to play." And Mike came through. He got the rebounds (offensive mostly). Billy D got the steals, and we got the championship.

As for Neil, Neil Walk had a great college career before becoming the first-round draft choice of the Phoenix Suns. He was the second overall pick in the draft right behind Lew Alcindor from UCLA (for you younger viewers, Lew later changed his name to Kareem Abdul Jabbar—sound more familiar now?). Neil played in the NBA for five years and currently works in the Phoenix Suns organization.

After the game, I congratulated our guys in the locker room and headed out to a stunned pressroom. The Hawks have a long history of shocking the press. (Phil Martelli might refer you to Billy Packer for validation.)

Billy D's Dropsy

"Coach, Coach!" Billy D was yelling. "They called me to come out and get the Gator Bowl MVP trophy! Can you believe it?! Me, Billy DeAngelis!"

I don't think Billy took a breath getting all that out. His selection certainly didn't surprise me. It seemed like Billy had 30 steals that night! I'm sure it seemed that way to Washington.

The 1952 team celebrates its 50th-year reunion in 2002—left to right: Father Rashford, Jack McKinney, Mike Fallon, Dan Dougherty, Bill Lynch, and the Hawk. *Photo courtesy of Jack McKinney*

I've never seen anyone so taken as Billy was that night! It seems ironic that I found myself yelling, "Billy! Walk with that trophy *so you don't drop it!*" to the guy with the surest hands I ever saw.

The Rest of the Cast

I don't mean to imply that Kelly and Hauer were a two-man show. They had a fine supporting cast. We had reliable guards like Buddy Gardler, Jack Snyder, Bobby Atene, and Jim McCallum. We also had one of our most unsung guys ever: Tom Lynch a former All-Catholic at Father Judge. We had Dave Pfahler, Mike Kempski, and John Connally inside. We had help on the boards from Ed Leonarczyk, Eric Mitchell, and Bruce Marks. And we had lots of success. The Kelly-Hauer years produced a Gator Bowl championship, a MAC crown, a Big Five title, and an NCAA bid.

No Bantom Weight

When the dynamic duo of Kelly-Hauer graduated, a strong nucleus of Atene, Snyder, McCallum, and Connelly remained. Pat McFarland and Mike Bantom came on board. Over the next three years, Bantom averaged 20.5 and McFarland 18.5. In their senior year (the 1972-1973 season), only one point separated the two for the season: Bantom netted 568 points, McFarland 569. Mike Moody was superb as well, and the Bantom-McFarland-Moody era culminated in 60 wins, a Quaker City Tournament Championship, two NCAA bids, and one NIT bid. Besides our successes against the "usual" Eastern powers, we knocked off national monsters like Utah, West Virginia, Purdue, Xavier, and Bowling Green.

Play It Again, Sam

An unexpected visitor showed up in Manhattan, Kansas, in December 1970. Sam the Drummer popped into the lobby, dragging his huge bass drum. Sam was a fixture at the Palestra and Fieldhouse. But we weren't in Philly anymore. We were in Kansas for the Jayhawk Classic—so Sam was a time zone away from his usual booming grounds.

Saint Joseph's basketball isn't a high-budget operation. Sam the Drummer was an integral part of the Hawk basketball scene, but we certainly didn't have funds in the budget to cover him on the trip. Sam funded his own trip to Kansas, flying to Kansas City with his bass drum (not as a carry-on item). When he landed, he put his drum over his shoulder, stuck his thumb out and got picked up by a truck full of girls. Details of that odyssey remain unknown to this day.

I asked the hotel to set a cot in manager Charlie Langtree's room, and we arranged to transport both Sam and his drum to the Kansas Fieldhouse.

We were playing Kansas in the second game. When we arrived at the Fieldhouse, the Villanova-Houston contest was in progress. Sam waited for a timeout, grabbed his drum, and settled into the St. Joe's cheering section with some of our players. Sam started, "Let's go Wildcats!" BOOM, BOOM, boom, boom, boom!

The Villanova players recognized Sam and got a kick out of seeing their traditional nemesis turn into an ally. Sam stoked it up till a guy approached him and demanded, "Son, you'll have to stop the drumming. It's getting too loud!" Sam said, "Who are you?" The guy said, "I'm Pepper Rogers, the football coach." Sam challenged: "You have any ID?" Pepper said: "No." Sam said: "Then you can't make me stop."

Pepper left, and another guy moseyed over with the same request. Sam said, "Who are you?" The guy answered, "I'm the athletic director." Sam challenged: "Do you have any ID?" The alleged athletic director snapped: "No, not on me." Sam finished: "Then you can't stop me."

When we took the floor for the second game, we heard Sam's drum booming away, "Let's go St. Joe!" BOOM, BOOM, boom, boom, boom! Villanova lost the first game, which had been sparsely attended. The place was full for the hometown Kansas Jayhawks. They did NOT want to hear Sam's drum.

The Villanova guys came into the arena and sat around their new best friend, Sam the Hawk Drummer. Sam rolled through all his Hawk cheers as the locals got restless. Catcalls and "Shut that drum down" started to reverberate. Eventually one very loud guy stood up and yelled, "If you don't stop beating that drum, I'm going to come over and make you wear it." At that point, the three Villanova guys sitting around Sam—6'7" Hank

Left to right: Jim O'Brien, Kevin Furey and Mike Moody. *Photo courtesy of Saint Joseph's University*

Siemontkowski, 6'8" Clarence Smith, and 6'9" Howard Porter—all stood up. The entire section got very quiet. Then Porter shouted, "Beat the drum, Sam!"

Sam played uninhibited and unprohibited the rest of the game—unfortunately to no avail. We lost the game.

After the game, the Villanova posse escorted Sam to our dressing room. Sam said, "Coach, you've always been my hero, but now you have to share that spot with Howard Porter."

And share it I did. We played Villanova the next night in the consolation game, which of course placed Sam on the horns of a dilemma. Sam handled it well. He went crazy as always for the Hawks. But when Porter made a sensational play, Sam would come out with, "Porter, Porter, he's the man. If he can't do it, no one can. BOOM, BOOM, boom, boom, boom. Let's go St. Joe. BOOM, BOOM, boom, boom, boom."

A Rocky Mountain "Hi"

It was December 1971. We were driving from the airport to Provo, Utah. The following day, Saint Joseph's College was scheduled to play in a tournament at Brigham Young's brand new William J. Marriott Arena. The area looked completely snow-bound. We couldn't imagine any spectators getting to the arena through this snowscape. But the next night, when we had the honor of christening this spectacular edifice, all 24,000 seats were filled. At the time, the Marriott Arena boasted the largest seating capacity of any college arena in the nation.

We upended College of the Pacific 64-58 on opening night for a memorable victory. But the most mind-blowing moment occurred during the pregame introductions. Being the visiting team, we were introduced first. The introduction went like this: "For the visiting Saint Joseph's Hawks from Philadelphia Pennsylvania, starting at guard, number 8, Jim O'Brien." As Jim trotted out to center court, 24,000 people hollered in unison, "Hi Jim!" Our whole squad was speechless. We were used to the indignities and catcalls we heard against eastern competition. This greeting was sincere, too. It wasn't a Bronx cheer. They greeted our entire lineup that way: guard Jim McCollum ("Hi Jim"), forward Bob Sabol ("Hi Bob"), forward Pat McFarland ("Hi Pat"), and center Mike Bantom ("Hi Mike").

After the game in the locker room, Jim O'Brien said he felt he should have shaken hands with everyone in the arena. I'm not so sure. Those Brigham Young fans were so polite, Jim might have come back a Mormon.

Marriott Clockwork

We ended up playing Brigham Young for the championship in front of a partisan BYU crowd at the Marriott Arena.

With seven seconds remaining, BYU scored to go ahead by one point, and we immediately called time out. When our team got to the bench, I noticed that only two seconds showed on the clock. I figured that if I had protested the "missing" five seconds, 24,000 people would have screamed in unison, "No Jack!" Twice in the huddle I tried to scream over the din and set up a play, and twice our whole squad said, "What?" There was such an uproar the team couldn't hear a word. As the horn sounded, I told everyone, "Go out and score." It wasn't my most inspired moment.

The guys ran an inbounds play for McFarland who got a decent shot off, but it didn't drop. We walked away with a 73-72 loss.

If time is money, and anyone at Marriott is reading this, you ought to knock $5 off my next stay—a dollar for each second you took away from me. Just five dollars. Time is money, you know.

Obie Gets His Man

In the first game of the 1972 NIT, we came up a little short against a tough Maryland team. In the second half Bobby Sabol got tangled up with a Maryland guy scrapping for a rebound. Bobby smacked down hard on the floor headfirst and was carried off on a stretcher. Father Ross, our chaplain, took him back to the hotel room.

After the game, the team was disappointed, but they decided to go out to McCann's Bar to celebrate an otherwise successful 19-8 season. When we arrived, we found out Bobby had a concussion and was out of commission for the night.

Jimmy O'Brien and John Zipp had other ideas.

They called Father Ross in Bobby's room and told Father there was an emergency in the lobby. Father Ross headed down to the lobby. Meanwhile, Jim and John scampered up to the room with Bobby's clothes, told him to get dressed and ferreted him over to McCann's.

Perhaps when he got back to the room, Father Ross thought the angels had come for Bobby. That would mark the first and last time anyone ever accused O'Brien or Zipp of being angels.

Grim, Grizzly, and Gruesome

The prospects for the upcoming 1973-1974 campaign were anything but promising. In Bantom, McFarland, and Bob Sabol, we were losing a trio who averaged 45 points and 25 boards a game. I didn't know what to expect with their departure, but I certainly got more than I bargained for. A collection of just "good" players jelled and gave me my most remarkable season ever. OK, I know coaches shouldn't play favorites, but here goes—they were my favorite team.

The summer before the 1973-1974 season, we had the opportunity to play in Europe, and the guys started to come together as a team. I thought we might do OK. But that's not what the Big Five preseason ratings predicted. One Philly pundit characterized our prospects as "grim, grizzly, and gruesome." Another thought we could count our 1973-1974 season as a success "if the Hawks carve out over .500."

That "Grim, Grizzly, and Gruesome" headline stuck. Literally. I stuck it on the bulletin board in the locker room, and there it stayed for the entire season. That article was a rallying point for everyone.

Our leader was Jimmy O'Brien. O'Brien was a coach's dream. It's no surprise to me that Jimmy was the latest in a long line of Hawks-turned-NBA coaches. When he played, Jim was a coach on the court. He never allowed anyone to slack off and never let anyone on our team accept that we were grim, gruesome, and grizzly.

Moody was a dependable number-two guard who ranked with Billy D as a defender. The front line was our big question mark. Center Kevin Furey emerged as a confident, dependable big man with the reliable John Zipp as his backup. At forward, Ron Righter, a transfer from Duke, was our shooter. The other forward slot was up for grabs, and Gene Prybella blossomed into a pleasant surprise.

We had a scrappy bench. Guard-forward Lou Peltzer was a "whenever you need me" shooter. Craig Kelly was our crunch-time foul shooter who iced several games away for us. Franny Rafferty, O'Brien's backup, was dependable and a good leader himself.

These guys slugged their way through the season, winning 20 games on guts and togetherness. Righter was our top scorer, averaging 12.1 a game. We won the Middle Atlantic Conference and an NCAA berth. So much for grim, grizzly, and gruesome.

The season ended in West Virginia when Pittsburgh beat us 54-42. It was over, but our band of overachievers had tons of fun shocking the critics. Harry Booth, my assistant coach, and I were beaming about what we considered an amazing season. I felt the most satisfied I had ever felt as a coach. That feeling didn't last very long.

The Shirt Off Lou's Back

"We had these T-shirts that we were supposed to turn back in, but I sneaked out with mine," Lou Peltzer laughs. "Don't you know I was thumbing down to the shore, and who stops to give me a lift? Jack McKinney. First thing he says when I hop in the car is, 'When you come to practice this fall, I want that shirt back.' I thought he was going to make me give it to him then and there, but he probably figured [correctly] I didn't have any other shirts with me for the weekend."

Converting The Explorers

Ron Righter recalls one of his sweetest memories: whipping the Explorers twice in one season.

"We beat La Salle twice when they were a Top 10 team by confusing them with our defense. Kevin Furey and I played zone in the frontcourt, and our guards played man. When LaSalle pushed the ball outside, Kevin and I would switch to man, and the guards would drop to zone. LaSalle's guards kept looking to their bench for help. Yeah, I'll never forget those games! I scored 19 points in one of them on some long jumpers, and the headline the *Philadelphia Daily News* ran the next day was 'Gospel According to St. Ron Converts LaSalle.' You don't forget things like that."

You're Fired

I was sitting at the desk in my office Tuesday morning after the season ended. The phone rang. It was the secretary in the athletic office telling me that Father Blee, the athletic director, wanted to see me. I hustled over right away. The secretary guided me into his office and shut the door as I sat down. Bad omen.

Father Blee didn't mince words. Our conversation lasted only two minutes—two minutes I'll never forget. Blee said simply, "Jack we're going to have to let you go." I was in shock. I stammered, "You mean I'm fired?" He looked at me and said, "Yes." I said, "Why?" He said, "I've been observing you for a year. I don't think you have any discipline or teaching value." All I could manage to say was, "And that's why I'm being fired? Does Father Toland know about this?" Father Toland was the college president at the time. Father Blee responded, "Yes."

As I got up to leave, Father Blee said to me, "I don't think you should mention this until you get another job."

I was in a state of shock. I drove immediately to Father Toland's office located across City Line Avenue from the main campus. I went to his office and explained what had just taken place. Father Toland responded simply, "Jack, if my athletic director makes a decision about athletics, I have to back him." I answered, "You mean you're not going to do anything about this—not call for a meeting or something?" Father Toland looked at me and said, "No I can't."

I returned to the basketball office. I gathered my assistant coaches Harry Booth and Mike Kempski in my office—well, what had been my office until my morning meeting with Father Blee. The two sat stunned and silent. None of us could make sense of the matter. We decided to call a team meeting in the locker room that afternoon. Each player was notified individually.

Everyone showed up. I didn't want them to read about it in the papers. When I gave them the news, no one said a word for what seemed an

Coaches Lynam, McKinney, Kelly and Booth during the 1970-1971 season.
Photo courtesy of Saint Joseph's University

eternity. Finally, Jimmy O'Brien spoke up: "Coach, are you serious?" I assured O'Brien and the team that I was serious. Serious, sad, and shocked.

I put off going home as long as possible. I dreaded having to tell Claire and our four children. But I did. As always, my family was there for me.

Early next morning, I drove to school, gathered my belongings, and left the campus before the news reached the students.

Leaving Hawk Hill

My visit to Hawk Hill the day after the firing, was the last time I would be back to Saint Joseph's University until the 1990s. I had known nothing but happiness at Saint Joseph's. With my sudden, confusing release, I left with an empty feeling in the pit of my stomach. My wife, Claire, was a Saint Joseph's student at that time. She left also. She couldn't bear to be on campus.

I grew to accept the fact that I had to get on with my life. I eventually got the opportunity to coach in the NBA, and with good breaks and good friends like Jack Ramsay, I had a successful coaching career post-St. Joe's.

On a positive note, the Jack McKinney years at Saint Joseph's ended with a terrific team, a terrific season, lifelong memories, and an Eastern College Coach of the Year Award.

Throwing Out The Book

A longtime Hawk fan sends us this story about the McKinney firing: "The 1974 Hawk basketball banquet was a tense affair. Father Blee had fired Jack McKinney a couple of weeks earlier. Jack had been selected as Eastern College Coach of the Year (20 wins and an NCAA berth). Harry Booth had been named as the new coach—and all three, Blee, McKinney, and Booth were at the banquet. Talk about surreal!

Philadelphia sportswriter Bob Vetrone was the emcee. He started his remarks out like this: "I had prepared a lot of material for tonight, but then I found out that there were going to be children present (Bob rips a page out of his book and tosses it on the floor). Then I found out there were going to be women present (he rips another page out and tosses it to the floor). And then I found out Father Blee was going to be here (Bob tosses the entire book down to the floor).

"It was classic Bob Vetrone. He met a tough subject head on, defused the situation as best he could, and even got in a velvet jab at Father Blee."

Joe Cabrey, the team manager, (who was then known as Pete) and now a loyal Hawk alumnus had this to offer about the firing and the banquet: "The team predicted to be 'Grim, Grizzly, and Gruesome' shocked everyone by winning their conference championship and playing their way back into the NCAA Tournament. Jack won the ECAC coach of the year award, and a few days later, we were summoned by the reps from the athletic department to report to the locker room immediately. We did. They told us Jack McKinney had been released. There were tears, shock, anger, and a sense of loss. Then there were student and alumni protests. The annual fundraising campaign was suspended. None of the media could believe the firing. How could a coach be dumped after he had such a successful season and a 100-percent graduation rate, with seven of his players on the Dean's List?

"I wrote a letter to *The Hawk*. I said that 'If Saint Joseph's allows Father Blee's decision to separate Jack McKinney from the school, job, and people that he loves so much, that the prospects were indeed grim, gruesome, and grizzly.'

"So I'll never forget that banquet that Bob Vetrone emceed. It was held atop the GSB Building. None of us knew how to react going to the banquet. I happened to be walking towards the building with my dad and saw Coach McKinney coming from another direction a few feet ahead of us. I ran ahead just to open the door for him out of respect. It was as though I wanted to keep doing for him because of all that he had done for us.

"We were angry that our coach had been fired. We were astonished that Father Blee was such a pompous ass that he thought he had the right to attend our banquet.

"But Bob Vetrone's opening remarks made us laugh—all of us—coaches, players, managers, and the Hawk himself. Bob made it OK to laugh. He set the tone for the dinner—a tone of celebration of the team—the team that gave McKinney, as he would later say, the most satisfying moments of a distinguished career."

Anniversary

Time heals. There we were on March 18, 2005—Jack McKinney and I—writing a book praising Saint Joseph's University, his former employer. The furthest thing from Jack's mind was the date, his personal day of infamy, his little Gethsemane. March 18 was the anniversary of the day he was fired in 1974.

He wasn't focused on the past. Much heavier on his mind was the upcoming NIT clash with visiting Buffalo. The Buffalo team was working out in the Fieldhouse. Their coach, Reggie Witherspoon, spotted Jack and me walking up to the athletic department office and hustled over yelling, "Hey, Coach!" In college, Reggie had played under Jimmy O'Brien, who was the captain of Jack McKinney's favorite Hawk squad.

Reggie requested Jack to say a few words to his Buffalo squad after their practice. Jack agreed and returned to the gym at three o'clock.

"Don't ever go out on the floor if you don't think you can win," Coach McKinney said softly. "Believe in yourself, and believe you're gonna succeed because then ... you can and you will."

Circled around him on the painted Hawk on the center-court hardwood, the Buffalo squad stood rapt. When Jack concluded, the kids pressed in to ogle his NBA championship ring and fire questions at him: "What was Magic like?" "Who was the greatest you coached?"

I was worried that he had pumped these Buffalo guys up too much. But the Hawks weren't about to lose this NIT clash. They battered Buffalo on March 19, a more propitious anniversary for Jack and Saint Joseph's University. On the Catholic calendar, March 19 is Saint Joseph's feast day. Sweet.

One Regret

Lee McIlvaine, a fanatic, and faithful fan recalls: "Jim O'Brien and Kevin Furey met at the Barbelin Tower, and off we went with the drum. BOOM. BOOM. BOOM. We zipped up to the third floor and knocked on the door of the first classroom. Dr. Bob Dunn waved us in. I asked him to dismiss his class so his students could join in the protest, and he balked, saying his students were preparing for a midterm. I told him if he didn't cooperate, I'd pound the drum so loud he wouldn't be able to teach anyway. He gave in, 'Class dismissed,' and we were off with our first protest enlistees.

"'WE WANT JACK BACK! WE WANT JACK BACK!' started to reverberate around the halls.

"We stopped at the next classroom and recruited some more protestors. In no time at all, a chanting army filled the corridors. We headed off to Villiger and then off to the Fieldhouse where we protested for hours. We ended the march on the front lawn of President Terrence Toland's residence. The Baker [one of our loyal fans] handed me a rock to toss through the window. I knew I'd be expelled if I threw it, so I didn't.

"To this day, not throwing that rock remains my single biggest regret as a St. Joe's student."

Susan McKinney de Ortega's
Letter to *Philadelphia Inquirer*

Susan McKinney de Ortega, Jack McKinney's daughter, is a writer living in San Miguel de Allende in the Mexican Central Highlands. She and her husband own Jasmine Day Spa and have two bilingual daughters.

"The occasion was big enough to bring family members from both coasts and another country. My father, Jack McKinney, former basketball coach and athlete at Saint Joseph's University, was to be inducted into the school's Athletic Hall of Fame.

"The ceremony took place on September 25. It was all very festive, but the next morning my brother Dennis had a somber question, 'Sue, why was Dad fired?'

"Dennis was eight in 1974 and I was 15 when my dad came home with a sad face on March 18, then went to the movies and stayed there until we were in bed. Late at night, I saw the *Philadelphia Evening Bulletin* headline my mother had tried to hide. It read 'St. Joe's Fires Jack McKinney After Team Wins MAC Title.'

"At the beginning of the season, sportswriters had predicted St. Joe's would not win half of its games. Yet by year's end, the Hawks had won 20 games and the team had competed in the NCAA postseason tournament. My father would be named Eastern College coach of the year.

"The athletic director, the Reverend Michael Blee, told my father his "discipline" and "teaching value" to the team were in question. 'How could we have had the season we had if we were anything but disciplined?' one player muttered.

"Students protested, demanding my father be rehired.

"Now maybe the school would reconsider, I prayed. But my Father remained an orphan, turned out by his alma mater, shunned by the school he loved.

"I had planned to go to Saint Joseph's—they would admit women by the time I was ready to enter, I was sure—and study English. Like my father, I never questioned that I would be a life-long Hawk. And then suddenly we weren't.

"That fall I started my junior year at Whitefish Bay High School on the shores of Lake Michigan and my father began an NBA career as the assistant coach of the Milwaukee Bucks. I almost forgot St. Joe's and the Big Five.

"I didn't realize what it meant to my father to be banned from the Saint Joseph's family until I walked amidst the school's ivy-covered buildings last month for the first time in 30 years.

"I remembered an athletic department employee telling me when I was a kid that he sprinkled salt on the Hawk's tail so it could fly. I remembered running on the court in my PF Flyers flapping my wings. I remembered knowing St. Joe's was a special place.

"That's why when my father told me that he would be inducted into the Athletics Hall of Fame, I knew it really meant something. I flew up from Mexico to attend.

"It was as if my father had never left. Everyone wanted to shake his hand. The Hawk flapped his wings throughout the cocktail party honoring the new Hall of Fame members. Former players told anecdotes. When my father entered for the awards ceremony, the room thundered with an ovation.

"On the morning after the ceremony, we went to the St. Joe's Student Union. There on the wall—along with Jack Ramsay and an early baseball team, along with the Rev. Dr. Martin Luther King, Jack Ramsay speaking on campus, along with other students and events depicting the school's last one hundred years—was a huge black-and-white cutout of 1957 track team member Jack McKinney clearing the high bar.

"My father belongs to four Halls of Fame. He owns two NBA championship rings and the 1981 NBA Coach of the Year trophy.

"Yet I can say that perhaps my father standing under that photo with his wife, children and grandchildren, having been chosen to represent a part of St. Joseph's history, has never felt prouder.

"For my part, I thought for the first time in my life, maybe St. Joe's is a place my children would someday like to study."

Father Lannon's Reply

Saint Joseph's University President Father Timothy Lannon, S.J. sent Susan McKinney the following reply to her letter.

October 14, 2004
Ms. Susan McKinney de Ortega

Dear Susan,
I just finished reading the article you wrote for the October 14, 2004 edition of the Philadelphia Inquirer. *I would like to compliment you on your captivating writing style. You conveyed your story with authenticity and frankness, and it was a pleasure to read.*

In chronicling your father's years with Saint Joseph's University, it's inevitable and inescapable that the firing be included. However, once past the difficult segment of the article, the story glows with the heartwarming reunion of a man and his alma mater. I'm happy to read that your father has a special place in his heart for Saint Joseph's University. The University certainly considers him one of our most celebrated and loved alumni. So there is mutual admiration between us.

I'd also like to thank you, Susan, for your positive portrayal of the University 30 years later. Thank you for stating that you remembered St. Joe's as a special place. As I conclude my first year as President, I must say that I agree with that assessment wholeheartedly. Saint Joseph's University is a wonderful place to work—a strong, caring community of great people.

Being inducted in the Athletic Hall of Fame at Saint Joseph's University is a well-deserved honor for your father. I am happy that I was able to share the joy of the evening with your family and to meet the legendary Jack McKinney. I hope you'll visit our campus again soon, and in the meantime I pray that God will continue to bless you and your family.

Best Wishes,
Timothy R. Lannon, S.J.
President

CHAPTER TEN

Mike Bantom

The Olympic Hawk

Mike Bantom was a power player who worked with finesse inside on the offense while excelling also as an outside shooter. He handled the boards superbly—so well in fact that he finished his career as the second top rebounder of all time at Saint Joseph's University. He also holds the distinction of being the only Hawk ever chosen for an Olympic team. Mike performed for the United States in the 1972 Olympiad.

Mike made his biggest national splash in 1973 when he was selected to the All-America team. However, he was stellar throughout his career, averaging 20 ppg and 13.7 rpg over a three-year span. At 6'9", Mike anchored the team from the center position and grabbed 1,151 career rebounds. He was twice selected to the All-Big Five squad and was a three-time selectee to the All-MAC squad. Mike was a two-time Hawk captain who posted double-double averages in each of his three varsity seasons in leading his team to three consecutive NCAA Tournament berths. In recognition of his many achievements, Mike was honored by his alma mater by having his jersey number 44 retired on March 1, 2003.

Statistically, Mike's best season came as a junior (1971-1972), when he averaged 21.8 ppg and 14.8 rebounds. He led the team in rebounding both as a sophomore (13.2) and a senior (13.1). As a sophomore he topped the squad in scoring. When Mike left college ball, he was second on the all-time Hawk scoring list (he's now seventh) and second on the all-time rebounding list—a position he retains.

After college, Mike was a first-round pick by the Phoenix Suns in 1973. He played nine seasons in the NBA, logging time with the Suns, Indiana, and Philadelphia. With the 76ers, he played in the 1982 NBA Finals.

Currently he's the NBA's senior vice president for player development.

Never Satisfied

COACH McKINNEY:

I remember Mike Bantom's heyday, too. I remember it well. When I roll the tape in my head, here's what I see. The side clears out as Moody and Furey vacate and leave Bantom in the low post with McFarland behind him. Then *Pin Down, Pop Out, Post Up* ... McFarland takes O'Bie's pass and O'Bie clears away, Then it's McFarland for a J or McFarland with a pass into Bantom, who makes his move. Then it's drop back on D, baby.

That formula worked successfully. What's more, it worked equitably. Yeah, equitably beyond belief! In their senior year, McFarland and Bantom finished the year *within one point of each other in points scored!* They had matching 20.3 points a game. They both ended up in the top 20 scorers all-time at St. Joe's for a single season!

Ah yes, I remember it well. What coach wouldn't?

The Hawks' Pat & Mike

I'll talk about Pat McFarland here for a moment. He's the other half of the Pat & Mike duo that frustrated so many opponents. Pat was a 6'5" forward who worked the frontcourt for the Hawks as magically as Jameer and Delonte worked the backcourt in the early 21st century.

Of his senior year in college, Pat has this to say: "Mike Bantom, Bobby Sabol, and I teamed up with juniors Jimmy O'Brien, Mike Moody, and Kevin Furey. My only regret is that I didn't know then what I know now. What I mean is, I feel I could have been a better team player. I think I had a good career here, but I realize now more than ever the reason I was good—it was my teammates. My teammates had the confidence in me to feed me the ball. And the biggest factor contributing to my personal achievements was the guy in the middle: Mike Bantom. I had the pleasure of teaming with Mike for four years. We really got to know each other on the court. We would work the ball into Mike, and if he couldn't get a good shot off, he'd get it back to me for a jumper.

"I got lots of help from the coaches as well. Every day, we split the big men off to one end of the gym. The coaches would work on something special, something new and helpful each day. Coach Mike Kempski was particularly helpful. He worked us hard, showing us what to do on each new move. It was fun and educational."

Co-MVPs of the 1972-1973 season, Pat McFarland (left) and Mike Bantom (right) with Coach McKinney (center). *Photo courtesy of Jack McKinney*

Pat was a model of consistency. To this day, he holds the Hawk record for most consecutive games in double figures. Pat hit double figures 45 straight games from January 11, 1972, through March 10, 1973. He also holds the Hawk record for most field goals in a season—a whopping 256.

In the 1973 NBA draft, Pat McFarland was the 10th player chosen in the second round. The New York Knicks picked him right after Atlanta chose fellow Big Fiver Tom Inglesby. Atlanta chose Inglesby three rounds ahead of future baseball Hall of Famer Dave Winfield, who never tried basketball. By the way, another Big Fiver was also selected in the second round. Boston drafted U of P star Phil Hankinson.

Life After Hawk Hill

Mike Bantom played on the 1972 U.S. Olympic silver-medal winning team. He played in the NABC East-West All-American Game. He went on to the NBA in 1974 and made the All-Rookie Team.

In a brief 33-game stint with the New York Nets in 1977, he averaged 18.3 ppg and 8.6 rebounds per game. Mike's finest NBA years, however, came with Indiana. He averaged 15.3 ppg for Indiana in 1978, 14.7 ppg in 1979, and 14 ppg in 1981. When the ex-Hawk reflects on his career, he feels his four-year stint at Indiana was his greatest period of personal growth. Mike was traded to Indiana in the summer of 1977 along with Adrian Dantley. He immediately became the Pacers' captain and player representative, serving four years in each of those capacities. He credits those experiences with refining his leadership skills and endowing him with a more acute sense of responsibility.

He finished his NBA career with 8,568 points, more points than any ex-Hawk ever scored in the NBA. Likewise, his 4,517 rebounds is the chart-topper for all ex-Hawks in NBA competition.

Mike spent seven more years on professional hardwoods after his NBA career was over. He played in Italy, an experience he feels broadens the perspective he brings to his new role. What is that role? Mike is the NBA's senior vice president of player development. Essentially he serves as guide and advisor to neophytes in the league. He educates them about prudent and proper behaviors. Mike views himself as a "gate keeper," the person at the gate who prepares young players to enter the new and baffling world that often swallows up young NBA talent. Mike and his associates strive to reach and teach players via a series of services from educational programming and support services to one-on-one mentoring. He and the NBA have developed rookie orientation programs. They've also established an 800-phone number that players can call at any time to get counseling anonymously.

Mike Bantom drives against a LaSalle defender in 1972.
Photo courtesy of Saint Joseph's University

The Roman Empire

Mike Bantom, Mike Moody, Jim O'Brien ... the Hawks, right? Correct, they were Hawks, but they were also Cahillites—Cahillites referring to Roman Catholic High School. Thomas E. Cahill was the school's founder, thus the "Cahillite" tag.

Bantom, Moody, and O'Brien accounted for three-fifths of the starting five for Philadelphia's Roman Catholic High School in 1969. Mike Bantom, who averaged 15.6 ppg, was first-team Philadelphia All-Catholic in the Southern Division, along with Tom Inglesby, who went on to stardom at Villanova, and Ed Hastings (Monsignor Bonner). Bob Sabol (Bonner) was also a first-teamer, while Mike Moody made second-team All-Catholic.

The 20th Olympiad

The U.S. squad breezed through its early rounds. It opened the Games with a 66-35 win over Czechoslovakia. Next, Ed Ratcliff tallied 18 points in a U.S. 81-55 romp over Australia. Next eventual third-place finisher Cuba fell 67-48 as Dwight Jones bucketed 18. In the following contest, the U.S. struggled with Brazil before finally battling to a 61-54 final advantage. Egypt was annihilated 96-31, as Mike Bantom poured in 17. Spain fell 72-56 before the U.S. drilled Japan 99-33, and seven U.S. players reached double digits.

Then tragedy struck. September 5 that year was a day that lives in infamy. Arab terrorists massacred 11 Israeli Olympic athletes. The tragedy put the Games on hold for nearly two days, but the Games went on.

When competition resumed, the U.S. trounced Italy by 30 points to advance to the gold-medal game and extend their all-time Olympic winning streak to an astounding 63 games. Dating back to 1936, the U.S. had never lost a single game.

But the Soviets had come a long way in a short amount of time in hoops. They, too, were cruising in the Olympics. They were 8-0 when they locked horns with the U.S. in the semifinal on September 10, 1972. The game started ominously as USSR jumped off to a 7-0 advantage. They carried a 26-21 lead into the locker room at halftime.

In the second half, the mood of the game started to turn ugly. With 12:18 to play and the Soviets holding a 38-34 lead, 6'8" Dwight Jones, the USA's top scorer and rebounder, and Soviet reserve Dvorni Edeshko were ejected after a loose-ball scuffle. On the ensuing jump ball, 6'9" Jim Brewer suffered a concussion. The U.S. chipped away and narrowed the gap to one point, 49-48 on Jim Forbes's jumper with 40 seconds remaining. The Soviets worked the clock down to 10 seconds, but Tom McMillen blocked Aleksander Belov's shot, and Doug Collins intercepted his pass as Belov attempted to toss it back out to center court. Collins drove to the basket and was fouled hard with three seconds left. The future 76er sank both charity shots to vault the USA into a 50-49 lead with three seconds left. Bizarrely, the horn sounded in the middle of his second attempt.

From then on, confusion reigned. Immediately following Collins's free throws, the Soviets inbounded the ball, but the referee, Renato Righetto of Brazil, blew the whistle with one second remaining on the clock. Following a conference with the officials, it was determined that Soviet head coach Vladimir Kondrashkin had called a time out. A decision was made to put three seconds back on the clock. At issue was the Soviets' contention that they had signaled for a time-out between Collins's two free throws. The funky part was that the game officials never acknowledged the time out.

After the Soviets in-bounded the ball a second time, the horn sounded, signaling an apparent American victory. Moments later, the teams were

Left to right: Coach McKinney with the three teammates from Roman Catholic High School—Jim O'Brien, Mike Bantom and Mike Moody. *Photo courtesy of Saint Joseph's University*

ordered back on the floor because the clock had not been properly reset to show three seconds remaining. Because of this mistake by the scorer's table, the celebrating Americans stood in disbelief when they were told they hadn't won. "We couldn't believe that they were giving them all these chances," Mike Bantom says. "It was like they were going to let them do it until they got it right."

On the third try, Soviet's Sergei Belov heaved the ball to Aleksander Belov (you'll read more about the Belov boys in the "Overseas Hawks" chapter) and the USA's Kevin Joyce and Jim Forbes went up for the pass. Unfortunately, Belov is the guy who came down with it. He hauled the ball in at the foul line as the two Americans went sprawling, Belov drove in for an easy layup and registered the winning points. Post-game, the U.S. filed a formal protest with the International Basketball Federation. A five-member panel ruled on the protest. Three of the five were Communist-bloc judges, all of whom voted for the Soviet Union. Final vote: 3-2, protest overruled. The Soviets were awarded the gold medals.

Over 30 years later, the American team's silver medals sit unclaimed in a vault in Lusanne, Switzerland. Several U.S. players expressed the same sentiment, "If we had gotten beat, we would be proud to display our silver medals today. But we didn't get beat. We got cheated!"

CHAPTER ELEVEN

The Hawks Overseas

Jack Ramsay Overseas

COACH McKINNEY:

In the summer of 1965, after Ramsay's Hawks finished the season 25-4, Jack got a call from the U.S. Department of State. No, he wasn't in trouble. The government simply wanted to know if Saint Joseph's College would represent the USA on its annual mission to foster better relationships with foreign countries through basketball. In previous years, some fine colleges had participated. It was an honor to be asked.

The itinerary changed yearly. This year's destination was South America. If St. Joe's participated, we would play 16 games all told in Brazil, Uruguay, Argentina, and Chile. The team would also provide a series of coaching clinics along the way. The trip would last the entire month of August.

Jack said "Yes" faster than an intelligent person can say, "Saint Joseph's University" (when an intelligent person is asked, "What's the best team in the Big Five?"). The State Department suggested Jack include a referee in the entourage. That's how Bill Davidson joined Dr. Jack's Traveling Show. Bill was a Youngstown, Ohio native who is now a podiatrist and part-time collegiate ref in western Pennsylvania.

Dr. Jack brushed up on his language skills. He knew a little French, but no Spanish, so he enrolled in a Spanish course. He wanted to be able to communicate on a basic level and maybe even negotiate if the situation arose.

The Hawks started their adventure in Brazil. They played their first three games there—one each in Sao Paolo, Rio de Janeiro, and Curetabo. Jack says, "The Basketball Federation treated us wonderfully. They tried to show us a great time, and they did—with niceties like treating us to sightseeing tours when we weren't playing. It was all new and magic to the kids who for the most part had never been out of Philly.

Different Times in Uruguay

"Then came Uruguay," Jack Ramsay says. "The great time we had in Brazil lulled us into a false sense of reality. We flat-out weren't ready for Uruguay, and vice versa. To begin with, the country was in a severe economic depression. The government was trying to cut costs and save money any way they could. To save electricity, they shut the elevators off all night long. Streetlights weren't turned on, and the city just about shut down at five in the afternoon.

"I remember a sobering drive the team took through the country. There were dead cattle lying all over the pastures. We found out that the farmers had no food to give them. Everywhere it was a depressing atmosphere and we were happy to leave. Next we went to Argentina. It was cold. The wintertime temperatures didn't deter the Argentineans. We played one game outdoors. It was football weather—like a great day for football in Green Bay in January. But we didn't have any heaters next to our bench like the football players do. We dressed for the game at the hotel and hauled blankets over from the hotel so we could bundle up on the bench and try to keep warm.

"In one city, we were dressing for the game when a guy knocked on the locker-room door. I opened the door and recognized one of my former St. Joe's students standing there. I invited the guy into the locker room and he promptly told us he was there on a Fulbright Scholarship. He continued, 'Look, I'm not trying to alarm you, but I've got to tell you they're not too friendly to Americans down here. Last week, one of our U.S. consulates was machine-gunned down right on the street.'

"'Not too friendly' is one way to describe a machine-gunning. But the guy had some more news for us: 'There's a strong anti-U.S. element in the stands at these games, and I think they'll demonstrate or disrupt the game.' Hopefully, by 'disrupt,' he meant something like yelling, not machine-gunning. The guy continued, 'I think if St. Joe's can dominate the game right from the start, the anti-American group will be embarrassed and dismiss the whole thing as an exhibition game. They'd let it go—no demonstration, nothing. But if the game is close, all hell could break loose.'"

Ramsay figured he had to make a good pregame speech. He relayed the ex-Hawk's message to the team exactly, with no sugar coating. Jack wanted to follow the guy's advice and take the competitive charm out of the game as quickly as possible by putting a 3-1-1 zone press in right from the start. He kept the pressure up the whole game long.

The strategy worked. The Hawks jumped out to a 20-3 lead and never looked back. The crowd was friendly and gracious. Machine guns were silent.

Coach Jack Ramsay and his team depart for South America with the sign: "Long Live the Hawks." *Photo courtesy of Saint Joseph's University*

Next the Gringos, er Hawks, headed for Resistencia, a remote Argentinean town. They didn't hear a word of English there. Summoning his hastily learned *un poquito* of Spanish, Jack tried to negotiate some decent living quarters. The team was sentenced, er housed, in a dingy dark hotel that would have creeped out Norman Bates. The food was horrible. As for the water... Ramsay forbade the team from drinking it. Coca Cola was the team drink.

Jack recalls, "One night we were served soup that looked like food stock mixed with something Jiffy Lube tossed out. Each guy did the same thing: he scanned everyone around the table to see who would try it first. It was one of those times when the first just might turn out to be the last. Finally Tom Duff decided to down it. Tom almost doubled up. He clutched his stomach, made a sickening ugly face, and said, 'My compliments to the chef!'"

Ramsay and the boys said goodbye to Resistencia feeling the same kind of joy that a business major feels when he says goodbye to his required calculus course. The whole crew headed home far more enlightened. They had played some good basketball and had seen lots of things they'd never see in Philly. They ended up 15-1 for the trip. They lost one game to a Brazilian team made up of guys on their Olympic team.

Jack McKinney Overseas

In the summer of 1972, I took a Hawk team overseas to play in Italy, Sicily, and Romania. We went without our top player, Mike Bantom, who was busy practicing with the U.S. Olympic team. We had hoped we could bring another key player, 6'8" Ron Righter. But Ron was a transfer student and wasn't eligible. So we did some creative recruiting. We picked up an old nemesis from Villanova, 6'8" strong forward Hank Siemontkowski. Hank had graduated and was available for duty. Jim O'Brien, our captain, recruited another big guy—6'9" Joe Gallagher, who was a friend of his family. Joe hailed from the Fairmount section of Philly and played for Pembroke State University in North Carolina as a collegian. Big Joe made it to the last cut in the 1968 Olympic trials and then completed a four-year stint in the Marines. Afterwards he coached at Pembroke. When Jim O'Brien graduated he started his coaching career at Pembroke as Joe Gallagher's assistant coach.

Anyway, with these additions, we had a respectable squad. I wasn't confident we had enough firepower to match up with competition of the caliber we were scheduled to face, but I was wrong. Our guys did great. Actually it almost wouldn't have mattered if we didn't match up. You couldn't put a price tag on the experience our guys gained. We got to meet people from all over the Old World. We traveled on buses with teams from Italy, Czechoslovakia, and the former Soviet Union. In fact, the Russian team we played was the same national team that Mike Bantom played in the Olympics. One month after our Hawks played these guys, the Russians would upset the USA for our country's first ever loss in Olympic competition.

We won four and lost six, but we played extremely well in my opinion. We also learned to play more physically—out of necessity. It was invaluable preparation for the upcoming collegiate season.

When in Rome

We landed in Rome and spent three days in what had been the U.S. Olympic Village in the 1966 Games. We practiced every morning, then came back to our hotel for a great Italian lunch. We didn't have any games scheduled in Rome, which gave us the chance to tour. We saw the Vatican, the Sistine Chapel, the Pieta, the Spanish Steps, the Coliseum, the Trevi Fountain, and other wonders of the Eternal City. Our boys knew we weren't in Philly anymore—if only because of all the nude statues everywhere they looked. The kids had a running joke about all the nude statues around the city. "Boy, you don't see that in Kensington!"

It was hot in Rome. There was a swimming pool by our hotel—another remnant of the 1960 Games. It was in great shape and looked really appealing after temperatures in the mid-90s all day long. Our guys couldn't wait to wrap up their morning outdoor practice and dive into the pool. Unfortunately, I was told we couldn't swim in the pool, and I had to relay that tragic news to my (suddenly) unhappy campers. They were crushed but plotting.

Roman Graffiti

One of the big movies out that summer was *American Graffiti*—a tale of a single bizarre night when a bunch of parallel adventures take place. Our last night in Rome was our version of Roman Graffiti.

We were heading to Sicily the next morning. Claire was joining me the following week, and I needed to find a hotel for her and make reservations. I strolled into town to take care of that little piece of business. I also needed to find a telegraph office to wire her where the hotel was located and give her the confirmation number. I figured I'd enjoy a quiet meal by myself while I went about it.

One of our new friends from the Olympic Village directed me toward the Spanish Steps, where I'd find several hotels. I set out on a hot, beautiful Roman evening. There were four or five large hotels in the area, and one seemed to fit the family budget. I reserved a room for three days. Claire was going to spend three days in Rome sightseeing and shopping—hopefully heavy on the sightseeing and light on the shopping—and then she was meeting me in Palermo, Sicily.

I wired her the particulars. She'd be staying at the hotel El Campo, which means "the Field." Mission accomplished, I walked back toward the Spanish Steps, hankering for a good meal. I spotted a café where people sat outside in tables set along the street. It looked like a good spot to sit and watch Roman life go by.

I sat at a table next to the curb. The waiter took my order for a beer and hustled up the steps to get it. I waited, entertained by the streetscape. There were several groups of fairly attractive ladies promenading along both sides of the streets. Many of them hollered to passing motorists. Some motorists stopped and chatted with them briefly.

As I was relaxing, a very attractive African lady decked out in a Cleopatra outfit and matching wig, happened by. Simultaneously my waiter, my beer in hand, scampered down the steps toward my table. He had his eyes on Cleopatra—he was no fool. He was no dancer, either. He missed the last step, tumbled, and doused me and everything around me with the beer.

Fran Rafferty (left), Lou Peetzer (center) and Coach McKinney flip coins into the Trevi fountain for good luck in Rome, Italy, in August 1972. *Photo courtesy of Jack McKinney*

Cleopatra got a huge kick out of the big spill. She helped with the clean up. It turned out that she was American, a refined, pleasant woman named Bettina who was a schoolteacher from San Francisco. She had been summering in Rome for the past few years to pick up credits for an advanced degree. I told her about our basketball itinerary, and mentioned that I had just reserved a room for my wife at El Campo. Bettina screeched, "Oh no, you don't want your wife staying there! That's where all the hookers stay!" I guess basketball coaches and hookers have similar budgets. She went on to say, "Go back to El Campo right now and get your money back. Then I'll direct you to another hotel four blocks from here called La Carriage. Your wife will really enjoy that one. I've stayed there in

the past and loved it. Ask for Georgio the concierge and tell him Bettina sent you. He'll set you up with a nice room."

I bought her a beer, thanked her for her help and headed to El Campo. They refunded my money without protest or fanfare. I headed back to the telegraph office, hoping it was still open. It was, so I sent Claire a brief note that I had changed hotels. I gave her the location of La Carriage and added cryptically "WILL EXPLAIN WHEN I SEE YOU"(they charge by the word).

I retraced my steps, now very hungry. As I walked past "Club Beer Spill," I was drooling for a Philly cheesesteak. Of course, there were none to be found. I settled for Plan B—pasta—and headed back to the Olympic Village. I got to my room about one a.m.

Someone had slid an envelope under my door. It contained a bizarre photo that begged explanation.

It was a really torrid night in Rome. The guys decided that since they were leaving the following day, they were going to sneak into the forbidden pool. Sure enough, they did. At 12 o'clock, they treated Rome to a taste of Midnight Madness, Hawk style. They spent a half-hour diving, dunking, cannon balling, and picture-taking. Then they sneaked back into their rooms undetected.

OK, back to the photo. It showed the whole group of Hawks standing and seated around the pool—a team picture of sorts. But not a team photo we could use in the media guide. In homage to the nude Roman statuary that had become the subject (I would say "butt" but ...) of our running joke, each guy had a towel wrapped around his head turban style and nothing else! Each guy assumed a different classic Italian nude pose—one of the poses they had seen around the city the past few days. In big black letters at the foot of the photo someone had printed, "When in Rome, do as the Romans do!"

Here's the kicker. The guys swear they've been searching for the photo for years just to prove that they "measured up" to the Romans. The photo remains missing in action, one of history's great mysteries. What became of the Ark of the Covenant, the Holy Grail, the 18 minutes of missing Watergate tapes? Did Oswald act alone? Who put the bop in the bop shebob shebop? Whenever we get together, we try to figure out what became of that photo! Everyone accuses everyone else, but no one 'fessing up. But I will accuse! My prime suspect is Dennis Bloh, manager who snapped and possibly snatched the infamous Polaroid.

We left Rome the next morning. The guys had several prior memories before we had even taken to the hardwood. I'll pass along random recollections from the guys.

Pat McFarland said: "They had no traffic lanes and the drivers like ticked off NY cabbies, but I never saw an accident." [Author I've spent a lot of time in Italy, and I have yet to see a car *without* it.]

Craig Kelly: "There were mosquitoes the size of half-dollars in Rome." [Author's Note: And those mosquitoes fly straighter than many of the local Italian pilots I've flown with.]

John Zipp: "I still liked all the statues." [Author's note: John, get over it.]

From Russia, with Water

Our train stopped in Reggio Calabreo. The train was moved onto a boat, and we sailed across the Straits of Messina to Messina, Sicily. There we took on the Russian National team, and they whipped us by 28 points. Alexander and Sergei Belov (not related) headed the onslaught. Vladimir reminded me of Billy Cunningham, so I nicknamed him, "Cunningham." I stopped calling him Cunningham when he sank the last-second shot to beat the U.S. Olympic team a month later. We nicknamed Sergei, Jerry West, because he was a brilliant ball handler and great passer and could score whenever he desired.

The Belovs

The following night, we lost again to the Czechoslovakian National team. Next morning, we boarded a bus with the Czechoslovakian team—destination Cantania, Sicily. That's where we registered our first win. It was there also that I befriended the Czech coach, Vladimir Heger, who later visited me when I was coaching Milwaukee in the NBA. Our next stop was Palermo. I wouldn't be accompanying the team on the bus trip to Palermo, because I had to meet Claire in Rome. I told the team I would catch up with them in the hotel in Palermo and gave them strict instructions to be up by 8:00 a.m. and on the bus by 9:00 a.m., or they'd be left behind.

My instructions apparently weren't strict enough. Lou Peltzer and Craig Kelly missed the bus—at least the *right* bus. When the two of them finally sauntered down and climbed aboard, they looked up and saw the Czech team on one side of the bus and the Russians on the other (the *left* side, I imagine). Lou and Craig spent the next three hours seated in different parts of the bus listening to unintelligible chitchat. The Russian coach spoke English, so he pumped them for the lowdown on the U.S. Olympic Basketball team. Lou and Craig knew a lot about Mike Bantom. But the way Bantom tore Lou and Craig up in practice, I figured whatever they told the Russian coach might actually benefit Mike. Anyway, neither Lou nor Craig was ever fingered as a Cold War spy.

We beat the Czech team in Palermo. On our second night there, we played Russia for the championship. These guys had clocked us by 28 points in the first encounter. The second time around, we pared the margin all the way down to 25.

John Zipp remembers: "After the game, Sergei [Jerry West] Belov, who spoke very good English, stopped me and Kevin Furey, pointed to our

wristbands and said, 'Can I trade you for them?' When we asked, 'For what?', Sergei replied, 'Our uniforms? We're finished with them. We're going home tomorrow.'

"Sergei invited us to his room, so John Zipp, Kevin Furey, Craig Kelly, and I went up. We knocked. The door swung open and a 6'11" bodyguard was standing there. The guy motioned us to sit down on the bed. Sergei/Jerry West yelled, 'I'll be right out.' Suddenly the front door flew open and in popped Aleksander [Billy C] wielding a scary-looking black revolver. He stared us down for two or three seconds and then pulled the trigger. Everyone got soaking wet. Then he laughed his butt off, turned and bolted out of the room. That was 'Jerry West's' signal to come into the room laughing. We gave him as many wrist bands as we had, and he gave us three red Russian uniforms with the big white CCCP on the front."

Palermo and Onwards

In Palermo, I was accosted on the street: "Hey, Coach McKinney!" I turned to see a tall, good-looking African-American man approaching. When he came into view, I recognized him as Jim Williams, a Temple great from the 1960s. The two of us talked old times awhile. Then he gave me some advice, "Coach, don't let the refs here upset you. They're different than what you're used to. I have never fouled out of a home game. You're going to see some really bad calls, but it's best to just laugh them off.'"

We played Jim's team—the team from Italy—the next night. He was right. The ref called one foul that was absolutely ridiculous. I leaped off the bench and yelled, "What is going on?" Then I looked over at Jim standing at the foul line. He had his hand over his mouth, holding back a laugh. I broke up laughing, too.

We lost that game but managed to beat the local Sicilian team the next night to pick up win number two for the trip.

Next we were on to Romania, which was under the Iron Curtain at the time. En route, aboard Romania's national airline, Claire dropped a spoon under the seats and couldn't retrieve it. Before we were about to land, after the food trays had been collected, the flight attendant walked back to Claire and said, "There was a spoon missing from your tray." Claire crawled down to the floor and eventually found it. No conversation, nothing—I shudder to think what would have happened had she come up spoonless. We might still be in a Romanian prison doing spoon time.

That prospect didn't seem far-fetched. Anti-aircraft guns flanked the runway. We were made to line up in twos and march to baggage claim surrounded by a military unit that carried rifles across their chests. We had to open not only all our luggage, but also every shaving kit, camera bag, and container inside. They checked everything out thoroughly as though they were looking for the king's jewels or a lost spoon.

In Bucharest, it seemed like there were young men armed with AK 47s on every street corner. We asked the interpreter, "Where are the police?" "Not needed," he said dryly. "How about your jails?" "No jails. Not needed. You get caught, you get shot. In this city, crime rate very low."

We won our first game against University of Bucharest before heading to the city of Cluj near Transylvania, Dracula's ancestral stomping, or actually sucking, grounds.

We had our first breakfast of hard cheese, hard bread, and salami. When we got back for lunch, we finished the leftovers from breakfast, which had grown even staler. The cuisine on this trip was a disappointment to our Villanova recruit, Hank Siemontkowski. Every place we went, Hank wanted a cheesesteak, and of course, he came up short. Hank returned to the States ten pounds lighter.

We lost our first game, a close one, against Cluj. All was not lost, though. They treated us to a soccer game that afternoon. Big-time stuff. The stadium was packed. The noise was deafening. And they loved their Cluj players—as long as they were winning.

In our return-court engagement with Cluj the next night, we had a tight game going. Our Romanian friends had one outstanding player—a 6'5" guy named Klugge who wore number 8. Klugge fouled out with about five minutes left, and with him out of the picture, we pulled ahead by five. Then with two and a half minutes remaining, Cluj brought a sub in who wore number 12. Jim O'Brien raced over to me, "Coach! That number 12 that just came in—that's number 8, the guy that fouled out!" I looked and sure enough, it was! I jumped up and screamed to the ref about the little piece of trickery. My wife, the only non-Cluj fan in the stands—was chiding me from behind the bench, "Sit down and stop acting like an ugly American."

The refs had their powwow and told Klugge he had to leave the court. A pall descended, but we held on and won by five. After the game, there weren't many friendly faces on either side in the gym.

Doctor Dracula

The match against Cluj had gotten heated. Lou Peltzer dove for a loose ball and took an elbow in the eye in the scramble.

Peltzer reconstructs the incident: "It sounded like a shotgun went off when I got hit. I put my hand up over my eye, and it felt like my cheekbone was hanging out. Jim O'Brien rushed over, and I asked him how it looked. Obie didn't offer much sympathy, 'It looks like your face threw up.'

"The Cluj trainer came out and said I had to go to the hospital. Craig Kelly accompanied me, along with Miki, our interpreter, who explained that the hospital I was going to was famous. 'It used to be Dracula's castle,' she said. Now there's a confidence booster! That was the worst news I'd heard since Coach McKinney told me I had to guard Calvin Murphy man to man. At least it only seemed like Murphy could fly. Dracula's a different story.

"When we got there, they told Craig to sit and wait in one of the rooms. They shouted to me: 'You! Come with us.' [Author's Note: we asked Lou if his nametag said 'Igor' or 'Renfield.' Lou didn't recall. Lou's eyes were closed the whole time.]

"I went into the operating room, and they instructed me to 'Climb up on the table.' They covered me with two sheets until the only thing visible was the area around my eye, which was covered with blood. I asked what they were doing and they told me, 'Sit here. Do not move.' They were walking back and forth from a stove (yes, a stove in the operating room) where they were sterilizing things in a bowl of boiling water (and maybe making some goulash for break time). One of the doctors (or Dracula's assistants) reached in and got a handful of instruments and came towards me. I screamed, 'Craig, get in here!' Then with no anesthesia, they stitched me up.

"As scary as it was, 'Dracula's grandson' did a great job. Right now, it's hard to even find a scar. Next time I'm in Cluj, I'd be happy to go to Drac's castle again to get treatment if I needed it."

Do that, Lou. Just don't offer to give blood.

The Banquet

That same evening (it was an afternoon game) we were the honored dinner guests of the University of Cluj in the school's banquet hall.

I walked into the hall and saw a single table set for 16 people on each side, with one setting at the head of the table. Our team arrived first and was seated on one side of the table. I sat next to the head of the table, which was eventually occupied by the university president. Claire sat next to me, followed by Miki, our translator, Dennis Bloh, our manager, and our captains, Bobby Sabol and Pat McFarland.

The Cluj squad filed in. Their coach sat directly across from me. Their trainer, their captain and 11 unhappy-looking Cluj hoopsters glowered across the table at our squad of equally unhappy Hawks. Only the Cluj captain could speak English. I thought, "Oh boy, bad seating arrangement!"

I could feel the tension mounting. Fortunately a couple of female servers—one thin and one NFL-husky—arrived and set a wine glass in front of each diner. They filled each glass with a heavy, opaque, mysterious liquid. The Cluj players were suddenly animated and smiling. I asked their coach what the mystery beverage was. He replied, "Eet ees swoika, a plum brandy. Ees very good."

The president stood up and said how happy he was to greet our friends from the United States. Then he picked up his wine glass, raised it and exclaimed, "I would like to make a toast to the wonderful University Saint

Joseph's from Philadelphia, Pennsylvania USA." He didn't say the three letters, U-S-A, successively. He pronounced it 'you-sah' like a single word. Then he added, "Noroc! (which is pronounced like 'na-rook' and means 'good luck')," and the entire Romanian contingent downed their goblets.

Our guys were all looking at me for the go-ahead. I gave it. Then they all gave it the old Hawk try and put the brandy down the hatch in one swig, Clujian style. Once it was downed, the waitresses refilled everyone's glass.

The Cluj coach stood up and said, "I would like to toast the wonderful coach of St. Joseph's basketball, Jack McKinney. Noroc!" and everyone, including my players and wife yelled, "Noroc!"

It didn't end there. The Cluj captain rose, holding his glass high, and said, "I would like to toast the wonderful captains of Saint Joseph's who knows how to lead their team and can really play this game. Noroc!" He was followed by the legendary number 8/number 12—Klugge, who stood and said, "I like toast team Saint Joseph's. Noroc!"

Now it was the Hawks' turn. Bobby Sabol, our captain, stood up and yelled, "I would like to make a toast to the wonderful team from Clujian University and their great coaches. Noroc! (or something like that)"

That was the final toast, and things settled down for a while. Inconspicuously I slipped over to Bobby and said, "Bobby, I don't want you to stand up and give any more toasts." He looked at me bleary-eyed and said, "Coach, I won't. I couldn't stand up if I wanted to."

Thank God for swoika! The two squads were now conversing—or something like that—across the table and having a great time. The difference in atmosphere was amazing.

As for the food, well, our provincial American palates went into shock. The servers gave us our first course. We recognized scrambled eggs, but from that course on, your guess would have been as good as mine.

The Cluj coach could see our puzzlement. He leaned over and said, "Coach, this is a delicacy. It is in your honor. It's scrambled eggs and chicken brains." Upon hearing that second ingredient, 14 U.S. heads snapped to me for guidance. I was suddenly demoted from coach to food tester (wasn't he the most expendable guy in the castle?). I had to hearken back to my own pre-trip pep talk. "We can't be ugly Americans. We'll have to eat some food that doesn't look very appetizing so as not to offend our hosts." I ate the entire serving as the team watched me like hawks (sorry). Then I turned my head towards our contingent and gave them the high sign right before I spun away, gagged, and turned purple.

Unfortunately, as soon as I was done I was served another full portion. I turned to see the NFL-type waitress staring at me, arms crossed, with a look that said, "You'd better eat all of that, or you'll be wearing it." So I did.

What a great evening! At the end, I had to work like crazy to get my team back to the dorm. The two opponents had bonded—laughing and joking, arms around each others' shoulders. Cluj players were giving their best rendition of "When the Hawk Comes Flying In"—a rendition that Simon and the *American Idol* judges would mercy kill in a nanosecond.

When I did safely gather the whole contingent, that's the song we sang on our way back to the dorm.

Hawks in Flight

The banquet proved a fitting end to our overseas trip. We orchestrated a few jeans-for-sneaks barter sessions before we left. They couldn't get jeans behind the Iron Curtain at the time, so they were a valuable commodity.

We had to fly from Cluj to Bucharest the next morning. When we saw the two ancient planes revving to transport us, I expected to see "Wilbur and Orville" scrawled on the propeller somewhere. Claire and I boarded the first plane, which seated five passengers on each side of the aisle. We were wishing we had stashed a case of swoika away for the trip.

Somebody asked one of the flight attendants, "How old are these planes?" He got a short answer, "Old." "How often do you replace them?" The reply? "When one of them goes down."

We landed in Bucharest safely. Our plane lived to fly another day, and so did all the Hawks in it. But that was *our* plane. The other plane gave the guys more thrills than a day at Dorney Park.

Bobby Sabol: "That prop plane was battered around unmercifully. All flight long we hit air pockets that dropped us straight down. It was scary.

"McFarland passed out. Craig Kelly was hugging Moody and whimpering, 'Mike, I love you, man!' Steve MacZinko turned green. Miki, our interpreter, got deathly sick. I felt my ear pop on one of our drops. When I got home, I found out I had ruptured my eardrum. The flight attendant handed out barf bags, and we needed them even more than we did the night before when we forced the chicken brains down.

"There was a couple onboard who lived in Cluj. They weren't bothered at all by the ride. Of course, it takes a lot to scare somebody who has Dracula for a neighbor.

"When the plane finally landed, Zipp kissed the ground. Craig Kelly said to Moody, 'Moody, remember what I said to you on board. Don't take it seriously. I was only kidding.'"

Craig apparently wanted to be clear that he was coming out of the clouds, not the closet.

Boyle—Overseas

Before the 1984-1985 season, Coach Jim Boyle got wind of a basketball tournament in Belgium that was to run from Christmas to New Year's Day. He found out that the tournament would pit three local Belgium teams and one visiting team. The tournament organizers were picking up all the expenses, so Jim figured he and his Hawks had nothing to lose, except maybe a couple games. He was right. Coach Bo was not aware that the "local teams" were actually national squads stocked with Belgium's finest players. These so-called amateur teams wound up blowing Saint Joseph's University out every game.

"The tournament looked like a men-against-boys proposition and we were the boys. I had gone into the tournament hoping I could interest a few of their guys in coming to St. Joe's. But these guys were NBA—not NCAA—candidates. One of my players, Ron Vercruyssen, later played in the Belgium league for about eight years.

Bo Knows Scouting—Not

Bo continues: "A lot of things backfired on that trip. I scouted a team we were scheduled to play and saw they had a bunch of older guys. One guy was over seven feet tall and weighed about 270 pounds. Rod Blake was our center, and I felt this guy would be too much for Rod to handle inside. I instructed Rod to let the guy take jumpers outside, even though it looked like he could shoot a bit. Rod followed my orders. Didn't work, not even a little bit—the guy had 30 points by halftime. He shot 10 for 10 from the three-point range."

Bo Knows Ping Pong

In the hotel the young Hawks were going crazy trying to occupy their time. They finally found an answer—a ping-pong table downstairs. Ping-pong was right up Bo's alley. He savored the chance to demonstrate another of his many skills, so he organized an impromptu ping-pong tournament. Bo blew through all the competition. Then Jack Concannon stepped up. Jack beat the coach. Bo couldn't handle that. He demanded a rematch—and lost again. He demanded another rematch and lost again—and again and again. Bo was determined to play all night to win if he had to. Finally, in the wee hours of the morning, Bo won. Jack did not ask for a rematch, just a late wake-up call.

A Gathering of Hawks

The year Boyle left St. Joe's, he was scheduled to take the A10 All-Star team to the Jones Cup in Taipai, Taiwan. Bo recalls: "Tony Costner had taken the trip a few years earlier as a player and was disappointed I wouldn't be part of the contingent. As fate would have it, I did go. Coach John Calipari from University of Massachusetts took the A10 All-Stars to the Jones Cup, and I happened to be there already, coaching the Chinese Junior Nationals in preparation for the All-Asian Games to be held in

Nagoya Japan. John Griffin was the assistant coach on the A10 All-Star team. Coach Calipari invited me to sit on the bench with the team during the tournament. At the same time, the USA Women's World Cup team was touring in preparation for the '92 Olympics. Both coaches of the women's team—Jim Foster and Theresa Shank-Grentz—were former Hawks. I ended up setting up a scrimmage schedule for their team when they got to Taipei. It was kind of amazing. Here I was a half a world away, and yet it was like a gathering of Hawks: Griff, Foster, Theresa, and I all wound up in Taipei at the same time.

John Griffin—Overseas

Griff flew the Hawks to Austria and Germany for six games. They came back a respectable 3-3. They didn't square off against national-caliber squads, but they did face some stiff competition.

As Griff relates: "Some of the guys we faced overseas were outstanding. The German team Levercruisen had a guy named Detlef Schremph who attended Washington College in 1985 before spending 15 years in the NBA where he split time between the Indiana Pacers, the Portland Trailblazers, the Seattle Supersonics, and the Dallas Mavericks. He was a two-time NBA All-Star.

"We played in some beautiful cities: Salzburg, Vienna, and Heidelberg. We also played in some pretty gloomy industrialized cities like Frankfort and Nuremberg, that had been bombed extensively during the War. Our players got to see the Dachau concentration camp, which was a sobering experience for all of us.

"I laugh now about complaining about how small our hotel rooms were. Those little rooms didn't bother my players at all. The players were 20-year-olds. They were used to rooms of that size. Our guys turned out to be a welcome hint of America to our soldiers stationed in Heidelberg. Our players befriended some of the soldiers' daughters and wound up with personal guides to show them around the city.

"Of course, Germany is Germany. Bamburg has more breweries than any other city in Germany. I used to warn my guys, 'Have fun. Just please don't get arrested.' They didn't. I was proud of them."

Puerto Rico

Jack Ramsay opened the door to Puerto Rico for a number of Hawk coaches. Jack had spent a few summers coaching in Ponce, a town in Puerto Rico. When Jack was the head coach at St. Joe's and I was his assistant, Ponce came calling again to see if Jack was planning to return that summer. Jack's schedule wouldn't allow it, so he recommended me as his replacement.

I was 26 years old when I made my first trip to the island. When I got there, I discovered that half of my players were older than I was. It didn't seem to matter. In fact, we jumped out to a 5-0 start in league competition. Then we lost our first game to Quebradillas. That's when our owner, Dr. Enrique [Coco] Vicens, stopped at my house to see me. To my surprise, the Dr. said, "Jack, I don't want you to get hurt. You're too nice. The team says, 'The coach—he ees too jong!' So I ask you now to go home. I weel pay you for thee season." I replied, "Coco, don't worry about me being hurt. You can fire me. That's your prerogative. But if you don't, I'm not going home until the season is over—and we've won the championship." Coco said, "I weel not fire you—so see you at practeece tonight."

We did win the championship and had one helluva celebration on championship night in Ponce. But I'll get to that story later.

The Tough Life in Puerto Rico

I coached seven summers in the Balconesto Superior of Puerto Rico. Eight of the 10 largest cities on the island sponsored teams. Puerto Rico's international team was drawn from this circuit. The league recruited U.S. coaches for their teams. Several Hawk coaches worked there, including Paul Westhead and Jimmy Lynam. There were non-Hawk coaches too, like PJ Carlesimo, Del Harris, Sam "Kiss it off the glass" Jones, Rollie Massimino, and Eric Geldart.

In 1962, I coached Ponce. In subsequent years I coached Santurce and Caguas. Most of the teams were clustered around San Juan in the northeast part of the island. About four teams were situated in the southeast, which often made for interesting transportation. One year I coached in Ponce and lived in San Juan. I had to fly daily over the mountain to get to practice and home games.

Most of the American coaches lived in the San Juan area in condos or motels on the beaches of San Juan. Our days were spent roughly like this—early morning on the tennis court (no one could beat Sam Jones) then off to the swimming pool or beach for a few hours before getting ready for practice or a game. After the game or practice, the "weary" coaches and wives would meet at a casino at about 10 or 11 p.m. and quaff a brew or two. We were constantly badgered by our assistant coaches—Puerto Rican natives—to drink the island specialty, rum. Great nights they were, those Puerto Rican nights—losing coaches crying about bad calls, winning coaches buying the rounds. What a tough life!

Mother's Day—The First Trip to San Juan

The whole McKinney family was booked to fly to San Juan on Mother's Day. I had to spend the weekend before our departure at the MAC track championship in Easton, Pennsylvania at Lafayette College since I was also the Hawks assistant track coach. When the meet ended on Saturday, I made tracks for Philly to pack.

I pulled into our driveway on the eve of our departure. Jack Ramsay and his wife, Jean, were at the house to bid us adios. After they left, Claire put the children in bed. When she came downstairs she looked pale and said, "I think I just had a miscarriage." We immediately called her obstetrician who told her to report to the hospital right away. Claire protested, "We're going to Puerto Rico tomorrow, and I've got to be on that plane!" The doctor said not to worry, that we'd make the plane, but we had to go to the hospital first. I called Claire's mother and asked her to come over and watch Susan and Ann, our two children. By the time Claire's mom arrived, it was after 11 p.m., and we left for the hospital. We met the doctor and voiced our concern about making our morning flight. He said, "I'll list her as an outpatient, and Claire will be ready to fly at 7 a.m." I left the hospital, got home and took two loads of clothes to the Laundromat (remember it was 1961). Then I packed my bags. I got to bed at 2:30.

At 6:30 I was up, rousing the girls (Susan was two, Ann was seven months). Claire's mother and I got them dressed, fed them breakfast, packed the car, and made it to the airport by eight. I was unaware of the adventure that had played out at the hospital all night long. After I left Claire that night, she waited in the emergency room corridor for hours. A big-time auto accident had occurred nearby and they rushed the victims into surgery. At 3:30 a.m., Claire was still waiting to be taken in for a D&C procedure. Her ordeal—waiting and then having the operation—lasted almost until dawn. Still she awoke at 6 a.m. and struggled to her feet. A nurse scurried into the room saying, "Where do you think you're going, young lady?" Claire insisted, "I'm going to Puerto Rico." An argument ensued. Finally Claire demanded, "Go get my doctor." The doctor had dutifully stayed all night, anticipating this situation. Claire got her wish. My parents went to the hospital and brought her to the airport at seven. Miraculously, we found ourselves jetting off to New York as scheduled, despite very worried looks from our mothers.

We relaxed in the waiting area in LaGuardia Airport waiting to board flight 521 to San Juan at 11:30 a.m. Then the flight was delayed till 2:10 p.m. So my situation was this—my wife had been under anesthesia five hours ago and my two-year old was hopping all over the airport greeting every person within earshot. We were practically the only Americans on a plane packed to the rafters with passengers—most of whom were Puerto Ricans headed home for Mother's Day. Practically every passenger had a brown bag full of food they were taking to Mom back home. Did I mention that my seven-month old seized the opportunity to test the questionable diaper-changing skills of her father? I changed diapers in between bouts of saving Claire from tumbling to the floor as she periodically slumped into a deep sleep.

When we got to Puerto Rico late in the day, it was too late to connect to Ponce. We needed lodging, so I asked the cabbie to take us to a good hotel. He did. He waited for me to make arrangements, and then took off—with my bag full of all my basketball notes and "stuff." The "stuff" was more critical. Our pacifier supply was in that bag. Now we had a crisis. I spent my first ever evening in Puerto Rico trying to find pacifiers in San Juan. The good news is I found them.

Next morning, we were off to Ponce, and everything went smooth as silk. Except that we were out of pacifiers again. Claire and I had used them all up.

Postscript—Coming Home

When we got home to Drexel Hill after our first summer in Puerto Rico, we had another surprise awaiting us. It turns out that our doctor had been brought before the hospital board and investigated. They thought he had performed an illegal abortion (this was 1961) and whisked the patient out of the country.

Help Yourself

Shopping could be an adventure in Puerto Rico as one of my fellow coaches discovered. Roy Rubin, who coached LIU and the Philadelphia 76ers was a bachelor in those days. One day he was food shopping. After packing the back seat of his car with groceries he headed back to his apartment. At a red light a Puerto Rican driver went through the light, slammed into Roy's car, never stopped, and left Roy with his car spinning in the intersection.

Despite Roy's cries of "Please help, broken leg, cannot move, please help," no one came to help him. Finally one young man slowly ventured over and asked sympathetically, *"You break leg?"* Roy answered, "Yes, look." The man looked into the car and said, *"You no can move?"* Roy said, "No. I cannot move. Please help." The man opened the back door, reached in, took the bags of groceries and calmly walked away.

Roy said, "Help," and the guy apparently thought he said, "Help yourself."

"Doctor McKinney"

I had a problem getting in to see Claire and our new baby. We played in the evening during visiting hours. By the time our games and practices were over, family and friends weren't allowed into the hospital. But doctors were.

I didn't think of that on my first visit. But it just so happened that I was still wearing my suit from the game that night. I went to the hospital after visiting hours and I figured I would make my way up to Claire's room until somebody stopped me. I never figured I'd actually get there. I didn't even speak Spanish, but I figured, "Why not give it a try?" I walked through the lobby, up the steps, down the corridor. All along the way, all I did was say the only Spanish I knew, "Buenos noches" to everyone I passed. Everybody smiled nicely and said, "Buenas noches" back to me. Nobody made any attempt to stop me, and I was the only non-medical person in the whole place. That's when it hit me. They thought I was a doctor because doctors were the only persons on the Island who wore suits. Doctors and basketball coaches.

Four Things Few Coaches Can Say

Those summers I spent coaching in Puerto Rico had a lot of impact on our lives. Our two daughters ended up studying Spanish in college and working for U.S. companies that dealt in the South American market. My daughter Susan now lives in Mexico. Our son Dennis was born in Puerto Rico, and we all made lots of friends there. The experience exposed our whole family to a different way of life.

As for basketball, were it not for coaching in Puerto Rico, I would never be able to say that:

1. I've been shot at in a car as we were driving out of an opponent's town after a game. The car had two bullet holes in it.
2. I've been in an arena that had been set afire by frustrated fans who couldn't get into the game.
3. I was made to lie on the floor of a car driven by the mayor of a town that we had just played and defeated. The mayor was driving through the hostile crowd smiling and waving, while I cowered on the floor under a blanket.
4. A referee convinced me to stop arguing by saying, "Jack, please don't argue again, because one of us could get shot if you do."

The Celebration

In 1962, just getting to our away games was an adventure. The games usually started at seven, so we would set out about five and rumble along twisty mountain roads that had no road barriers paralleling the cliffs. En route, we usually stopped for refreshments. I'd get a Coke. My players would be goading me to drink rum or scotch or beer. I promised them I'd have some only when we won the championship. Well, we won.

The night we won, the town went wild. We were driven all over town as screaming fans lined the streets beating pots and pans. Claire left the celebration early because we were flying back to Philly at eight o'clock the following morning. We needed to get home before Saturday afternoon because her sister was getting married.

The parade spilled into one of Ponce's popular watering holes. Inside, the team started working me over, "Coach, you promised you'd have a drink with us when we won. Tonight's the night. Drink up!" Every single one came up to me with a glassful of something. I was *not* a drinker. I had—and still have—no idea what they were handing me. All I know is that, too many times, I had to toast, "Ponce becomes champion," and chug a glassful down the hatch. Not once, but several times. Definitely too many times—just ask Claire. On second thought, don't.

At about one o'clock, some of my team half-carried me out of the watering hole and stuffed me into a car. They took me home, dumped me on the doorstep, rang the bell, and vanished into the night. Claire opened the door, saw me, and somehow got me to bed. She was not a happy camper. And I was one sleepy camper. Compared to me, Rip Van Winkle would have seemed wired. When seven o'clock struck, I tried valiantly (sort of) to get out of bed, but I couldn't find the floor even though I was sure it was down there somewhere. I told Claire I couldn't make the plane.

When I finally managed to get both feet out of bed and pointed in the same direction, I limped into town and booked a flight for the next morning. We made that plane with no problem. We landed in Philly one hour before the wedding and had a great time *dancing*—just dancing. I'm told they had a great open bar, but I didn't get anywhere near it.

Puerto Rico Farewell

When Claire and I reminisce about Puerto Rico, three sentences come to mind:

1. "The coach, he ees too jong (young)."
2. "He meesed thee turn."
3. "Eet ees covered in your contract."

You already know about the "Coach, he ees too jong" episode. As for the second quote, Claire and I heard that one night after we had dinner with Coco and his brother, Willie, the team's co-owner. As the car was coming down the mountains on the way home, Claire and I noticed a lot of white crosses on the sharp curves along the road. We asked what they were, and Coco said there was a cross for each driver who disappeared when "He meesed thee turn."

Then Willie gave us a suggestion. He said, "And Jack, if you are riding along thees road late at night and you are alone and some hombre steps in front of you to flag you down, do not stop, run over him, keel him. If you stop, he will rob you and he will keel you. Isn't that right, Coco?" Coco nodded: "Willie ees right. Do not stop. Run over him and keep going!" Claire and I were sitting in the back seat frozen with fear at that point, squeezing each other's hand hard enough to stop the blood flow. I was thinking, "Run over him. *Keel him,* or *he will keel you*—holy shit, where am I?"

The third sentence relates to a 1961 incident. I had put my daughter Ann to bed for her afternoon nap but forgot to pull up the side of the crib. About an hour later, we heard a thud on the tile (gulp!) floor. We also heard a crying baby. The side of her head started to swell. In a panic we called Leana, Coco's wife. She immediately called Coco, who in addition to being the team owner, was an ear and nose specialist. She told Coco we'd bring Ann over right away. Coco examined Ann and X-rayed her. Ten minutes later, he was showing me the crack on her skull in the X-ray. *"Eet ees cracked,"* he said, *"But do not worry. Eet ees covered in your contract."*

Puerto Rico, land of enchantment, land of (almost) firings, baby births, fractured skulls, dead man's curves, crazy airport misadventures, radical fans, basketball championships, and crazy celebrations. We survived it. And we loved it.

CHAPTER TWELVE

The Super-Guards as Coaches—The Booth-Lynam Era

Jack McKinney's Replacement

COACH McKINNEY:

The next order of business for St. Joe's was to find a good coach. They made an excellent choice in Harry Booth, one of my assistant coaches. I knew Harry for a long time—from my early assistant coaching days to my head coaching days. As a player, Harry was as good a defender and as tenacious a competitor as I've ever seen. He was a good, solid basketball player and an even better baseball player.

Looking back these days, Harry confesses that he wondered at the time if taking the head coach job was a good career move for him, given the shape the basketball program was in. Back then, he thought long and hard before he finally accepted.

While Harry had doubts, I didn't. Harry had paid his dues as an assistant coach for eight years. In my mind, he was ready to step in. He was the guy I would have recommended if I had been asked for input.

If Harry could get his charges to play with the mental and physical toughness that he himself brought to the gym, he would do well. However, as coaches know firsthand, the quality of a coach is generally measured by the quality of the players. I hadn't left a very good crop for Harry to work with in the 1974-1975 season. And to be honest, my firing left the recruiting program in turmoil. Many recruits changed their minds and went to college elsewhere.

Six seniors graduated in my final year. That left Harry with only one veteran, Ron Righter. Ron, aided by a good point guard, Fran Rafferty, struggled to get the job done. An incoming freshman named Michael Thomas added some firepower. Michael averaged more than ten points a game over a four-year career. That's right—four-year career. Michael was the beneficiary of a new NCAA ruling that allowed freshmen to play varsity ball.

Graduation Stats

I have mixed feelings about freshman eligibility for varsity competition. If experience proves that more players graduate with this rule in effect, then I suppose it's a good rule. But it's scary to me to see the appalling record so many major college sports programs have in graduating their athletes. I'll share a frightening statistic with you, just a little tidbit I caught in the news last year. The *Los Angeles Times* reported that 27 of the 56 teams playing in the 2004 football Bowl games, including five of the eight representatives in the Bowl Championship series, fail to graduate half their players.

I am proud to say that is not the case at Saint Joseph's University, which fields 20 different men's and women's varsity teams. Eighty-one percent of Saint Joseph's athletes graduate. That rate exceeds the University's overall rate of 76 percent. The graduation rate from the men's basketball program matches that 76 percent rate. Here's another uplifting statistic: 97 percent of the basketball players who exhaust their four years of varsity eligibility graduate.

That's why I'll always consider St. Joe's a wonderful place for the legitimate student-athlete. They know they won't receive special treatment, and they'll be expected to attend all their classes in order to graduate on time.

Big Booth Star

Besides Mike Thomas, Harry Booth eventually picked up some talent—guys like Norman Black and Zane Major. Harry also picked up a guy who would be instrumental in keeping the Hawk flying into the 1990s. John Griffin played for Harry for four years and picked up a lot from his mentor. Griff served as an assistant under Jim Lynam and Jim Boyle before eventually taking the reins himself in 1990-1991.

Norman Black

From the 1975-1976 campaign through the 1978-1979 season, the same player led the Hawks in scoring average every year. Norman Black remains the only Hawk who can make that claim.

Did I mention that Norman also led his team in the category of average rebounds per game? He only did that for three years, though—no big deal.

After college, Norman played in Venezuela, where he was MVP on a championship team. He then went to play in the Philippines for 10 years and coach 17. In that span of 27 years, he has ten national championships to show.

Norman is coaching yet. He also does TV work as a basketball analyst.

Norman says: "I've had ups and downs in my basketball career, but when the basketball was over, I realized how valuable my education was to me. I don't consider St. Joe's like other schools. If you didn't study there, you were out. I know too many other players at other schools who majored in basketball. That's sad. My education prepared me for life, not basketball.

"That said, I was fortunate enough to enjoy an exciting basketball career. Leading the team in scoring and rebounding for four years was gratifying. Harry Booth and Jimmy Lynam made the whole experience fun for me.

"But one of the most gratifying memories I have was the NIT game against Ohio State in my senior year. We were getting crushed. With six seconds left, Coach Lynam called a timeout. At that point in the game, I needed two points to tie Mike Bantom for the SJU scoring record. Zane Major needed two more points to reach 1,000 for his career. The whole team was aware of the situation, so Coach Lynam said, 'We've only got time for one more shot...who's it gonna be?'

"It was quiet for a few seconds and I was thinking, 'If I tie Bantom for that record, it's just going to be broken somewhere down the line—and probably soon. If Zane gets 1,000, he will have accomplished something that will always be his. That thousand-point milestone can never be taken away.' So I said, 'Zane should take the last shot.' He did, and he sank it. I don't think anyone was happier for him than me.

"Zane and I are still good friends. Over the years, he worked for Delta Airlines and came down to the Philippines twice to visit me."

Norman Black just lets it happen and appreciates the moment—each moment—from his days on Hawk Hill to the present. He especially savors the SJU Athlete of the Year trophy he won as a senior. Norman was a star on the 440-relay team that year, so he was selected not only for his exploits on the hardwood but also in track and field—a man after my own heart.

Eight Men Out or And Then There Was One

Harry's era saw one of the most nightmarish SJU games ever. Harry suffered through a miserable night on the bench watching it. Misery, they say, loves company. And Harry had plenty of company on the bench that night.

St. Joe's lost 109-96 at Schmidt Fieldhouse in Cincinnati that January 10, 1976, in double overtime. Astute fans will be thinking: 13 points ... that's a pretty steep differential for an overtime game. There *is* an explanation, though not a palatable one. The Hawks were whistled for 44 fouls while the hometown Xavier squad was whistled for a mere 19. By the end of regulation, the Hawks couldn't field five eligible players, because so many guys had fouled out. Amazingly, they almost won the first overtime with only four men on the court. Xavier missed a free throw with 12 seconds left. The Hawks then had the ball and a chance to win. St. Joe's called timeout and was charged with a technical. The Musketeers from Xavier missed the technical as well as a follow-up desperation jumper, so the game extended into a second overtime.

St. Joe's started the second OT with four players on the court: Borski, Cakert, Thomas, and Vassalotti. Vassalotti soon fouled out, followed by Thomas. That left Borski and Cakert on the court to match up against the Xavier five. Cakert scored two points on two foul shots as something strange happened. The hometown fans cheered. Shortly afterwards, he too fouled out. That left Borski as the sole survivor.

"We had smoke coming out our ears," Borski said. "It was basically— just give me the ball. I went down at full speed, barreled into one of their players and handed the ref the ball. I told him he might as well call that, too."

After the game, the NCAA summoned an emergency meeting and overturned the rule that limited the number of players a team could travel with to 10. Henceforth they allowed teams to travel with a full complement of players.

A Decent Season Goes Down the Drain

Harry's Hawks were in the midst of a decent run in 1975-1976. They were 9-8 with eight games remaining when Harry had to confront a difficult situation. He had to discipline his two top players, Zane Major and Willie Taylor, by dropping both men from the team. That killed the season. His Hawks won only one more game after that and finished with a disappointing 10-16 mark.

Fortunately there's a happy postscript to the episode. Zane Major later returned to the basketball program and completed an outstanding career.

Harry Booth

Harry Booth was a Hawk assistant coach for eight years before ascending to the head coach position. He had attended Bishop Neuman High School in Philadelphia where he played under Jack Kraft, former Villanova and URI head coach. He entered St. Joe's in 1958 without a grant-in-aid. Harry played varsity baseball and basketball for three years. As a senior in the 1961-1962 season, he co-captained the Hawks basketball squad.

Harry was Middle Atlantic Conference All-Star in baseball in both his junior and senior years. After graduation, he coached for three years at Bishop McDevitt in Wyncote and fashioned a 46-28 record. In 1966, he joined the St. Joe's basketball staff, where he performed recruiting and scouting duties. He became the frosh basketball coach in 1970. His teams went 46-19. Then in 1973 he became the number-one assistant to the varsity basketball coach.

Meanwhile, he compiled a 51-29 record in an interrupted six-year stint as baseball coach from 1967-1969. Harry was working in the business world as well during this period. His commitments forced him to relinquish the head baseball job the following year, but he continued to serve as the assistant baseball coach. After vacating the spot for a year, Harry resumed head baseball coaching duties and compiled a 44-27-1 record over a three-year period. His Hawks won a Mid Atlantic Conference Championship and a berth in the NCAAs under his leadership.

Harry continued his education after graduation, earning a BS in business administration in 1962 and MA in education in 1973.

Harry served as a volunteer assistant coach on Rollie Massimino's staff when Villanova won the 1984-1985 NCAA championship.

Lynam's Four to Score

Coach Jim Lynam made a big splash in 1978, his rookie year as a coach. Jim made his team successful with his four-to-score offense. He had some talent to work with in returnees Norman Black, Zane Major, Bob Valderia, Luke Griffin, Jeffery Clark, and John Smith. But he also had some brilliant newcomers in Tony Costner and Lonnie McFarland.

The four-to-score concept was to keep passing the ball and force a slow, sloughing-off defense to spread apart until the Hawks managed a one-on-one matchup. Once the Hawks had the D spread all over the court, the defense had few opportunities to double up the man with the ball without giving up an easy layup to the man left open for the double-team. If the Hawks faced a zone defense, they simply positioned themselves in four corners. The point guard stayed out front with the ball and waited for the defense to come out to play him.

The major drawback to the four-to-score was that it couldn't be used unless you had the lead. But Lynam's guys managed to get the lead frequently. As a result, a lot of game scores were low.

Patriot Games

They're calling the New England Patriots a dynasty because the Pats won three Super Bowl titles in four years. Their margin of victory in each of their three wins was three points. The Pats have taken a page from the 1979-1980 Hawks' book. Saint Joseph's won the Big Five title outright that season. They swept the series but won every contest except one by a single point.

Norman Black drives to the basket against Mt. St. Mary. *Photo courtesy of Saint Joseph's University*

Black to the Rack

John Smith recalls the St. Joe's-Georgetown game in 1979:

"Georgetown was ranked No. 11. John Thompson was the coach, and Sleepy Floyd was the big star. We played the game in a bandbox high school gym packed to the rafters with 3,000 screaming Hoya fans. We weren't supposed to have a prayer. But we managed to get an early lead so we went into the four-to-score. We ran it and ran it, and those Hoya fans booed louder and louder.

"When the game wound down, we were down by a point. Coach Lynam, in our timeout huddle, said to our star player, Norman Black, 'Take it right to the rack—and hard.'

"Fortunately, we didn't need the foul and won 39-38. Those fans were shocked. I don't think they ever got over that game."

A Hoya Be-Heading

John Smith of the 1978-1979 squad recalls: "While we were in the locker room celebrating the win over Georgetown, we noticed that Kevin Quirk, the Hawk mascot, was missing. Those Hoya fans were all over us the whole game long. Anyway, out of nowhere in walks Kevin. The Georgetown fans had jumped him and decapitated him. Kevin ran into the locker room with a bloody nose chanting, 'The Hawk will never die!'"

Dethroned DePaul

On March 14, 1981, the Hawks took on No. 1-ranked DePaul University in the second round of the NCAA Tournament. DePaul was led by All-Americans Mark Aguirre and Terry Cummings. The whole country anticipated a big DePaul win, but the evening ended with the canonization of the Hawks' John Smith. John Smith recalls his biggest moment:

"With 15 seconds to go, we were down by three and we missed a shot. I ended up wrestling for the ball on the floor with Terry Grubbs. Grubbs was a 6'8" jumping jack. I was 6'5" and I don't have any doubt that he could probably just jump right over me. Well, on the tap, I figured I had to do something to have a fighting chance. I broke about five rules. I jumped too soon. I jumped over the line and into Grubbs—but it was the only way I could get to the ball [Author's note: John claims to have broken five rules, but he's only divulged three.] My desperation tactics worked—the ref didn't call anything on me, and I ended up tapping the ball back to Byron Warrick, who immediately drilled a jumper. Now we were down by one with ten seconds left.

"DePaul inbounded the ball, and we immediately fouled the guy with the ball, Skip Dillard, which didn't seem like a good thing at the time. Skip was their best foul shooter. He was shooting free throws with something like

88 percent accuracy, and we had just sent him to the line for a one-and-one. Eight seconds remained. There was no three-point line then, so if Skip canned one of the two fouls, we could still tie with a field goal, but if he made both–and he was averaging nine of 10–we were pretty much cooked. Coach Lynam called time. He said, 'If Dillard misses, *do not* call timeout. Just run the fast break exactly the way we practice it every day.' Then he added, 'And score!'

"We take the floor again. Dillard's foul shot clangs off the rim to the left. Bryan Warrick grabs it and pushes up court. The rest of the Hawks fill their lanes–one on each sideline with the four and five men racing down the middle.

"At that point, Bryan gives a little NBA show. As the first DePaul defender tries to stop him, Bryan freezes him with a crossover dribble, then blasts by him. Bryan gives the next defender a between-the-legs dribble that causes the guy to trip. As he brings the ball up from between his legs he streamlines a half-court chest pass down the sidelines to Lonnie McFarland who immediately goes up for a jumper. Both defenders react to the ball, so as Lonnie goes up, he spots Tony Costner and me–the four and five men on the break. There we are alone under the hoop! Lonnie hits to me. I put it in with one second left, and we win 49-48."

That's John Smith's description of one of the Hawks' most historic plays. He called it his "Fourth and Shunk" layup. That was the South Philly playground where Smith played as a kid.

Don't Leave Home Without Howard

Phil Jasner of the *Philadelphia Daily News* recalls:

"Before the game, Jim Lynam and I were relaxing in the whirlpool listening to two other guys going on about how St. Joe's had no chance against DePaul. Jimmy just sat stonefaced the whole episode. But the whole country felt the way these two guys did, 'Why bother to play the game? St. Joe's had no chance.'

"After the big upset we went back to the hotel. Jim Boyle telephoned a Chinese restaurant and arranged a celebration dinner for the team, the coaches, and the Philadelphia press corps. Before the food order was taken, everyone clasped hands and said grace. It was truly a moving experience. I sat there and wondered, 'How many of the big schools ever do anything like this–something intimate and personal and real and not pretentious? *This* is what it's all about.' Honest, that memory has always been very special to me.

"The Hawks spent that dinner replaying the game. Then Lynam went to pay and came up short on cash. Philly sportscaster Howard Eskin saved the day by putting it on his American Express card." Don't leave home without Howard.

Tony Costner offers this insight: "We knew if we kept certain people at bay, we had a legitimate shot at beating DePaul in Dayton. The group of players we had my freshman year was as good as any in the country. The year before, I played in a high school program that was really dominant. When I got to Hawk Hill, I expected the same thing. I wasn't disappointed. So when we went up against DePaul, we had the personnel and we had the game plan. All we needed was some good old-fashioned luck. When Skip Dillard missed that free throw, history was about to be created. And it was!"

It's Dei-Lightful, It's Dei-Lovely, It's Dei Lynam

In the euphoria of the win over Dayton, the national TV audience was tuned into Coach Lynam's 15-year-old daughter running up the sidelines and leaping into his arms.

Daughter Dei was a Hawk basketball junkie. She went with her dad to all his summer basketball clinics and lectures. She happened to be the only one of the Lynam children at the arena that night. Her older brother and sister were both away on school class outings. Dei pleaded to go on the trip and won her case. She even offered her dad the $100 she had stashed away "for emergencies."

So Jim let Dei make the trip and stay with her grandmom at the hotel. Jim couldn't wangle a seat for Dei in the sold-out arena, so he put her to work. He told her to sit at the end of the Hawk bench and keep statistics.

Dei put both her statistician experience and TV experience from that night to good use. She grew up to become the statistician for the Los Angeles Clippers. And because of all the basketball savvy she picked up (and inherited) from her dad, Dei Lynam became a sports reporter for Comcast Sportsnet.

As we were going to press, Bob Gordon was a guest on the *Daily News Live* show. He was there to talk about his latest book (at the time), *Legends of the Philadelphia Phillies*. Dei Lynam was the host. Bob said, "We should talk about the book I'm writing right now with a good friend of your dad's." Dei said, "Must be something to do with the Hawks." Ah, those daughters of Saint Joseph's coaches—living proof that the Hawk will never die.

Nightmare on Lynam Street

Joey Meyers, Ray Meyers's assistant coach, thought he was having a nightmare.

"I was still reeling from that loss to St. Joe's a few weeks afterwards when I went to the finals—as a spectator obviously—thanks to St. Joe's. I was in my hotel room about one in the morning. I had just dozed off and I kept hearing this loud voice. The guy was speaking a mile a minute. As I started to get more alert, I could hear every word he was saying. He was giving this other guy a blow-by-blow description of the game I was trying to forget. Then it hit me. I recognized that voice. 'That's Jimmy Lynam!' I thought. I got up, went to the door, and saw Lynam and some other guy starting down the steps at the end of the hall. Lynam was *still* chirping away. And I thought, 'You little ****. You're gonna make me lose sleep forever!'"

Hoop Dreams

It's a shame someone had to lose such a great, evenly contested game. But it's only a game. It's devastating when players and coaches lose sight of that. That's what happened to Skip Dillard after he missed the foul shot that set up the Hawk win.

He had to watch his miss again and again on TV. He started obsessing about it, spending all his time in the gym and sloughing off classes. Coach Ray Meyers confronted him about cutting class. Skip told Ray he didn't need the education because he was going to the NBA. Skip's teammates from Westinghouse High School and some other friends from Chicago had all made it to the NBA—guys like Isiah Thomas, Eddie Johnson, and Mark Aguirre. Skip's whole existence was built around playing in the NBA, but it didn't happen. Skip didn't even get an invitation to an NBA camp.

His life took a horrible downturn. He turned to drugs. He robbed a gas station and was sent to prison for ten years. While he was in prison, *60 Minutes* did a segment on him—on the aftermath of missing the foul shot and not making the NBA—and how he ended up resorting to a life of crime and drugs.

Before he turned to drugs, Skip used to seek the counsel of his coach, Ray Meyers. Skip continued to seek counsel from Ray even while he was on drugs. While he was in prison, he got off the drugs and turned into a model prisoner. The coach and a friend named Dick Heise promised he'd try to get Skip an early release and a job when he got out of prison. Dick came through on both counts.

Ray Meyers is one of the warmest, most compassionate coaches I've had to compete against. Ray told me, "It was devastating to see Skip. He apologized to me for the state he was in when he was doing drugs. I'm happy to say he's really improved now."

One Point

Remember Jack Palance as Curly in *City Slickers*? "One thing." That was Curly's philosophy. Well Jimmy Lynam is basketball's answer to Curly. One point ... that was what Lynam teams shot for. That was the margin of victory in 16 games over Jim Lynam's three-year coaching span. In other words, in almost one of every five games he coached, the game was decided by one point.

Discretion Is the Better Part of Valor

Mike Hauer was one of the roughest, most physical players ever to don a Hawk uniform. Never one to back away from a fight, Mike recalls a time when coach Jimmy Lynam just let Mike be Mike. Or maybe there was another reason.

"We were playing Seton Hall in a freshman game at the Palestra, before the varsity game," Mike recalls. "I got into a fight with one of the Seton Hall guys. Coach Lynam, all 5'8" of him, and Seton Hall's coach, who was about 6'8", were just watching. Coach Lynam suggested they should step in and break it up. The giant from Seton Hall said, 'No. Let them fight it out.' Lynam just said, 'OK.' I think Coach Lynam agreed because he had visions of rolling around the hardwood at the Palestra with this big monster if he had tried to step in. Anyway, he didn't bother. He let the Palestra security crew break it up."

Jim Lynam Moves to the NBA

In his final season as the head Hawk, Jim Lynam spun a gem of a season—25 wins. After three successful years on Hawk Hill, Jim Lynam, had an opportunity to take the next step up. The Portland Trailblazers' head coach, Jack Ramsay, offered Jim an assistant coach position—a position that became available when a guy named Jack McKinney vacated it. McKinney had just accepted the head-coaching job for the Los Angeles Lakers.

CHAPTER THIRTEEN

The Bo and Griff Years

COACH McKINNEY:

Jim Lynam's 25-win season in 1980-1981 was a tough act to follow. The guy who took on the challenge was a former high school and college teammate of Jim's, Jim Boyle. Bo Chang—or simply Bo—as he was nicknamed, quickly proved he was up to the task. Bo matched Lynam's 25 wins. Of course, Bo had the good fortune to inherit Jeffrey Clark, Tony Costner, Bob Lajewski, Lonnie McFarlan, and Bryan Warrick. Scoring was evenly distributed among Costner (14.5 ppg), McFarlan (14.3 ppg), and Warrick (14.9). The Hawks earned an NCAA berth but were eliminated when they lost a squeaker to Northeastern 63-62 in front of 15,225 spectators.

The 1981-1982 team managed to score an historical first when they became the first team other than Syracuse ever to win the Carrier Classic in Syracuse. They beat North Texas State 73-69 in the opening round before closing out Syracuse 59-57 for the title. Also for the second consecutive year, St. Joe's captured the East Coast Conference Tournament.

Bo's boys slipped to 15-13 in 1982-1983, though they did cop the top prize in the Atlantic City Classic with a 99-73 trouncing of Northeastern. Again in 1982-1983, the Hawks were led by Tony Costner (15.7 ppg) and Lonnie McFarlan (16.1 ppg).

The resurgent Hawks enjoyed a 20-9 season in 1983-84 as Costner (18.6 ppg) teamed with Bob Lojewski (15.4 ppg) for a potent one-two punch. The Hawks got an NIT bid but were eliminated in the first round 73-63 by Boston College at the Palestra.

The 1984-1985 squad turned in a solid 19-12 season, with Lojewski and Maurice Martin carrying the lion's share of the scoring load. Rodney Blake treated the Hawk faithful to an all-time moment that year against Missouri in the NIT. St. Joe's had just relinquished the lead, 67-66. As the

Hawks set up for the last shot, Rodney worked for a good inside shot and launched it with about two seconds left on the clock. The ball missed the mark, and all seemed lost till he followed with a tip-in at the buzzer for a hair-raising 68-67 victory.

Led by Blake and Martin, the 1985-1986 team fashioned a glitzy 25-6 record—the last super squad of the Boyle regime. They wrapped up the Far West Classic in Portland, Oregon, downing Kansas State, Oregon State, and Iowa in succession. They also bested West Virginia 72-64 to win the Atlantic 10 crown at the Brendan Byrne Arena in East Rutherford, New Jersey. Unfortunately, their march in the NCAA Tournament sputtered in the second round when Cleveland State bested them.

Bo's Hawks managed winning records of 16-13 and 15-14 in 1986-1987 and 1987-1988, but these seasons were to be the last winning ones in the Boyle regime. The 1988-1989 team finished 8-21 while the 1989-1990 edition limped across the finish line at 7-21. The 1988-1989 squad had two legacies. Freshman Matt Guokas III is the son of Hawk great Matty Guokas, Jr. (and grandson of Matt Guokas, Sr.) while Mike Kempski is the son of Mike Kempski, former Cardinal Dougherty star who played for me from 1966 through 1968.

Those final two seasons blemished what would have been an extraordinary record for Bo. As it is, Boyle's 151-114 record (.570) ranks him eighth by winning percentage among 14 SJU coaches. With those seasons deleted, however, his record becomes 136-72 (.654), which would zoom him up to third place on that same list. Under that scenario, he would displace the current occupant of the number-three slot—a guy named Jack McKinney (.652).

Shakin' The Sheiks

Jim Boyle boils about a time when his team had to rescue the Hawk: "We were playing against Duquesne about 1983. The Dukes had a cheering section called the Sheiks that sat under the basket not far from our bench. These people dressed like the Taliban, with one major difference. The Sheiks were partial to drinking beer and whiskey during the games. As the game progressed, they took to harassing our mascot, who was Dennis Sheehan at the time.

"The Sheiks decided to attack the Hawk during a timeout. It was a serious attack. The Hawk seemed in danger to me, so I ordered an assault on the Sheiks. Our guys rushed over and started a donnybrook in the stands to save the Hawk. The game was on ESPN, so the whole nation saw the rescue.

"Next morning, Father MacLaine at SJU called me into his office. I was wincing, expecting to be fired. Know what he did? He complimented me for saving the Hawk!"

Coach Jim Boyle directs the team from courtside. *Photo courtesy of Saint Joseph's University*

Downsizing

Jim Boyle can chuckle now about some practical jokes from his coaching days: "One night we won a big game against Fordham, a rival Jesuit school. The next morning, I was told to report to the college president's office to see Father MacLaine. I went over beaming. I thought maybe he wanted to give me a raise.

"When I walked in, he looked at me and said, 'I read the box score and saw that you only used six guys last night.' I figured he'd tell me I was a genius, winning with only six guys. Not.

"'Why would I pay for 12 guys to go to New York when you only played six? 'Father MacLaine said sternly.' "From now on you can only take six guys to away games.'

"I didn't know what to say. Then he laughed, and I realized he was just busting my chops."

Samurai Coach

Tony Costner, 1984, laughs about Coach Boyle's samurai instincts: "Coach Boyle always believed he could compete with his players. So it's Saturday morning practice, and he pulls out that damn cushion. We all think the same thing, 'Time for Coach Boyle to get out all his frustrations in the 'Big Man Drills' again.'

"We're doing a wing fake and one dribble into the lane for a lay-up or dunk. Coach Boyle is standing there with this cushion, ready to take on each guy as he does the move. Lonnie went first. He was 6'6", 230 pounds, and strong as a bull. Wham! Right into Coach Boyle. Lonnie backed him up a bit, but Coach was still holding his own. Then Kevin Springman—6'11", 250 pounds—and not the most graceful guy—goes. Bam! He slams into Coach Boyle with his elbows high. Now the Coach has a cut on his head. It's bleeding and he's winded. But he's not about to stop. He decided he wanted me to demonstrate the proper way to attack the basket. I'm telling him he needs medical attention. He's telling me, 'No, not till after the drill.' I'm 6'11", 265 pounds and really not caring who is standing in front of me. I only care that someone is standing in front of me. My goal was always to make whoever was in front of me feel bad when I came to the bucket and scored. The first time I hit that cushion, Coach Boyle lifted up off his feet. I asked him if he was OK and he growled, 'Sure, bring it on.' The second time I hit the cushion, he hit the floor. I asked, 'Coach, you OK?' He said, 'Is that the best you got?' Now he was challenging me. So I reached deep for a move Moses Malone taught me. Moses said to drive up through the defender's torso to back him up. That's what I did, and Coach Boyle went flying across the floor. When he got up—beat up, battered, bruised, and bleeding—I asked if he was OK. He looked me straight in the eye and said, 'Samurais do not complain.'"

Coach John Griffin talks to Bernard Jones during a game in the 1991-1992 season.
Photo courtesy of Saint Joseph's University

Eat Your Heart Out, Mr. Myagi

Ex-Hawk Bruiser Flint recalls some psychological ploys that Coach Boyle used to employ: "Coach Boyle was always psychological in his approach to basketball. He drilled us on how to visualize our shots going in—especially foul shots. He also tried to show us how to utilize pressure points in shooting.

"We were playing an away game at West Virginia in 1984, leading by one point with 10 seconds left. I was fouled and went to the line for a one-and-one. I could ice the game if I sank both. Coach Boyle motioned me to the bench and said, 'Give me your hand. I want to squeeze an important pressure point.' Then he grabbed my hand, separated the thumb and forefinger, and squeezed. 'OK, you're set,' he said, and sent me back out.

"I hit both shots and iced the game for a 75-72 win.

"I still don't know what he did. On the way back home that night on the plane, I was playing with my fingers and hand all night trying to find the spot."

Reprising DePaul

Bo knew how to utilize the Lynam four-to-score strategy. He rolled it out against DePaul, the No. 2 team in the nation at the time. The entire game, St. Joe's held the ball outside, forcing the defender to come out and take it away. The Hawks worked it to perfection and downed DePaul 58-45.

Scrapping It Out

When John Griffin took over the head coaching position in 1990-1991, he inherited a program that had been struggling for a couple of years. At the start of his tenure, Bernard Blunt, an outstanding freshman, was the star of the team. Bernard averaged a lusty 18.8 ppg, which still rates as the best ever for an SJU freshman. Craig Amos, Chris Gardler, Rap Curry, and Matt Guokas III rounded out the quintet.

The Hawks scrapped their way through the season, registering six more victories than the previous year—including four of six overtime contests. Moreover, they tied for first in the Big Five—their first Big Five crown since 1985-1986.

In his second year as head coach, Griff missed a .500 season by one decision. Bernard Blunt improved on his freshman year performance, upping his scoring average to 19.7 ppg. Bernard led the team in scoring average his first three years. In his senior year, he relinquished the crown to Carlin Warley.

Griff's third year proved the most successful of his career, as the Hawks soared to 18-11, a second consecutive Big Five crown, and an NIT bid.

Griff's squad won the first ever Hawk Tip-Off Tournament at the Fieldhouse on a 93-69 laugher over Hartford in the finals. They also finished runner-up at the Sugar Bowl Tournament—their first engagement there since finishing third in 1972. The Hawks surprised Texas A&M in the opener and then lost a 68-65 heartbreaker to Notre Dame in the final.

The Hawks dropped off to .500 the following season. The highlight was their amazing one-point upset over number-ten-ranked Massachusetts. The next year they rebounded to 17-12 while staking claim to another Big Five title.

All in all, Griff ran into some bad luck in his coaching career. One year all his best players disappeared. Rap Curry and Bernard Blunt ended up on the injured list, and Carlton Warley was academically ineligible. Despite such setbacks, Griff managed to exceed the .500 mark in career winning percentage. Griff opted to forsake his coaching career to return to the business world in 1995.

Bernard Blunt

"Bernard blossomed into a team player as he matured," John Griffin says of his former star, Bernard Blunt. "He was a warrior on the court. He had an aggressive personality and believed he was the best of all time. That was the good news. The bad news was that he was stubborn and set in his ways. I watched him develop, day by day. He made the necessary changes with a little guidance on my part and a little understanding on his part. Gradually he became a leader. Watching him achieve his potential as a player and a person was one of my most pleasant rewards."

Turnaround Is Zone Play

The 1992-1993 season featured a great Hawk victory over the Wildcats. Steve Lappas, the Villanova mentor, was in his rookie season as coach. His 'Cats had jumped off to a 19-point lead after 10 minutes at the Spectrum when Griff pulled the switcheroo on him—in reverse.

Griff recalls: "We were playing man to man and switched to zone. Normally it's the other way around. You switch to man D so you can go out after the ball. Zone tends to slow the game down. So they didn't expect us to use any tactic that would slow a game down when we had 10 points to make up. But the tactic got us back into the game. Villanova kept missing. We kept getting the defensive rebound, making the outlet pass, starting a fast break, and scoring. We went into the locker room up by three and went on to win the game by 11."

Bernard Blunt at the Palestra in 1994. *Photo courtesy of Saint Joseph's University*

Blunt Ending

Griff: "We were playing George Washington at the Fieldhouse, down one point with one second left. Demetrius Poles inbounds the ball to Bernard Blunt on the right wing. Bernard is about even with the foul stripe when he catches the ball and in the same motion heaves a desperation shot that goes right through the hoop for a win."

That ending rivaled the St. Steve Donches of Bethlehem ending from years before, but Bernard from Chagrine Falls didn't get equal acclaim. He would have if he had saved that little miracle for Villanova.

Some Coaching Wisdom

Griff reflects: "While fundamentals are of the utmost importance, I would spend more time getting to know the athletes. The players were only a few years younger than me when I was coaching, but I realize now how much they look up to the coach. They're young guys who want direction and leadership. A coach is their on-court 'father.' Next time around, I would try to get closer to my players and be able to put my arms around them and offer understanding, warmth, and counsel. I'm a parent now myself, and I see the coaching role in a different light.

"I think one of the best experiences I had was coaching overseas. It's a different experience. You get to live with the players and see them in a different setting. It strengthens the player-coach relationship and bond. I'd recommend any coach taking a trip like that. It makes you a better person and coach.

"Another important thing—something that deserves a lot of emphasis—is choosing a good assistant. I did. I had Phil Martelli, and it made all the difference. Phil's the best I could have hoped for. His success as head coach doesn't surprise me one bit."

CHAPTER FOURTEEN

The Phil Martelli Years

The Ramsay Heritage

COACH McKINNEY:

Phil Martelli continues the tradition of excellence started more than a half-century ago by Dr. Jack Ramsay. At this point in history, the two Hawk coaches stand as illustrious bookends in a marvelous era of Hawk basketball. I think a lot of successful chapters remain in this era before we close the book on the Phil Martelli era.

Phil is only the third coach in the Saint Joseph's University's long hardwood tradition who did not matriculate there as an underclassman. He got his job in the time-honored Hawk fashion, rising from the assistant coaching ranks to head coach. That was my career path. It was also Harry Booth's and Jim Lynam's and—well, you've read the book! Thus, when coach John Griffin changed his career in 1995 from coaching to financial services, Saint Joseph's University glanced Phil's way. They wisely looked no further.

Phil had served as Hawk assistant coach for 11 years. When selection time rolled around, he got rave reviews and endorsements from each mentor he served under. As for Phil's not listing "former Hawk hardwood star" on his resume, he had the next most acceptable entry in its place. He had been a "junior Hawk." Like Matt Guokas and so many other Hawks, he played high school ball at Saint Joseph's Prep. He went on to play college ball at Widener University in Chester, Pennsylvania.

Phil dove into the coaching profession right after college, accepting the junior varsity coaching job at Cardinal O'Hara in Springfield, Pennsylvania. He stayed a year before advancing to assistant coach at Widener. After a year at his alma mater, Phil was off to a head-coaching job at Bishop Kenrick High in Norristown, Pennsylvania. At Kenrick he attracted lots of attention from basketball insiders. Phil made Catholic League playoffs six

168

straight times. He owns the school mark yet for career coaching victories with 108. In 1982, he was awarded the Catholic League Coach of the Year.

Before graduating from Widener, Phil got engaged to Judy Marra, who had played basketball for Cathy Rush at Immaculata on three national championship teams and later was a Villanova coaching assistant. Phil met Buddy Gardler at a basketball camp and got to be his assistant at Cardinal O'Hara. At the same time, he secured a job teaching at Philadelphia's St. Martin of Tours on Roosevelt Boulevard (the parish school that former Phil pitching coach Joe Kerrigan attended). He lived in Clifton Heights, taught daily at St. Martins, rode out to Cardinal O'Hara for practices and games, then went home. He quips that he spent more on gas and oil than the $5,000 he earned teaching. The next year he was an assistant at Widener and the following year the head coach at Bishop Kenrick.

In the summer of 1985, Hawk mentor Jim Boyle wooed Phil to Hawk Hill as his assistant. Phil remained an assistant through both Boyle's and Griffin's reign.

Bryant Takes a Dive

Upon Griff's departure in 1995, Phil took the reins, and what a run he's having! Even without the magic of 2004's practically perfect season and SJU's No. 1 ranking, Phil Martelli has already accumulated a lifetime of memories.

Phil is suited to success. He's a gifted guy. He's different from the average bear, and he's the first to admit it.

When I asked Phil, "What play won't you ever forget?" Phil reflected and said, 'At Dayton in the A-10 series in 2003, we were losing big when all of a sudden we started to come back. Someone knocked a ball loose, and the Dayton guy was reaching down to pick it up. Out of nowhere came John Bryant diving in headfirst and swatting the ball toward the bucket where Jameer outran everyone on the floor, scooped up the ball, and put it in the hole. To me, that one little play illustrates Saint Joseph's spirit in the flesh. You ask, "What's so distinct about this school, this team's spirit, and the whole St. Joe's mystique?" and ... well that play is what it's about. It's just one little five-second segment of one game, but I'll never forget it because it says so much about what makes our people and this place special."

Less Than Mo

"It was obvious as soon as Phil became an assistant coach that he had all the right stuff," Don DiJulia recalls. "He had a knack for breaking down the game as a strategist, but more important, he could communicate his strategy clearly to his players. And Phil handled—and handles—the public and the media better than anyone I've ever seen. And he has a tremendous sense of humor."

Especially around the Quaker City, Phil is renowned for his sense of humor and self-deprecating style. He doesn't take himself nearly as seriously as his post seems to befit. A *Los Angeles Times* article during the perfect season described him as a "quirky" coach and expressed amazement at his humble office and environment. Martelli told the reporter, "The ceiling in his office drops off to 6'4". That's why we have guards."

Phil was a guard himself at St. Joe's Prep, where he played for Eddie Burke. His backcourt mate was Mo Howard. A not-to-be-named Hawk informs me that Phil tells everybody that his high school backcourt averaged 30 points. What he doesn't tell them is that Mo Howard averaged 28 of them.

Breaking Down Phil

Let me take a look at Phil Martelli as a coach. There are some things that some coaches never learn. The most important is that you simply can't get everything from every player, and the things you can't get, you have to let go. Everyone can't handle the ball like Jameer. Few can shoot like Delonte or Pat Carroll. You can't make a ballplayer do things he can't do, and you can't transform him into something he's not. But some things you can and must get from everyone. Like defense. *Everyone* can play defense. Everyone can, should, and must give 100 percent. And *everyone* can adopt a winning attitude. *Everyone* can, should, and must walk on to that court every game expecting to win. Those are the "musts." Phil knows how to make those musts work in his favor. Many coaches never learn those little truths, and consequently spend a lot of their time banging their heads against the wall.

Let's talk defense. I marvel at Phil's approach to D, how he gets his guys to play aggressively, intelligently, and relentlessly. The off-the-ball help is awesome. Everyone knows his responsibility. I can see why opposing teams collapse late in the game against the Hawks. It's defense.

As Don DiJulia says, "A lot of Phil's' success owes to his being a true Philly guy. Philly's unique. It's not New York or Boston. It's a small big city, very ethnic. It's all about neighborhoods and parishes and remembering your roots. Phil understands where the kids here are coming from."

Coach Phil Martelli talks to Delonte West during a game in the 2003-2004 season. Pat Carroll (#33) looks on. *Photo courtesy of Saint Joseph's University/Sideline Photos*

Hawk Talk

Phil Martelli hosts a hit TV show, *Hawk Talk*. The show has become a showcase for his off-kilter sense of humor.

"When I was first approached about doing a talk show, I wasn't excited. I didn't want to do the same type of format that I've seen coaches do," Phil reveals. "I said I would do a show if they were ready to let me do something different. I look on it as being 'fun' more than 'funny.'"

Phil pulled off his somewhat nebulous concept swimmingly. He interviews some unusual guests—people like the team bus driver and manager.

"I had the bus driver on 'cause he became such a fan of the team," Phil chuckles. "He's the guy who drove the team to the airport and games. So we did the show on the bus, driving from the campus to the studio.

"It's funny. Lots of wives of other coaches come up to me and say, 'I want my husband to relax and do his show the way you do it.'"

Phil also taped a show in black and white during a losing streak just to try to break the streak of bad luck. He had his 12-year-old daughter on as his guest one night (she's now 18). He's done quirky shtick like opening the show lying in a coffin to parody the fact that his team had been given up for dead. Once he stationed a heckler behind him to heckle him all show long in order to toughen up for a raucous road trip.

It's (Almost) A Family Affair

Phil Martelli's dad sits in the top of the bleachers and watches every practice. His wife buys a block of tickets—*28* tickets—every game, so the entire extended family can attend. Well *almost* the entire family.

"My brother-in-law jinxed us a couple of years ago," Phil confesses. "We stopped giving him a ticket. But he's back again. I relented."

Philly Phil

When Phil Martelli was born, his parents lived in a row home on Shields Street between 66th and 67th Streets. His dad worked at the nearby DuPont factory. They soon moved, and Phil grew up in Drexel Hill, home of another Big Five legend, Fran Dunphy. He played guard for St. Philomena's in Lansdowne in the CYO league. His team won the CYO championship when he was in seventh and eighth grade. Phil attracted the attention of Saint Joseph's Prep, but not necessarily because of his basketball exploits.

"I won an academic scholarship to Saint Joseph's Prep," Phil explains. "Otherwise I would have gone to Monsignor Bonner. But I loved basketball—lived and died for it. Looking back, those days were really important in my path toward being a coach. I actually started coaching then in the sense that I learned a lot about conflict resolution, leadership, and other relationship aspects that are important for a coach to know. And I think the most positive influence on me was my parents. They taught me not to be judgmental. They taught me to respect others. To this day, people come up to me and tell me that my dad's a 'great guy' whenever they meet him. He was good to me. He and my mom raised seven kids in an era when moms didn't work. They both worked hard and were totally dedicated to their family."

Four-Guard Offense

As Phil Martelli assessed his 2003-04 team, his greatest strength was at the guard position. He took a bold step and instituted a four-guard offense on a team that national pundits criticized as weak under the boards.

"We had to get out of the box a bit," Phil assesses. "Our strength was with Jameer, Delonte, Pat Carroll, Tyrone Barkley, and Chet Stachitas— all guards. I decided to leverage that strength with a four-guard offense. It was tough for the guys to accept at first. I told them you've got to forget how we guard the opponent and focus on how they stop us. Mentally and conceptually, I met some resistance. No one really wanted to be considered a forward. Some of the experts thought we couldn't possibly win without any rebounders. But we used it against Gonzaga with great success and Gonzaga was supposed to have—well they did have—a great front line.

It would have worked against Oklahoma State, too, except we shot terribly that night. Yes it was unconventional and yes it was a stretch, but it worked well all year, because we had guys like Jameer and Delonte who made sure it worked."

Doing It Big

Of the perfect season, Don DiJulia says: "Where do you find a school that doesn't have a Division I-A football team helping to subsidize the basketball program? And to skeptics who say the Atlantic 10 is weak, member teams played the toughest non-conference schedule four of the five past years [up to and including the 2003-2004 season]."

From the Jack Ramsay period onward, St. Joe's has achieved disproportionate results from the money invested in the program. The recruiting expense in 2003 was $58,028, a sum that Tom DeLay couldn't make stretch to President's Day. The only other school in the Top 10 that spent less than $100,000 was Gonzaga. In contrast, North Carolina spent $586,935.

Gate revenues are smaller, too. SJU has the smallest arena of any team in the Top 25.

Up Where Hawks Fly—
the Almost Perfect Season Begins

"This season has all the ingredients of a good movie. It's Seabiscuit and Hoosiers all wrapped up into one." —*Don DiJulia*

In the 2003-2004 season opener, SJU upended No. 10-ranked Gonzaga—a doubly sweet victory because it marked Phil Martelli's 150th career win as a coach. It was also the first of his team's unprecedented 11 national TV appearances that season.

St. Joe's followed that victory with a series of games they won by considerable margins—topping Boston University by 15, San Francisco by 22, U of P by eight, Boston College by 10, and Drexel by 22. Only Old Dominion gave them a run for their money but still lost 75-72.

The Hawks were cruising along until the California game at the Pete Newell Challenge. With the contest up for grabs, Nelson took matters in his own hands in the final seconds, and SJU won the game by a bucket.

By the holidays, Saint Joseph's University, with a 10-0 record, was ranked No. 10 in the nation.

Rankings

The 2003-04 team's 20 weeks in the Top 25 set the school record for most weeks in a season in the Top 25. They also set the SJU record for most consecutive years in the Top 25—four. As a testament to the quality of Phil Martelli's program, five of the nine teams in SJU history that have been nationally ranked came during Martelli's tenure.

In mid-January, the Hawks had their 14-0 overall record and 4-0 conference record on the line. Xavier had them down by six points at half. But Delonte West picked this night to be perfect. He made every shot he took, 12 from the field, three from the arc, and six from the line for a career-high 33 points. The following day, the Hawks moved up to number three in the nation.

Staying Perfect

The Hawks were winning without a lot of muscle under the boards. Martelli flipped that apparent deficiency from a negative to a positive. By inserting a four-guard lineup—complementing Jameer and Delonte with sixth-man Tyrone Barley and Dwayne Lee, the guy who so effectively inherited the point guard position after Jameer left.

Not many No. 3 teams have four walk-ons. The Hawks did. Seniors Brian Jesiolowski and Robert Hartshorn proved to be valuable practice players, as was sophomore Rob Sullivan and freshman Andrew Koefer.

The Hawks entered February ranked number three with a nationally televised game against archrival Villanova. It was Groundhog Day, and copying what Punxsutawney Phil did earlier that day, the Wildcats never saw the light.

Dayton, leader of the Atlantic 10's West Division, came to town the very day that Jameer Nelson landed on the cover of *Sports Illustrated*. Jameer and his mates, however, shattered that old jinx. West, Nelson, and Barley combined for 54 points in a relatively easy victory. Within the week, the Hawks usurped Duke's No. 2 slot in the polls, trailing only fellow unbeaten Stanford.

Temple had designs on upending the Hawks at the Palestra. St. Joe's blew the Owls out by 23. The blowout gave St. Joe's a sweep of the Big Five for the second consecutive year. It extended their string of victories against city opponents to 13. Their average margin of victory during that streak was 17.5 points.

The Hawks routed St. Bonaventure's 82-50 to close out their season undefeated at 27-0. Their unblemished record earned them their first ever No. 1 national ranking. They did succumb to Xavier in the opening round of the Atlantic 10 playoffs, but they received a number-one seed in the NCAA Tournament.

The NCAA Tournament

SJU shuffled off to Buffalo, New York. For the first time in history, a Hawk team was seeded number one in the NCAA. In the first round of Tournament play they routed Liberty 82-63. In round two, they locked horns with Texas Tech and their volatile coach, Bobby Knight. Texas Tech grabbed an early lead, but the Hawks rallied for a 24-2 run and an eventual 70-65 win. Jameer canned 24 points, while Delonte West chipped in 15 and Pat Carroll 14 on his 4-5 marksmanship from three-point range.

The victory advanced the Hawks to the Sweet 16. They jetted back to the more familiar confines of East Rutherford, New Jersey, where they hung a dramatic 84-80 loss on Wake Forest. Nelson and West each contributed 24. Carroll threw in 17 on the strength of 5-7 shooting from beyond the three-point arc.

The Hawks took on Oklahoma State, led by John Lucas, son of the former NBA star with the same name. The Hawks came within seven seconds of a trip to the Final Four. The game was a nail-biter from start to finish. After Pat Carroll hit a three-pointer to give the Hawks the lead with 29.9 seconds to go, Lucas swished a jumper to push Oklahoma State into the lead with 6.9 ticks remaining. Jameer sped down three-quarters of the court, battling Oklahoma State defenders and the clock en route, and launched a jumper that missed the target and halted the Hawks' championship hopes.

Better, Better, Best

Don DiJulia had this to say in the spring of 2004: "On January 17, we beat Xavier on national TV. On January 18, a certain football team [the Philadelphia Eagles] lost an NFC Championship game. Starting January 19, every week has been Super Bowl week. I said in 1996 when we got to the NIT Finals, 'It can't get any better than this.' And I'm sure I said in 1997, 'It can't get any better than the Sweet 16.' I hope I'm here on this earth if it gets any better than what's happened in 2003-2004."

Taking a Toll

"They called me on it, so I had to do it," Phil Martelli joked. Prior to the 2004-2005 season, Phil had made a remark on a WIP talk radio show about looking for a less stressful job like becoming a toll collector on a bridge. Delaware Department of Transportation's (DelDOT) Chief Traffic Engineer Don Weber, heard the comment while driving to work. He called the radio station and challenged Martelli to try being a toll collector to appreciate their problems. Martelli accepted. So when the season was over, there was St. Joe's Phil yukking it up with all the toll payers and telling everyone the TV cameras were there because they were looking for the best driver on I-95. The story made all the local news broadcasts.

He then spoke to the DelDOT staff as his appearance coincided with an employee appreciation day. "I really enjoyed myself," he chuckled. "But the most enjoyable part was the people. The people here were terrific, and I definitely have a great appreciation for what they do day in and day out."

CHAPTER FIFTEEN

Jameer Nelson

Jameer Nelson's record speaks for itself. What he did and does for the SJU basketball program is priceless. In the four years before he stepped onto the Fieldhouse floor, St. Joe's was 36-51. Over his four-year stint, the Hawks racked up 98 wins—almost three times as many as the class before him. Jameer and teammate Tyrone Barley are the elite members of that class—the winningest class in Hawk history. Jameer netted 2,094 points in that stretch, most ever by a Hawk. He also tops the list for career assists (bettering the number-two guy, Rap Curry, by 133) and career steals. He's third all-time in three-point goals.

The Jameer Nelson name appears in both the first and second slot on the list for most assists in a season, and he's second for most steals in a season behind the legendary Billy DeAngelis. Twice he dished out a dozen assists in a single game. He handed off 11 in one game and 10 on five other occasions. His 39 points versus Dayton on March 14, 2003, rank him fifth on most points scored in a single game by a Hawk, and his 659 points in his senior year place him third on the list of most points scored in a single season.

Jameer is the only one ever to lead the Atlantic 10 in assists two straight years. Scoring, leading, dishing off all those assists, Jameer was the catalyst for the Hawks' magical 30-2 season in 2003-2004. The 5'11" point guard swept all of the national postseason awards. He was named the National Player of the Year by the Associated Press, CollegeInsider.com, the U.S. Basketball Writers Association (USBWA), the Naismith and Wooden Committees, *Basketball Times, The Sporting News,* CBS Sports/Chevrolet, and the National Association of Basketball

Coaches (NABC). Jameer also became the charter recipient of the Bob Cousy Award, presented by the Naismith Memorial Basketball Hall of Fame to the country's best point guard. He won the Senior CLASS Award from the Kansas City Club, and the Frances Pomeroy Naismith Award, which goes to the best player under six feet tall. He won the Hawks' John P. Hilferty Award (team's co-MVP), the Big Five Player of the Year Award, and the Atlantic 10 Player of the Week (eight times).

"Jameer arguably received more awards than anybody in the NCAA's history," Don DiJulia points out. "One reason for that is practical. There's a lot more awards these days than there used to be when Oscar Robertson was playing. Awards like the Bob Cousy Award weren't around in the past. And admittedly, the guys like Walton and Jabbar were dominant, but they were giants, and they don't have special awards for the centers like that Cousy Award. But besides all that, Jameer was clearly the college player of the year. That seldom happens. So he won all the big traditional awards plus a slew of others that are of more recent vintage."

Jameer's number 14 now belongs to the ages. Retired on April 23, 2004, it now hangs in the rafters.

The Waterboy

What do Adam Sandler and Jameer Nelson have in common? Former SNL cast member Sandler starred in the movie, *The Waterboy*. As for Jameer …

"We were in the airport at Cincinnati," Jameer laughs. "The security lady was speaking with me and she said, 'So you're on the swimming team?' I told her I was on the basketball team. She checked out all the guys and noticed I was only 5'11" so she said, 'And you must be the waterboy.' I told her, 'Lady, I'm the best waterboy you ever saw!'"

The Early Years

COACH McKINNEY:

Jameer grew up with only one love greater than basketball. That would be his mom, Linda Billings. As for Linda, the sun rises and sets on her "Baby." These days, Jameer is just as crazy about his own baby, Jameer II, as Linda was about Jameer I.

"Jameer was the baby of the family," Linda beams. "He got lots of attention. "Even his brother Floyd Jr. and sister Althea showered him with attention and took good care of their little baby brother.

"Jameer was a good boy and a loving son. When he was three and four, he loved to break dance. He'd spin around on his head and we'd all die laughing. I shouldn't tell you this cause it might embarrass Jameer, but our family and friends called him 'Boobie' and it stuck.

"Then when he hit eight or nine, the basketball bug hit. If that boy could find an open hoop, he'd probably shoot anything he had in his hands through it—socks, tennis balls, baseballs, candy bars. And from then on that was Jameer, playing sports all the time—mostly basketball and baseball."

When we asked Linda if Jameer was always a star, she thought for a moment and said: "I guess he was, but I never thought of him as a star. He was just always one of the best at everything from the time he started in Biddy Basketball. That's when he got his first trophy."

Dr. Earl Pearsall, director of the Chester Biddy Basketball League: "You could tell Jameer had a special talent on the court. He wasn't the best player, but he had basketball intellect and a bent for leadership. He was slipping down that slippery slope a bit when he reached the age of about 14. He was staying out late at night, and he was starting to let his schoolwork go unattended. His grades began to drop. I spent a year trying to convince him to come work with me so I could set him in the right direction. He continually refused, telling me I was too strict. When he was 15, thanks to some benevolent intervention from his Biddy basketball coach, Joe Griffin, Jameer finally started to work with us.

"We focused on school. His final grade point average (GPA) as a sophomore was a shaky 1.6. But as a junior and senior, he had some semesters where he got a 3.0 or better. He graduated with an overall 2.3, which was good enough for college.

"On the court, he really started maturing. He never looked to be the great scorer. He was a leader. Jameer was naturally sort of shy and quiet, but that wasn't his court persona. He was always talking, always directing. I watched him grow in that role.

"The team would rally around Jameer. And once we got him on track with school, he became a good listener—a pleasure for his coaches."

Mentoring Jameer became a Pearsall family project.

Dr. Pearsall: "My son Ernest [St. Joseph's '88], who is now the director of basketball operations at Columbia University, got very involved with Jameer. He tutored him five days a week at his house. Many's the night when Jameer's mom made Ernest sleep over because it was too late or the weather was too treacherous."

Jameer had a great high school career. In his senior year, his Chester High team won the state championship. In fact, his high school, the Chester High Clippers, have played in more title games than any school in Pennsylvania. Hundreds of programs around the country wooed Jameer. He was most interested in Notre Dame, UMass, Texas Tech, Maryland, Temple and St. Joe's.

Coach John Wooden and Jameer Nelson pose together after Jameer won the John R. Wooden Award in April 2004. *Photo courtesy of Saint Joseph's University/Sideline Photos*

"Team Jameer" which consisted of his mom, his Uncle Joe Griffin, and Jameer's dad (Linda and Jameer's dad broke up when Jameer was 14), turned to Dr. Earl Pearsall for guidance in choosing a college.

Location, Location, Location

When it came down to it, Jameer placed the major emphasis on where to attend college on one factor: location. He wanted his family and friends to be able to see him play. He wanted to be able to go home whenever he wanted. I've got to think mom's cooking had something to do with that stipulation.

That line of thinking narrowed things down to Temple and St. Joe's. He had one visit from Phil Martelli, and that was all she wrote.

Dr. Pearsall: "Phil Martelli was fantastic at explaining what Jameer could do for Saint Joseph's University and vice versa. When Phil left Linda's house, Jameer said, 'That's it. I'm going to St. Joe's. No more visits. I've made my mind up.'"

A Touch of Class

Phil Martelli says: "In many ways, I think what distinguishes Jameer Nelson is that he was a kid who was loved not because of basketball. His family was loving and nurturing. That's what shaped his personality. I look on Jameer as being a better person than basketball player. He was shaped in the right way growing up, and he was wise enough to choose a wholesome path.

"Jameer did things that were considerate—things other kids don't think of. I remember when we won the Pete Newell Challenge, he went back out on the court to pay his respects to Pete Newell. It was warm and natural—that's what Jameer is. I've seen him that way so many times. I was inducted into the Philadelphia CYO Hall of Fame, and Jameer was there. We auctioned off one of his jerseys and it went for a few thousand dollars. On his own, Jameer sought the winning bidder out and made his way over to his table to thank him for his charity and chat with the guy. Jameer wasn't getting anything out of it, and was only at the event as my guest, but he showed graciousness and class that is rare these days."

Scouting Jameer

Phil used to go to Jameer's high school games. He'd sit in the stands after the game was over just to nod a "hello" to Jameer when he emerged from the locker room. Phil never made a pest of himself, just a presence.

Phil Martelli: "One night Jameer had one point in the first half, yet completely dominated the game. I was completely sold on him. I knew he had the talent to be the best in the country.

"I had watched Jameer play in the Youth Interlock Society in Chester—a program that stressed academics and athletics. He played three years, so I got to see a lot of him. Dwayne Jones played too, and he and Jameer got to be friends."

Deciding on the NBA

When Jameer was a junior at St. Joe's, he had to do what NBA guys do: get an agent. Steve Mountain was an agent from Villanova, not far from St. Joe's. Steve owned the Summit Sport Center. He represented numerous professional athletes, mostly from the National Hockey League.

Jameer Nelson is one of the most coveted players in the history of Saint Joseph's basketball. *Photo courtesy of Saint Joseph's University/Sideline Photos*

Pat Croce was a Steve Mountain client. Croce was also a friend of Phil Martelli and suggested Mountain as a possible agent for Jameer.

Steve Mountain: "I told Jameer he'd get picked in the first or second round. But that wouldn't guarantee him playing time. He'd be living the good life of an NBA player, but I felt he'd be better off waiting and going back to Saint Joseph's to complete his degree. He'd come out better in the end waiting for next year's draft. Once money starts getting thrown at them, kids normally don't listen to that line of reasoning. But Jameer listened. It all worked out great for him 'cause he listened."

Jameer reflects: "I wanted a great education. I wanted to be a role model. St. Joe's made all this come true. Coming back to school for senior year was the best decision I ever made in my life."

The NBA Jameer

Despite all his fame and fortune, the good things in Jameer Nelson's life go on, same as they always did. When the Magic play the 76ers in Philly, Jameer spends half his time in Philadelphia with his kid, "Meer Meer" and Meer Meer's mom. He spends the other half in Chester with his mom, Linda. Linda ends up cooking a huge feast for Jameer and a half dozen of his Magic mates every time Orlando comes to town.

Linda lives in a little row home in Chester with tiny rooms. Once there was a giant dining room in the house, but she turned it into a trophy room that houses 100 trophies. So when the Magic team descends on Chester, she cooks up a storm and jams 10 guys into a kitchen that might normally accommodate five. Don't forget that the five people it's designed to accommodate are not the size of NBA basketball players. Anyway, you get the picture. It's crowded and animated inside that little Chester house. I asked Linda what the players talk about. She said, "They don't talk. They just eat."

And doesn't Linda wish she had her old big dining room back for these types of occasions? If she could just move all those trophies somewhere else ...

"Having Jameer here with me means more than all the trophies in the world. He's never brought me anything but happiness, and he still does."

CHAPTER SIXTEEN

Delonte West

Jameer's Sidekick

T he other half of the Hawks' 2003-04 killer tandem was Delonte West. We've talked about some dynamite duos in Hawks history like Guokas-Anderson and Bantom-McFarland, but none as ballyhooed as Nelson-West. The two Hawks were pretty much universally acclaimed as the best one-two guard punch in college basketball. Old-timers in the Quaker City likened them to the duo of Guy Rodgers and Hal (King) Lear—the Temple terrors that Jack Ramsay's Hawks defeated for the first Big Five championship.

"Delonte was Metro Washington's Player of the Year as picked by the *Washington Post*," Don DiJulia says. "He was probably over-recruited for a while in high school, then people backed off because he was one of those 'tweeners—too small for forward and too big for guard."

'Tweener or not, Delonte had a superb senior year at Roosevelt High in Washington. He averaged 20.3 ppg and 6.5 rebounds and 5.0 assists and 4.0 steals the year he left Roosevelt High.

Don DiJulia continues: "We were lucky to get him. And once he got here, he worked so well with Jameer. It was like magic from the beginning with those two."

Jameer was not a one-man show. He's the Hawks' all-time assist leader. That means he had to be dishing the ball out to someone.

"Yeah," DiJules continues, "Jameer was the rare ballplayer who could make ordinary players look good, and good players look great. And in the case of Delonte, he had a great player that he helped make even greater."

As Phil Martelli looks at it, Delonte and Jameer were about as perfectly paired as guards can be.

"The main thing these two have in common is the desire to win. But not just the desire to win, the commitment to do whatever they had to do, fulfill any role necessary for the team to win. And that's the other part of it. They both realized that *teams* win. Individual statistics don't win games. A lot of players never catch on. Delonte and Jameer had the strongest drives to win of any players I've ever coached. They were more willing than any players I've coached to subjugate their own games for the good of the team and forego individual accolades. They were both completely unselfish. And Delonte made himself into a deadly shooter through hard work. That was his role and his objective."

Delonte could (can) flat-out shoot. He showed that talent from the start, but he showed lots of other court smarts, too. As a frosh, he averaged 5.9 ppg and 3.0 rpg as a spot player on a good team. Despite his non-starting role that year, he managed to lead his team in rebounds three times and assists twice. And when he was rewarded with a start against North Carolina, he shined, earning A-10 Rookie of the Week honors with a stellar performance.

Phil Martelli was impressed from the start with Delonte's work ethic.

"The difference between Jameer and Delonte was that Jameer *wanted* to be great, while Delonte *needed* to be great. Jameer's pursuit of that goal was rational and Delonte's was emotional. Delonte grew up on some mean streets in DC. From the time he was a little kid, he viewed basketball as his ticket out. He set playing professional basketball as a goal when he was in high school, and he became the most driven individual I've ever seen trying to achieve it. He also became his own harshest critic. My challenge was to get him to ease up on himself. Delonte rarely showed emotion. He was so focused on trying to do everything perfectly.

"So where did that work ethic show up in his game? His role developed into the shooting guard. You know, Delonte only hit three three-pointers as a freshman, but when he had to step up into that role, he worked and worked to become one of the best three-point shooters in our history."

On Track

As a sophomore, Delonte set himself on the fast track to achieve his dream. He became the marksman his role demanded. Delonte made the first-team Atlantic 10 and first-team Big Five All-Star teams. He was also named Most Improved Player in the A-10 and the Big Five.

From sophomore year on, his accuracy was uncanny. He finished his career as the second most accurate free-throw shooter in Hawk history. Delonte's .831 percentage from the charity stripe trails only Jeffrey Clark, who shot .837. Delonte's single-season free-throw percentage of .892 in 2003-04 tops that list.

Delonte was a sure shot from the field as well. He led his team in field-goal percentage in his sophomore and junior years, wresting the spot from the guy who led the previous two seasons, Jameer Nelson. He left Hawk Hill as the 10th most accurate shooter from the floor in Hawk history.

On January 17, 2004, Delonte showcased his accuracy as no Hawk before or since. In front of a nationwide TV audience, he elevated his game to the level of pure art. Delonte poured in 33 points—an impressive total in itself, but astounding considering he pitched a perfect game to do it.

You can't beat perfect. You can pull down 30 rebounds and fret about the two that you let get away. You can dish off 15 assists and cry about that one open guy you missed all alone under the boards. But you can't top perfect. Delonte shot 12-12 from the field that night. He hit three of three three-pointers and went six for six from the foul line.

In the perfect Hawk regular 2003-2004 season, Delonte was the leading scorer before he suffered a stress fracture on his right fibula. Over a four-game stretch prior to the injury, he was averaging 28.5 ppg and shooting 56.7 percent from field. He had two 30-point games consecutively—one against Fordham (31) on February 8 and the other against Temple (32) on February 13. The injury he sustained diminished what would have been even more spectacular statistics. As it is, he finished the year second in scoring behind Jameer averaging 17.3 ppg. He finished second in assists with 83, second in steals with 41, second in three-point percentage at .374, third in rebounding with 4.3 rpg, and third in three-pointers made with 55. All in all, Delonte was a vital cog in SJU's most successful juggernaut of all time. And his coach, Phil Martelli, credits his fierce single-mindedness and competitive flame.

"I took Delonte out of the Xavier game that we lost," Phil explains. "We were out of the game at that point, and it was clear we were going to lose. I wanted to keep these guys unhurt for the NCAA tournament. Delonte was really upset and angry. He never gives in until the horn sounds. He wants to win every game and win in every aspect of the game.

Delonte West was the other half of the killer tandem during the 2003-2004 season.
Photo courtesy of Saint Joseph's University/Sideline Photos

"That's Delonte's personality. The tough neighborhoods he grew up in shaped him into being mistrustful. But once people gained his trust, he had a great sense of humor and a great knack for imitation. Delonte was a little irreverent and a jokester once you knew him. He made a lot of good friendships on the team. Brian Jesiolowski, who was a walk-on, and Delonte became close and hung around together. Brian's a white kid from Lancaster. They were sort of an odd couple, but they appreciated each other's sense of humor. Delonte and Jameer were good friends, too. They had a great relationship on and off the court. But Jameer's time was taken up with his son, Meer Meer, and a lot of his local friends.

"As for going on to the NBA, Delonte is entering that phase of his career with the same singularity of focus. He wants to be the best player in the NBA. I've spoken with him this year, and he's feeling comfortable with the league, the level of competition and his role.

Phil has no qualms about Delonte's physical strength playing in the bang bang physical NBA game.

"Delonte has 'country strength,'" Phil continues. "He's deceptively strong. His body is taut and tight. Delonte is careful with his diet and true to his conditioning regimen. He never missed his late-night workouts and strength training. No, he's strong enough for the NBA game, and I'm sure he'll do what he has to do to become an NBA star."

CHAPTER SEVENTEEN

The Big Five

Fun Times at Penn's Place

W riter Bob Lyons tells the history of the Big Five eloquently in his book, *Palestra—a History of the Big Five Pandemonium.* We're not going to delve into the league's history, just a little Hawk lore about the Palestra.

The Palestra opened in the 1926-1927 season. Since then, the 8,722-seat arena has played host to 50 NCAA Tournament games as part of 19 national championship competitions. The University of Pennsylvania's place has also been the site of numerous NIT contests, a season of women's professional basketball games (American Basketball League), and early NBA games. But more than anything, the Palestra is the home of Big Five basketball.

The Big Five was officially organized on November 23, 1954. The original agreement called for five teams—Saint Joseph's, Villanova, LaSalle, Temple and Penn to play a round robin each year to determine a city champion. Unlike some other famous college leagues like the Big Ten, where the number "10" has been more a guideline than a rule for the number of members, the Big Five has remained a league of five. The same five. And all five come from the same city.

The Big Five played its first contest on December 14, 1955, when St. Joe's downed Villanova. In 1979, the Big Five competition was extended to women's basketball teams.

And the main stage for these dramas remains the Palestra. Saint Joseph's University has fared well on that stage—making it a home away from home. The Hawks have won 68 percent of their Palestra battles (307-143). They've won several of them in style, too—like setting the record for most points scored at the Palestra on December 15, 1971, when they rolled up 128 against Nevada-Reno. They also set the Palestra record for most rebounds in a single game when they grabbed 83 against St. Peter's on February 2, 1962.

The Hawks' finest year at the Palestra was 1964-1965, when they went 15-0—their only perfect Palestra record till 1995-1996, when they went 1-0 (15 wins or one, undefeated is undefeated). They followed with a 2-0 season in 1996-1997, then flashed a 6-0 and 5-0 record the next two seasons. The Hawks have done so well at the Palestra that they hold a winning edge against every Big 5 opponent except Villanova.

The Glory of Its Time

COACH McKINNEY:

Jack Ramsay says: "In its heyday, Big Five ranking meant more in the Philadelphia area than a national ranking. No team—no matter how strong—is immune from being upset by one of their local underdog rivals. City rivalries were so intense that if I were given a choice of coaching my team to either the Big Five title or the national championship—but not both—I would have taken the Big Five title in a heartbeat.

"In the 1960s, the Big Five became THE winter sporting event in the Philadelphia area, especially since the Philadelphia Warriors had moved to San Francisco, and the 76ers had not yet made the scene. The Philadelphia Basketball Writers hosted weekly luncheons at the Sheraton Hotel, which was located on 39th Street at the time. The principals of that group—Bob Vetrone, Herb Good, and Stan Hochman loved the sport of college basketball and promoted it in their daily columns. They honored the Big Five and the small college Player of the Week at the luncheons, and then called each coach to the podium to recount the glories or woes of the previous week.

"The coaches (Al Severance—Villanova, Ray Stanley—Penn, Basketball Hall of Famer Jim Pollard—LaSalle, Harry Litwack—Temple, and Jack Ramsay) were a close, friendly group in that first year."

You're Cliff's Brother? Yes I Am!

When they were high school freshmen, Lou Peltzer and a friend went to the Palestra to watch a Saint Joseph's University game. Lou and his friend were both Caucasians.

"We saw Al Grundy and Cliff Anderson outside and ran up to them for tickets," Lou chuckles. "They told us they didn't have any. But Cliff said, 'Carry my bag in with me.' So we went walking through the door with them. A guy stopped us and asked who we were. Cliff jumped in and said, 'That's my little brother,' and the guy said, 'OK, you can go in then.'"

Les Is the Bomb

Mention any of these phrases—"ring-tailed howitzer," "in again out again Finnegan," and "tickles the twine"—to Philly fans who are long of tooth and they'll tell you right away "Les Keiter." Les Keiter is a Philly broadcasting legend. I consider Les as instrumental as anyone in putting Big Five basketball on the Philly map.

If Les were calling the games today, the kids would be saying, "Les is the bomb." Back when he was broadcasting, however, Les was almost the bomb—literally. He got a little too close for comfort to a real bomb on February 20, 1965.

St. Joe's was squaring off against Villanova at the Palestra in front of 9,200 fans. Les was perched high up in his broadcasting booth, a little cubbyhole he shared with his statistician, Tony DeLuca. At halftime, Les was scheduled to interview Lou Eisenstein the referee.

Lou had just climbed up to Les's aerial quarters and started his interview. Keep in mind that this was all taking place in the pioneer days of broadcasting before shoulder cameras had made the scene. Les was forced to do the interviews way up there in his little perch, because that's where the cameras were set up and they couldn't be moved. In fact, Les's room was so tiny he couldn't fit three bodies inside. Whenever Les did an interview, Toby D had to vacate the booth to make room for the guest.

The interview had just started when the Palestra public address announcer, Mike Morgan, a Temple student, directed everyone to vacate the premises, "Please leave your coats and bags on your seats, and in an orderly fashion go outside the Palestra." Mike kept repeating the announcement in a steady, unruffled tone. As for the players, they were directed to a corridor outside Hutchinson Gym where they spent the next 30 minutes in confusion.

As the fans piled out, cops stormed in, assisting in the evacuation. Then the Bomb Squad burst in. We found out later that someone had phoned in a bomb threat. The Bomb Squad went about their business, searching everywhere, including inside coats and bags that had been left behind.

Up in the TV booth, Les Keiter was confused: "I had to ad lib. I told the viewing audience that the Palestra was being evacuated because of a bomb scare and I myself would be leaving and returning the viewers to the studio. Toby and I were putting on our coats when I got a call from the station manager back at the studio. He told me, 'Les, stay right where you are! This is the biggest viewing audience we've ever had and it's growing! And good luck to both of you!'

"In my mind's eye, I was picturing Philadelphia's last glimpse of Les Keiter. I'd be blasting through the Palestra roof, a human ring-tailed howitzer. We followed orders though, good soldiers that we were. We stayed and manned the post. We broadcast the blow-by-blow of what the Bomb Squad was doing.

"Two Bomb Squad guys who looked really ticked tried to get us to leave, but we ignored them. Then a cop shook his fist at us and yelled, 'Get outta there now before I come up and get you—and I've got a gun.' We never left, though. The Bomb Squad checked out the whole place, found nothing, and eventually let everyone back in while we broadcast the whole drama."

The players returned, took layup practice and started the game again. And everyone lived happily ever after—well, at least on Hawk Hill. The Hawks were the bomb that night, whipping the Wildcats 69-61.

City Line March

St. Joe's was gearing up for a mega on-campus pep rally. Then the Booster Club received an upsetting phone call. Ernie Accorsi, former St. Joe's Sports Information Director who is currently the GM of the New York Giants (yes, some Hawks do go over to the Dark Side) called and said he couldn't attend. The parking lot was packed with Booster Club members, students, and fans itching for some fun. So the rally leader decided they'd move the rally down City Line Avenue to the offices of the WFIL TV station. They figured Les Keiter would be the speaker. Les, of course, was unaware of the honor.

So led by a non-stop flapping Hawk mascot, the procession marched on foot the few miles down to the station where the entourage camped out 1960s-style, chanting, "We want Les! We want Les!"

Les Keiter recalls the march: "The manager of WFIL was in a panic. He yelled, 'Les, get out there or they'll storm the place.' I went out, said a little something positive about the Hawks and then apologized and said I had to leave 'cause I had work to do!"

The procession was on a roll, however. They continued the march all the way down to the Palestra.

The Booster Club Booms

The famous St. Joe's bass drum (the one that Sam made famous) had been banned for over a year. It was considered too disruptive, in polite terms—obnoxious in blunt terms. The Hawk Booster Club was determined to sneak the drum into the Villanova-St. Joe's game, though. The Hawks hadn't beaten Villanova since 1974, Jack McKinney's last season at the Hawk helm. The Booster Club met at 7:30 p.m. at the Bulletin Building (next to the 30th Street Station, for those who are not old-time Philadelphians) and marched to the Palestra—with no drum. Once there, they marched into the Palestra with no drum, circled the corridor twice and ascended to the Hawk nest in section NB. Once the game got underway, they opened the side window, tossed down a rope, and hoisted the drum into the Palestra. The drum was in and the Wildcats were out. The Hawks boomed their way to a 54-50 victory over Villanova that night.

Big Five Reception

John Smith, class of 1981 remembers watching Big Five basketball as a young Philadelphian, "I was a Philadelphia and Big Five superfan as a kid. That's why the Palestra always gave me chills. Those Big Five players were my idols. To watch my favorite players growing up, I would adjust my TV antenna [metal hanger] and hit the black and white TV two good shots on its right-hand side. Then I'd get pretty good reception. Getting clear reception on Channel 17 in those UHF days was always a problem on Second Street in Philly."

Wright's Wrong Time to Leave

It was the Wright place, but it was the wrong time—to leave.

"I was in my first year as assistant coach at Villanova (1987-1988)," recalls Jay Wright. "We were playing St. Joe's at home at the Pavilion. They didn't have a particularly strong team that year, and we were outstanding. We had Doug West, Mark Plansky, Gary Massey and Kenny Wilson.

"In those days, we were allowed to scout anyone at any time. Our next game was against LaSalle, so Coach Massimino sent me to Fordham to watch them play LaSalle. I left our game at halftime. We had rolled up a big lead, and it sure seemed like St. Joe's was cooked.

"As I drove the New Jersey Turnpike, I listened to the game on the radio. St. Joe's waged this enormous second-half comeback, but it still seemed as though there was no way we could lose. Our Doug West went to the foul line with six seconds left. We had a one-point lead. Doug missed the front end of a one-and-one. St. Joe's grabbed the rebound, but they had no timeouts left. Ivan "Pick" Brown drove the length of the floor, tossed up a shot at the buzzer, and it went in. St. Joe's took its first lead of the night as the game ended.

"I was stunned. I actually had to pull off the Turnpike at the Vince Lombardi rest stop and sit for a second. I know now Villanova-St. Joe's games aren't over till they're over."

Palestra Pride

Tony Costner loves the Palestra for its sheer magic.

"I was on the Overbrook team that won the last two Philadelphia City Championships ever played there. Then I spent four years at St. Joe's. Unbelievable! The atmosphere, the fans, my family coming to watch me play every home game—it was a dream come true. That last game—the final time I played in the Palestra as a Hawk—was tough emotionally. We lost to American University. I had so many emotions running through my mind— then, to lose the game—it really hurt. You know, I'm so proud to have been part of that place and that tradition. The teams that played there during the early 1980s made for the best competition in the northeast part of the U.S. And I'm proud to have been a part."

The Big Five's Greatest Backcourts

I figured we had to pay homage to the great/greatest Big Five guard tandems someplace in this book. Of all the great ones, the two that stand out for me are Temple's Rodgers & Lear and St. Joe's Nelson & West. I was unfortunate enough to play against Rodgers and Lear and fortunate enough to catch Nelson and West on TV in a number of games. Guy Rodgers was the consummate point guard—the leader, director, pusher, runner—the guy who made things happen. He could score, too. Hal Lear was a super shooter who ran with Guy on the fast break. He knew anytime he got open Guy would get him the ball and he could launch one of his soft jumpers.

After I graduated from St. Joseph's, I was in the Army Reserves assigned to Fort Holabird, Maryland. I ran into Hal Lear my first day there. He immediately took me to the commander and had me assigned to his unit, where I joined the basketball team. We played other Army camps and Hal got to realize that I was not Guy Rodgers. But we had fun, and since he had a car we drove home together every weekend.

Jameer and Delonte were the modern version of Guy and Hal. No one could ask for a better guard tandem—ask anyone associated with the NCAA in 2004. Jameer ran the show in a quiet fashion—scoring, rebounding, running, passing—he did it all. He was a nonpareil leader who could take the ball to the hoop and challenge the big guys like few others. He also possessed extraordinarily quick hands on defense. He could score, too, but was unselfish dishing the ball out—usually to Delonte West. Delonte was a superb shooter, probably a little better even than Jameer.

So now I'm being pushed to pick the best ever. My answer is this: if you gave me Rodgers & Lear or Jameer & Delonte or Rodgers & Delonte or Jameer & Lear, I'd be such a happy coach I'd never ask for a raise.

Jack McKinney Speech on His
Big Five Hall of Fame Induction

I got a call from Dan Baker: "I want to congratulate you for being voted into the Big Five Hall of Fame."

Me: "You mean the same group that houses Ken Durette, Guy Rogers, Jack Ramsay, Wally Jones, and Harry Litwack?"

Dan: "Yes, and now you are one of them."

Me: "I said, 'Holy shit!'"

For me, this is a very special honor simply because in my basketball career, my fondest memories are of the days in the Big Five as a player and coach. There were great wins and naturally some heartbreaking losses, and they are all stored up in the memory bank and will never be forgotten.

When you get an award like this, there is always someone to thank—and if you didn't, they would probably get ticked off, so I would like to thank three parties:

Jack Ramsay—my teacher, my coach, confidante, guru, and very good friend. He coached me in high school and college and taught me what coaching is. He recommended coaching to me and got me started. He invited me back to coach with him, and I learned. Then he set me adrift and said, "Go coach—you're ready." It was an education equivalent to a Ph.D. from Oxford.

Eighty outstanding young men at St. Joe's who made my coaching career in the Big Five a cherished event.

To all the other coaches and players in the Big Five and the rest of the Big Five family who made it such a friendly, fun-filled, memorable time.

Recently, while working for AmPro Sportswear, I was with two customers, one my age and one much younger. The older man noticed my watch and starting reading, Villanova, LaSalle, Penn. "Oh, the Big Five! Do you remember the Big Five?" and the younger man said, "What's the Big Five?"

An avalanche of memories flooded my brain and absorbed my mind for the next half-hour.

Do you remember the Big Five? What is the Big Five?

To me, the Big Five was the Explorers, the Hawks, the Owls, the Quakers, the Wildcats, Jim Henry, George Bertelsman, Josh Cody, Jerry Ford, Bud Dudley.

And it was also Doo-rette, Clifford, Guy, Wali, Corky, John Smith, John Zipp, Joe Rapczynski, Sam Iorio, Decker Uhlhorn.

It was Harry Litwack, Jack McCloskey, Jack Kraft, Tom Gola, Jack Ramsay. And it was Philadelphia court generals, Jim Lynam, Jim Huggard, Jeff Neuman, Pickles Kennedy, Fran Dunphy.

It was the dynamic duos. Rodgers and Lear, Jones and Leftwich, Williams and Taylor, Hauer and Kelly, Bilsky and Wohl. It was high-ranking national powers—Western Kentucky, Columbia, West Virginia, Brigham

Young and Kentucky—all who came into the Palestra like lions and left like lambs.

It was going to the Palestra to see Wilt Chamberlain, Bill Bradley, Oscar Robertson, Calvin Murphy and Julius Erving. It was drives to the city, no parking, miniature locker rooms, compressed crowds on top of players, hometown court atmosphere, pressing high-fives, rejecting, diving on the floor.

And it was pep rallies, marches, motorcades, parades, victory parties, streamers, rollouts, bands, cheerleaders, mascots. It was victory, jubilation, celebration, Cavanaugh's, summer bragging rights, defeat, frustration, humiliation, Cavanaugh's, summer excuses.

It was Bob Vetrone, Stan Hochman, John Dell, Frank Dolson, Herb Good, Steve Honzo, Les Keiter, Bob McKee, Al Shrier, Big Al Meltzer. It was ring-tailed howitzer, in-again-out-again-Finnegan, bomb scare, Charlie Frank, Yo Yo. And it was dynamic, competitive, exciting, nerve-racking, friendly.

It was Penn, Temple, LaSalle, Saint Joe's, Villanova. It was college basketball at its best. It was Philadelphia. It was the Palestra. It was the Big Five. It was beautiful. And it's worth saving. Don't let it get away."

CHAPTER EIGHTEEN

The Chapter We Didn't Plan to Write

(But Just Had to and We're Glad We Did):

The 2004-2005 Season

The Team of the Year After

Damn those 2004-05 Hawks. You know what they say about the ruined best-laid plans of mice and men. It applies to this book. We didn't plan a chapter on the 2004-2005 team—primarily because of production deadlines. Besides, in their heart of hearts, even the most ardent of the glass-half-full contingent probably anticipated a rebuilding year in 2004-05.

The 2003-04 Hawks made the most ballyhooed run to glory in the school's history. They achieved the first ever, in-season No. 1 ranking. They just missed making the Final Four. They featured the most acclaimed college ballplayer in recent memory.

The Hawks were engaging the 2004-05 season *sans* 40 percent of their offensive attack. Considering that both guys they were losing were gobbled up in the first round of the NBA draft, the actual loss far exceeded 40 percent.

The prospects for a good season seemed slim. But these Hawks had a different idea. Did they ever.

So we had to cover the just completed season. We're starting to catch on … maybe this book should be titled *The Never-Ending Story.*

Dwayne Jones

Dwayne Jones emerged as a major force in the 2004-2005 season. Arguably Dwayne had the most daunting, most mundane, and most

Dwayne Jones drives to the hoop. *Photo courtesy of Saint Joseph's University/Sideline Photos*

imperative job. He took charge of the boards. What a job he did! He did so well on the college boards (the fiberglass ones), that as we go to print, he's testing the waters in professional basketball.

Dwayne starred in high school, earning first-team All-Tri-State Christian Athletic Conference honors three times at American Christian. In 2001, he was the TSCAC Player of the Year, averaging 25.8 points, 17.8 rebounds, and 6.4 blocks per game.

Dwayne was named Atlantic 10 Defensive Player of the Year and earned a berth on both the All-Big Five and Atlantic 10 Second Teams. He became the first Hawk since 1995-1996 to average a double-double with 10.1 points and a team-high 11.6 rebounds and the 27th player in Atlantic 10 history to achieve the feat. More impressively, he ranked fifth in the nation in both rebounding (11.6) and blocked shots with his average of 3.0 per game. The junior was also named to the Atlantic 10 All-Championship Team and the NIT All-Tournament Team. He set Saint Joseph's postseason records for career rebounds (105) and blocks (33).

He was the co-recipient of SJU's John P. Hilferty Award for the team's Most Valuable Player in 2004-2005. His 418 rebounds is the second best single-season mark in school history, while his 109 blocks is the third best single-season total.

Chet Stachytis

Chet led Nease High to the Florida Class 3A state title, while earning Most Valuable Player honors. He finished his high school career as Nease's leading scorer with 2,505 points. His No. 13 uniform was retired. Meanwhile in his best imitation of the second coming of Jack McKinney, he placed second in the high jump (with a 6'6" leap) in the state championships.

"I only looked at St. Joe's," Chet says echoing a recurring theme. "I was sold when I got here, and I'm happy with the decision."

Chet's parents both attended Penn. Both were jocks. His father, Len, ran track while his mother, Martha, played field hockey, lacrosse, and fenced. Both were good students, another trait they passed along. In 2004-2005, Chet was named to the Atlantic 10 All-Academic Team and earned SJU's Student-Athlete Award in 2004. He schooled a lot of defenders this past season, posting double figures in all but five games including a career-high 27 points against UC-Davis. He also scorched Davidson for 25.

As a sophomore, he was named the team's Most Improved Player as a role player who consistently came off the bench to provide a big offensive boost. In that role, he hit double figures nine times.

In the 2004-05 season, he came off the bench in the season opener, but started every game thereafter.

Chet will be a key player and big scorer in the upcoming season as he and Dwayne Lee move into the leadership positions.

The Hawk Half-Century

COACH McKINNEY:

This year the curtain descended on 50 years of Hawk basketball that spanned from the 1955 arrival of Jack Ramsay to Phil Martelli's superb 2005 season. Jack launched that 50-year run with 23 wins and a third-place NIT finish. Phil wrapped it up with a 24-win season and a second-place finish in the NIT. Pretty impressive bookends to a pretty impressive half-century.

To be sure, the more recent bookend—the 2004-2005 team—was *not* the slick machine of 2003-2004 that purred through the season undefeated on the high-octane superblend of Jameer and Delonte. The 2004-2005 edition was an unproven gang with guys like Chet and Pat and John and a pair of Dwaynes and a Dave. This crew was suspect to the eyes of the basketball experts but not to themselves. These guys filled up their tanks on confidence and camaraderie and teamwork and optimism and positive thinking and defense. Oh yeah, a few guys named Phil and Monte and Mike and Mark had something to do with that fabulous season, too. They taught this team to believe in themselves and not to accept losing.

As Coach Martelli states, "This team was saddled with the tag 'The Team of the Year (After).' To their credit, they shed that tag and developed their own identity."

While I still have my pen in hand, let me give credit to *all* the people who helped make that 2004-2005 season happen. The team was awesome, but so was the student cheering section (aren't they always awesome?). I thought the fans might have a letdown after 2004. Silly me. Even though it's tough to sustain the rollicking enthusiasm of 2004, Hawk fans never let up. They came back ready to rock in 2004-2005 and never doubted their Hawks. Not even when their guys got out to a 3-6 start. The fans were still rocking that Fieldhouse—the students, the Hawk, the cheerleaders and the dance team. And while I'm at it, let me say a word about those Hawk cheerleaders, too.

We didn't have female cheerleaders in my coaching days (I knew I was born too early). The cheerleaders are fabulous, but guys, be careful on those tosses! They scare me more than facing a roster full of Dr. Js. Those young ladies are much too pretty not to catch on those high tosses, so please be careful.

I'll sum up by congratulating the entire Saint Joseph's University community. You did a great job as the sixth man in 2004-2005. Fact: March 31, 2005, 11,500 people in attendance at the Madison Square Garden, and 8,000 of them were Philadelphians and Hawk fans. Many times, Coach Martelli has recognized the contribution of Hawk fans, and I second him. I tip my hat to all of you. You make an old player, coach, and current alumnus very proud to be on your team up in the stands.

And as for next year, it's not, "Wait 'til next year," it's, "I can't wait 'til next year!" Sure, we lose super shooter Pat Carroll (that kid can flat-out shoot!) and super tough John Bryant. But there's a big contingent of veterans returning. And—oh yeah—Martelli will be back. So I couldn't be more bullish—well, hawkish—on the next half-century. I think we'll be off to a dynamite start.

How 'Bout Them Hawks?

"When people walk up to me or anyone else on the team, they're like, 'How are you guys going to be this year?'" said Pat Carroll, high-scoring senior of the 2004-2005 squad. "It's like a negative. That's not how I feel. I'm going into this season like we're going to win. I'm going to Kansas and I'm expecting to win at Kansas. I think we can win that game, and we're going to win that game."

Oops ... Pat might have to ask for a refund on his crystal ball. Kansas was red hot. St. Joe's didn't start the fire. The squeaker Kansas had just lost to unranked Vermont that dropped the Jaybirds from No. 1 to No. 2 in the national rankings did—and playing a nationally televised game against the most media-celebrated team of the previous season. The Jaybirds shellacked the Hawks, and Pat Carroll couldn't do a thing about it. He was sidelined with a shoulder injury. So bad was the defeat that the Hawks came within four points of matching the school record for their worst loss, a 123-79 blowout by Cincinnati on December 28, 1959. That Cincinnati team had a guy named Oscar Robertson on it.

For the first nine games, the 2004-2005 squad looked very much like the Team of the Year After. In game two, they got themselves on the winning track by beating Davidson 76-61 at the Palestra. Then Drexel upended them before they whipped Fairfield and UC Davis. At that point the roof caved in. They got an old-fashioned 80-54 butt-kicking from San Francisco and slumped to four straight losses. When their head stopped spinning, they had a 3-6 record. Nine games into the season, they had lost three times as many games as the previous year. A weak team would have caved in. This was anything but a weak team.

They turned the season around by beating Fordham, Rhode Island, Massachusetts, and LaSalle in succession. After a loss, they ran off a trio of wins over Xavier, St. Bonaventure, and Duquesne as January turned into February. After a single setback from Villanova, they rolled again to four straight victories and upped their record to 15-9. An ugly incident that captured national attention colored the final win in that skein, a 63-56 win over Temple. After a technical foul was called on Temple coach John Chaney at 15:24, the Hawks expanded their lead to 39-31. In the next three minutes, the Owls' Nehemiah Ingram picked up four personal fouls plus a technical as the physical play escalated. Ingram fouled out after just five minutes with a hard foul on the Hawks' John Bryant, who injured his arm on the play and missed a few games. Chaney was suspended as a result of these tactics and spent a few embarrassing weeks discussing the episode with the local and national press.

The Temple mugging seemed to ignite the Hawks. They sped out to eight wins in the next nine games. They were riding the crest of another four-game tear when they entered the A-10 Tournament, but George Washington surprised them in the first round.

The GW loss killed their chances for the NCAA, but they did get an invitation to the NIT. And they showed up bright eyed and bushy tailed—or I suppose more appropriately, ready to shake a tail feather.

Pat Carroll

"Just call him a great person and very coachable kid," Phil Martelli says of Pat Carroll.

A long-distance sharpshooter extraordinaire, Pat finished his career as SJU's all-time leader in three-point field goals (294), three-point percentage (44.5) and three-point attempts (661). He is also the Atlantic 10's leader in career three-point percentage (44.5). He fared impressively nationally, too, ranking third with 3.9 three-point field goals per game and 12th with a 43.4 three-point percentage.

Pat ranks 22nd on St. Joe's all-time scoring list with 1,324 career points. His teams compiled a 96-32 career record. He leaves Hawk Hill as a stalwart of the second winningest class in school history. His teams earned four consecutive postseason berths.

Carroll became the fourth Hawk in as many years to receive the Robert V. Geasey Award as the Big Five's Most Valuable Player. Jameer copped the

Pat Carroll was a big part of the second-winningest class in St. Joe's history.
Photo courtesy of Saint Joseph's University/Sideline Photos

honor the previous two years while Marvin O'Connor won it four years before. Pat had made the second-team All-Big Five the previous two seasons. His credentials for the honor included being the Big Five's top scorer (with 640 points) and selection to the All-Big Five First Team (rounded out by Steven Smith of La Salle, Mardy Collins of Temple, and Allan Ray and Curtis Sumpter of Villanova).

Carroll was the Atlantic 10 Co-Player of the Year and an Associated Press Honorable Mention All-American. He was named to the All-District Teams by both the USBWA and the NABC, and was the Most Outstanding Player of the Atlantic 10 Championship. Pat and Dwayne Jones were co-recipients of the John P. Hilferty Memorial Award, given to the Most Valuable Player of the Saint Joseph's basketball team.

Pat Carroll mixes three generations of sports in his gene pool. His grandfather, Don Graham, coached Pittsburgh North Catholic H.S. to 801 basketball victories to make him the winningest high school basketball coach in Pennsylvania history. Pat's father (John) was a quarterback for Penn State, while his uncle, Tom Carroll, was a pitcher for the world- champion Cincinnati Reds. His brother, Matt, was the two-time Pennsylvania State Player of the Year before starring at the University of Notre Dame. Matt played for the San Antonio Spurs in 2003-2004 and Charlotte in 2004-2005. As we go to press, Pat and Tom are hoping the basketball gods somehow team them up.

Pat says, "I'd like to play professional basketball either in the NBA or abroad. That's been my lifelong goal, but I've got fallback plans if it doesn't happen—I'll use my degree in Information Systems. I do dream of playing against my brother in the NBA! It would be even more awesome to play on the same team. I don't think that'll happen, though. Our styles are too similar. But who knows? Maybe there's a team out there that needs two shooters. That would be great!"

Fieldhouse Victories

While Villanova was gyrating at the big NCAA dance, St. Joe's was dancing at the local ball in the NIT. Instead of letting bruised pride take their game away, the Hawks went about the business of winning the still-highly competitive National Invitational Tournament.

The Hawks packed the Fieldhouse. They opened with a 53-44 victory over Hofstra and followed with a big 55-50 win over a tenacious Buffalo squad. The Hawks earned another game in the Fieldhouse and bested Holy Cross 68-60.

Pat Carroll was superb in all three games despite defenses that were focused almost entirely on stopping him. Dwayne Jones totally dominated the boards, while Dwayne Lee proved that he had stepped up and admirably filled the largest shoes in all of college basketball.

Dwayne Lee

It was a surprise to no one when the 2004-2005 Big Five's Most Improved Player award was announced. Hawk junior point guard Dwayne Lee received it on the heels of being named SJU's 2004-2005 Robert F. O'Neill Award recipient as his team's Most Improved Player.

Dwayne is also proud of the off-court honor he received when he was selected to the Athletic Director's Honor Roll in the Spring 2004.

From Team of the Year After to Team of the Year Ever After

The Hawks flew off to College Station, Texas, to take on Texas A&M in their own backyard. With the eyes of Texas upon them, they recorded a convincing 58-51 win. The Hawks winged their way back to Philly as the darlings of Philadelphia. Villanova had lost a heartbreaker to eventual champion North Carolina in the NCAA Tournament.

In Madison Square Garden, the Hawks outpointed Memphis 70-58 in the semifinal. "Only" talent-laden South Carolina separated the Hawks from their first NIT championship ever, but they fell short in a hotly contested 60-57 loss.

What a season! The only strike against Phil's group of likeable young gentlemen is the stunt they pulled on next year's team. They passed along all their dirty laundry to them. Now the 2005-2006 team will have to wear those shirts that say, "The Team of the Year (After)."

Those shirts might be passed along forever, until they change it to the proper tagline: "The Team of the Year Ever After." After all, the Hawk will never die.

CHAPTER NINETEEN

Where Are They Now?

In Coach's Words

Craig Amos, '92

Craig played for a month with a team in Istanbul but left because he missed home too much. He played semipro with the Newark Blue Bombers and became a guidance counselor while coaching basketball at Pikesville High and Millford High. He was inducted into the SJU Sports HOF in 2000. Craig still sees Rap Curry and Marlon Miller.

Craig lives with wife, Tracey, and seven-year old, Milan, and five-year old, Regan.

Cliff Anderson, '67

Following his pro basketball career, Cliff was a wine salesman in New York, a Pillsbury marketing man in California, and a district sales manager in Atlanta. Currently he's a probation officer in Philadelphia. Cliff is unmarried. In his leisure time, he plays tennis and pinochle.

Mike Bantom, '73

Mike played with Phoenix for two years before going to the Seattle Supersonics, the New Jersey Nets, the Indiana Pacers, and the 76ers. After nine and a half years in the NBA, he played for Italy for seven years.

Mike wound up working for the NBA, first in International Marketing, now in player development.

Mike and his wife, Bonita, have three children—Robbie, Misha, Brenda, and Allen. Mike still plays in a league for over-fifties in NYC. He keeps up with Pat McFarland, Jim McCollum, Bruce Marks, Cliff Anderson, and Jim O'Brien.

Norman Black, '79

Norman played a year in Venezuela, then to the Eastern League with the Lancaster Lightning and the Philadelphia Kings. He played with the Detroit Pistons in 1980-1981.

Norman returned to the Philippines and averaged 40 points and 19 rebounds per game over the next ten years. One year he averaged 51 points per game and 24.5 rebounds. In his top game, he scored 76 points. Holy Wilt! He followed with a 17-year coaching career (six as player-coach). In '94 he coached the Philippine National Team.

These days he does TV basketball analyst work and runs his own Junior Philippine Basketball Association.

Rodney Blake, '88

Rodney was drafted by the Houston Rockets but ended up playing in the CBA for the West Virginia Gunners. OK follow along, here's Rodney's odyssey in pro basketball: Italy (one year), Cologne, Germany (one year), Wichita Falls, Texas (one year), Nicosira, Cypress (one year), Gent, Belgium (one year), Chicago Rockets (one year), Estco, Finland (one year), Bayereuth Germany (one year), Fribourg Switzerland (two years), Lugano Italy (one year), Madrid Spain (three months).

Rodney returned to the USA in 2001 and became a math teacher. For the past three years he has worked for the Philadelphia Electrical Tech Charter School. He loves teaching. In the summer, he runs a World Sports Camp where he teaches basketball fundamentals to children between the ages of eight and ten.

Rodney and wife Shelly live with daughter Elizabeth, now nine years old, in Yeadon, Pennsylvania.

Rodney reports that he still sees Jameer Nelson but has stopped playing one on one with him: "He goes by me so fast now, I get whiplash!"

Tony Costner, '84

The Washington Bullets drafted Tony who was the last guy cut in '85. He went to Naples Italy for one season; then played one season in Spain, before hooking up with the 76ers. Unfortunately knee surgery forced him to the sidelines.

He played in France for one year followed by a year with the city of Limoges, where he teamed with LaSalle's Michael Brooks. Tony played in the Global Basketball Association as well as for Albany, Georgia in the CBL. He played on the USBL team and won one championship before putting in a seven-year stint in Athens, Greece.

When his basketball career ended, he came back to the U.S. and worked for IKON in New Jersey.

Tony lives with his wife, Stacey, and children, Brandon and Jordan, in Montclair, New Jersey.

Steve Courtin, '64

After graduation, "Weaver" as he was called, played a year with the 76ers. He followed his 76er career with stints with the Harrisburg Patriots and the Wilmington Blue Bombers in the Eastern League.

He launched his workaday career with Boeing, working at the Philly Airport for a year. Next he began a career in radio, starting on WEEZ in Chester and moving to WRMS in Wilmington where he worked for twenty years in sales. For the past 15 years Steve has been the Director of marketing and advertising for the Carman Auto Group.

Steve has three daughters—Barbara, Teri, and Nancy, and six grandchildren. He's living in Wilmington, Delaware.

John Doogan, '53

John entered St. Charles Seminary and was ordained as a priest in 1962. He left the priesthood in 1970, and went to Lansdale Catholic as an administrator. In 1971, he married Teresa Marie. Teresa was a standout basketballer at Millersville where she averaged 25 points a game. The couple has been married ever since and had two children—John Patrick and Kevin Brendan.

He left Lansdale Catholic and ran a teenage anti-drug program for the City of Philadelphia for five years. He switched careers, working for Prudential Insurance for six years. After suffering a heart attack, he started working at the YMCA as an instructor in weight training. John still works out three times a week. He is also politically active, trying to get people out to vote—and if they're not sure how to vote, he teaches them how to spell "Democrat!"

Dan Dougherty, '57

Doc spent a year as a financial analyst for the government. He quit and spent ten years with St. Pius X in Pottstown. Doc moved on to Malvern Prep. He spent five years as assistant coach at Villanova before accepting the head coach position at West Point. He returned to the high school ranks after West Point—first at Penncrest, then at Episcopal Academy across from the SJU campus.

Currently, Dan is finishing 29 years of coaching and teaching math at Episcopal Academy. He has won ten Inter-Ac titles there and has taught math and coached now for 47 years. With all his background in math, he has never been able to figure out how Jack Savage scored two points in zero seconds.

Ed Garrity, '53

Ed is now retired from his insurance job with All State. These days he plays golf in the morning, tennis in the afternoon, and watches TV / sports in the evening. Daughter Mary Sue was the first female athlete to receive a basketball scholarship from Saint Joseph's University and immediately set school scoring and assist records. Ed now has a grand-daughter Lynne at St. Joe's.

Ed and wife Cass have lived for the past 40 years in Narberth Pennsylvania. They have 11 children.

Mike Hauer, '70

Mike played briefly with the ABA Pittsburgh Condors and the Eastern League's Wilkes Barre Barons. He then pursued a sales career with Eli Lily and Smith Klein and French. Next he spent a few years as a restaurateur in the Jersey Casinos. Currently he's in Florida working in sales in the commercial and customized packaging industry.

Mike lives in Sarasota, Florida with his wife, Doris. They have three children. Michael and Katie are both in their thirties, while Jake is 15.

Dan Kelly drives to the hoop for an easy bucket. *Photo courtesy of Saint Joseph's University*

Dan Kelly, '70

Dan played with the Scranton Apollos in the Eastern League for two years. He taught and coached at Malvern Prep for three years and then went into sales working in Chicago, Milwaukee, St. Louis, and Chicago. In '83, he joined High Steel in Lancaster and in '93 became division president. Later he became president of the Trade Association.

Dan and his wife, Mary Ann, have been married for 34 years and have three children—Andrea, Mike, and Megan.

Jack Lister, '51

Jack was stationed in the South Pacific during World War II. He returned and graduated from Saint Joseph's College in 1951. As an Army reservist in '51, he was recalled into the Korean War. He joined the Marine Reserves and stayed there till 1976, finishing as a Lieutenant Colonel.

He graduated with a law degree from Villanova in '56 and spent 49 years in corporate law. Jack still does actuarial work on a consulting basis.

Jack started refereeing basketball games in high school, and eventually refereed volleyball, girls' softball, and boy' baseball. In '53, he started refereeing wheelchair basketball and continues doing so to this day.

Jack and his wife, Ellen, live in Villanova. He and his first wife, Mary Agnes, had six children. Jack and second-wife Ellen adopted three children. Together they have 23 grandchildren—busy Hawk!

Pat McFarland, '73

Pat was drafted by the ABA Denver Rockets. He played there for a year and then went to San Diego for a year.

Pat worked with the Retirement Capital Group, a consulting firm. From there, he moved to the Group Health Insurance Company. Besides insurance and consulting duties, Pat has found a new love—meditating.

Pat lives in Cleveland and has three children—investment banker Jennifer and twin boys Brian (banker) and John (fireman).

Bob McNeill, '60

Bob spent a year with the New York Knicks before going to the LA Lakers. His Laker team lost to the Celtics in overtime in the seventh game of the NBA championship after Frank Selvy missed a 12-foot jumper at the buzzer in regulation.

Bob left the Lakers and returned to Philly to work for IBM. He now works for McKeeson as group president of sales. He has offices in Villanova and Atlanta—quite a commute!

Bob played with the Camden Bullets and Allentown Jets for seven years in the Eastern League.

Bob lives in Villanova with wife Eileen and children Bob, Chris, Leeann, and Patrick.

Jim O'Brien, '74

Jim took some assistant coaching jobs, eventually landing the head-coaching job at Dayton. He then went to Kentucky as Rick Pitino's assistant where he won a national championship in 1996. His team was runner up in 1997. Jim moved on to the NBA where he served as Pitino's assistant on the Knicks and Celtics. He took over the head-coaching job for the Celtics before moving on to the hometown 76ers. Jim left that post after one year.

O'Bie lives with his wife, Sharon (Jack Ramsay's daughter), and children Shannon, Jack, and Caitlin in Newtown Square Pennsylvania.

Ray Radziszewski, '57

Ray spent a short stint with the Philadelphia Warriors, followed by the Scranton Miners of the Eastern League.

Ray is now retired from All State where he was an insurance adjuster for forty years. He continues to consult part time on litigation. He used to coach basketball in Wayne and now coaches the Hackettstown High Tigers.

What does Ray do for excitement these days? "I'd like to say I climb Mt. Everest, but actually my biggest excitement nowadays is pitching horseshoes in the local horseshoe league."

Jack Ramsay, '49

A true snowbird, Coach shuttles between Ocean City, New Jersey, and Naples, Florida. Children Sharon, Chris, John, and Caroline have produced 13 grandchildren. When Dr. Jack is not writing or broadcasting

NBA games for ESPN, he's playing golf. Though no longer a triathlete, Jack swims daily in the Gulf of Mexico located just across the street from his home.

Ron Righter, '75

Ron played in Luxembourg for two years. He returned to become assistant coach at Lafayette College, followed by a year at Lehigh University as assistant coach. Meanwhile he earned an MBA in education counseling. He spent two years as head coach at Wilkes College, followed by seven years as assistant at Washington State, Iowa, and USC. He then took the reins at Clarion, where he has spent the past 17 years. His Clarion teams have made the playoffs nine times. In 2000, Clarion went to the NCAAs for the first time in history.

Ron and wife Julie have lived in Clarion, Pennsylvania, for the past 17 years with son Matt and daughter Emily. Ron's son Matt was drafted by the Detroit Tigers and is carrying a 2.91 ERA in the minors as of this writing. Emily graduated Carnegie Mellon and is now studying classical opera.

Joe Spratt, '59

The Philadelphia Warriors drafted Joe along with a guy named Wilt Chamberlain. Joe was married at the time with two children, so he opted not to play pro ball but to stay with Philco in their computer division. Joe had graduated with a degree in Electronics-Physics. Joe says, "In '59, pro ball was grueling. It didn't pay well and there was so much traveling. You truly had to love the game and be single and unattached to choose that lifestyle. I don't know if I would have made it through tryouts. I've often wondered about it but I knew for sure that wasn't the life for my family and me."

Joe played in the Eastern League for four months ("I earned a whopping $35 a game!").

Joe stayed in computer manufacturing for forty-five years. For part of that time he ran his own consulting business. He is now selling real estate for Weichert Realtors in Doylestown, Pennsylvania and residing in Warminster, Pennsylvania.

Joe married Donna Weston after his sophomore year at SJU and has been married ever since. They have two daughters: Donna and Shawn.

John Tiller, '64

John taught for several years before engaging a public service career. After serving as a state congressional administrative assistant for a couple of years, he embarked on a series of assignments that culminated in his becoming special Assistant to the Secretary of State, Alexander Haig in 1981-1982. Afterwards he became White House liaison for Ronald Reagan before accepting the position of assistant director of land management for eight years. He and wife Sydney continue to spend their life shuttling between D.C. and Philly.

Tom Wynne, '63

Tom worked for Akron Goodyear and played for the Akron Wingfoots when they won the US AAU title in '64. He also played briefly with the Allentown Jets in the Eastern League.

He was a VP with MCI, spending several years in Chicago and Denver. He then became president and CEO of LCI International, which was acquired in '98 by Quest Communications.

Tom is currently chairman of the Small Ventures Capital Group in Philadelphia. Tom and his wife shuttle back and forth between homes in Malvern, Pennsylvania and Naples, Florida.